D0086151

The
Green
Office
Manual

A Guide to Responsible Practice

2nd edition

Earthscan Publications Ltd, London and Sterling, VA

Second edition first published in the UK and USA in 2000
by Earthscan Publications Ltd

First edition 1997

A catalogue record for this book is available from the British Library

ISBN: 1 85383 679 6

Typesetting and page design by PCS Mapping & DTP, Newcastle upon Tyne
Printed and bound in the UK by Redwood Books Ltd, Trowbridge, Wiltshire
Cover design by Danny Gillespie
Cover photograph courtesy of Herman Miller, Inc (www.hermanmiller.com)

For a full list of publications please contact:

Earthscan Publications Ltd
120 Pentonville Road
London, N1 9JN, UK
Tel: +44 (0)20 7278 0433
Fax: +44 (0)20 7278 1142
Email: earthinfo@earthscan.co.uk
http://www.earthscan.co.uk

22883 Quicksilver Drive, Sterling, VA 20166–2012, USA

Earthscan is an editorially independent subsidiary of Kogan Page Ltd and publishes in
association with WWF-UK and the International Institute for Environment and Development

Printed on Repeat Offset, 100 per cent recycled paper from a mill with environmental
management systems standard ISO 14001 and Forest Stewardship Council (FSC)
certification. Front cover finished with a biodegradable varnish

Contents

List of Figures, Tables, Case Studies and Guest Articles

FIGURES

TABLES

CASE STUDIES

GUEST ARTICLES

About Wastebusters

Wastebusters is the leading UK environmental consultancy specialising in greening the office. The consultancy was established in 1991 by Lesley Millett in response to a market need for a practical approach to green office auditing and environmental programmes.

We produce concise and jargon-free advice and information to make good environmental practice possible for all organisations and individuals. We are best known for our work in the office; our experience also extends to publishing, utilities, hospitality, retail and the public sector.

Wastebusters also manages Waste Alert, a network of waste minimisation clubs helping small businesses to reduce costs through improved waste management and materials exchange.

Wastebusters has worked with a wide range of organisations: small companies, multinational organisations, local and central government and schools. Wastebusters felt that this information could be made available on a nationwide basis in a form that would be relevant to all offices and so published *The Green Office Handbook* in October 1994. This was the first guide of its kind to offer practical advice for organisations intending to manage the environmental effects of their buildings and office activities.

The Handbook was revised and updated in 1997 when it was first published by Earthscan as *The Green Office Manual: A Guide to Responsible Practice*. This second edition of the Manual is once more the result of substantial revisions and new and updated case studies, guidelines and advice.

Our business is based on strong ethical principles. We are a limited company which does not distribute profits and a registered Environment Body under the Landfill Tax Regulations. As part of our commitment to encouraging environmental improvement, we aim to minimise our own environmental impacts. We have recently published our first environmental report detailing what we as a company are doing. For copies of the report and further guidance on greening your own operations, contact us at:

Wastebusters Limited
3rd Floor
Brighton House
9 Brighton Terrace
London, SW9 8DJ, UK
Email: lesley@wastebusters.co.uk
Tel: +44 (0)20 7207 3434

LESLEY MILLETT MBE – AUTHOR

Lesley is a sales and marketing professional and established Wastebusters in 1991. She was awarded an MBE for services to the environment in June 1999. Her particular strengths are balancing environmental concerns with the practicalities and financial considerations of introducing sound environmental practice into offices. Lesley is Director of Wastebusters.

Lesley works with leading organisations involved in improving environmental performance and is an Advisor on the Environmental Technology Best Practice Programme (ETBPP), a government initiative which aims to promote better environmental performance while increasing the competitiveness of UK industry and commerce. In this capacity, Lesley has extensive experience of helping a wide range of organisations to implement environmental initiatives which are cost effective and result in environmental improvement. This experience has covered a wide range of industry sectors including: the prison service, theme parks, museums, architect's practice, telecommunications, the financial sector, retailing and NGOs. Lesley is a recognised speaker at industry seminars.

Lesley's experience includes advising Reed Elsevier and Schroders London Group on the development of their environmental reporting in line with current best practice. She advised the BBC and National Grid on their waste management contracts to ensure the integration of environmental criteria.

Acknowledgements

The author would like to acknowledge the help of the following people and organisations in the preparation of this Manual, particularly our guest authors:

Rachel Jackson from ACCA (Association of Certified Chartered Accountants) for her article on Environmental Reporting and Dr Ruth Hillary from the Network for Environmental Management and Auditing UK for her article on environmental management for small businesses.

Barbara Morton from the Environmental Supply Chain Forum at UMIST, Edwin Datschefski at Biothinking International, and Justin Keeble at Dudley UK Ltd for their contributions to the purchasing chapter.

All Wastebusters clients and Waste Alert members who provided case study material. The Waste Alert team for their best practice case study contributions, particularly Christine Bentley, Steve Dulmage and Jason Langrish.

Special thanks go to Emma Burlow and Chris Knight at Wastebusters for their hard work and commitment to this project; Emma particularly for her contributions and research on waste and building management and for coordinating the project, Chris for his work on environmental management and reporting and collating good practice case studies.

Kogan Page and Earthscan for supporting us.

CASE STUDY ORGANISATIONS FEATURED

Barclays
British Airports Authority
British Hospitality Association
Castle Homes Ltd
Cheshire Business Supplies/Cheshire
    County Council
Chesswood School
The Co-operative Bank
Crofton Halls
Dudley Stationery Ltd
EMI Group plc
Environment Agency
HM Customs & Excise
Horniman Museum and Gardens
Inveresk plc
Joanna's Restaurant

Kodak Ltd
National Grid
NHS supplies
Paperback
Ravens Wood School
Reclign
Reed Business Information
Schroders plc (now Schroder Salomon
    Smith Barney)
Shell International Ltd
Shot in the Dark
Stockley Park
Three Valleys Water
Unilever
Waste Alert Club Network
Wilkin and Sons Ltd

Acronyms and Abbreviations

ACCA	Association of Certified Chartered Accountants
BiE	Business in the Environment
BOD	biochemical oxygen demand
BRE	Building Research Establishment
BRECSU	Building Research Energy Conservation Support Unit
BREEAM	Building Research Establishment Environmental Assessment Method
BSEN	British Standards Euro Norm
BSI	British Standards Institute
BSRIA	Building Services Research and Information Association
CBI	Confederation of British Industry
CFC	chlorofluorocarbon
CHP	combined heat and power
CIRIA	Construction Industry Research and Information Association
CNG	compressed natural gas
CO_2	carbon dioxide
COD	chemical oxygen demand
COSHH	control of substances hazardous to health
DETR	Department of the Environment, Transport and the Regions
DTI	Department of Trade and Industry
EA	Environment Agency
ECF	elemental chlorine-free
EEBPP	Energy Efficiency Best Practice Programme
EfW	energy from waste
EIRIS	Ethical Investment Research Service
EMAS	Eco-Management and Audit Scheme
EMF	electric magnetic field
EMS	environmental management system
EPA	Environmental Protection Act
EPI	environmental performance indicators
ERA	Environmental Reporting Awards
ETBPP	Environmental Technology Best Practice Programme
FSC	Forest Stewardship Council
FTSE	Financial Times Stock Exchange
GDP	gross domestic product
GRI	Global Reporting Initiative
GWP	global warming potential
HCFC	hydrochlorofluorocarbon
HFC	hydrofluorocarbon

HSE	Health and Safety Executive
ICC	International Chamber of Commerce
ICER	Industry Council for Electronic Equipment Recycling
IPCC	International Panel on Climate Change
ISO	International Standards Organisation
LCA	life cycle analysis
LPG	liquid petroleum gas
MACC	make a corporate commitment
M&E	mechanical and electrical
MRF	materials recovery facility
NASA	National Aeronautical and Space Agency
NFFO	non-fossil fuel obligation
NGO	non-governmental organisation
NiCd	nickel cadmium
NO_x	nitrogen oxides
NSCA	National Society for Clean Air and Environmental Protection
NWDMC	National Water Demand Management Centre
OBA	optical brightening agent
ODP	ozone depletion potential
PFC	perfluorocarbon
PIRC	Pensions and Investment Research Consultants
RUG	Refrigerant Users Group
SAD	seasonal affective disorder
SEPA	Scottish Environment Protection Agency
SMEs	small- and medium-sized enterprises
SO_2	sulphur dioxide
TCF	totally chlorine free
TBL	triple bottom line
TRI	toxic release inventory
VDU	visual display unit
VOC	volatile organic compound

CHAPTER 1

Why Green Your Office?

INTRODUCTION

Responsible environmental practice makes good business sense and is synonymous with a well-managed organisation.

Despite keen interest to develop environmental initiatives, the pressures of an organisation's core business often result in a lack of time and resources necessary to research and implement environmental practice. There is plenty of information available telling organisations what they should be doing, but a lack of practical information on how to do it.

Wastebusters' *Green Office Manual* aims to solve these problems by giving clear, concise information about environmental issues and listing the practical steps needed to create a greener office environment and cut costs at the same time.

The Manual is aimed at the person responsible for running the office – generally the office or facilities manager. It will assist all types of organisations, from a large manufacturing company wishing to ensure the office is not ignored in its environmental programme, to a small organisation where there is no one specifically appointed to take care of environmental issues. The Manual is therefore designed for people who are extremely busy, have very little time to spare and are probably already struggling to try to work their way through all their existing reading material!

Although the Manual is aimed at offices, the principles are equally applicable to other sectors, particularly schools, retailers, hospitality and small businesses.

The Manual will enable you to structure your own environmental programme including: self-audits to assess your current environmental performance, preparing an environmental policy and simple action plans. There is also guidance on environmental management systems and how to report on your environmental performance. The Manual will help you to:

- Identify what can be done, how it can be done and who will help.
- Plan a successful and cost-effective approach to environmental issues.
- Produce an environment report which is relevant to your business and of interest to your stakeholders.

Wastebusters' experience of implementing successful environmental programmes has enabled us to highlight common problems and make sure you avoid them!

THE BUSINESS CASE

Improving environmental performance is no longer optional. The minimum standards demanded by legislation require an awareness of the impacts of a business on its wider environment. However, the range of pressures is wider than legislation. Stakeholders are increasingly demanding of organisations and there are potentially substantial cost savings from cutting energy and waste. Non-financial data such as community involvement and environmental impacts, are increasingly incorporated into mainstream financial decision-making by ethical fund managers and concerned investors. These pressures and opportunities can combine to exert a powerful influence on organisations.

Increased costs of legislation

The last 20 years have seen environmental legislation grow from a few specific measures to a comprehensive programme of regulation. The European Union has enacted over two hundred pieces of legislation covering pollution of the atmosphere, water and soil, waste management, chemicals and biotechnology safeguards, product standards, environmental impact assessments and protection of nature. In the UK the role of the Environment Agency is to protect and enhance the environment and it is one of the most powerful regulators in the world.

Failing to comply with legislation is expensive and does major damage to an organisation's reputation. There is also the prospect of directors being held responsible for their company's action and receiving jail sentences. The principle of making the polluter pay is being implemented through taxes and duties on pollution. This affects every business and organisation that uses resources or creates waste.

A Better Quality of Life

In May 1999, the UK Government published *A Better Quality of Life: A Strategy for Sustainable Development for the UK* (DETR, 1999). This strategy aims to meet four objectives: social progress which recognises the needs of everyone; effective protection of the environment; prudent use of natural resources; and maintenance of high and stable levels of economic growth and employment.

In order to meet these objectives, the Government will require businesses, local authorities and all organisations to take action.

Waste minimisation is one area in which everyone can make significant improvements through simple steps. Waste minimisation does not stop at the rubbish bin, it includes utilities such as energy and water, transport and purchasing. Everything you buy in is an asset to your company; wastage of resources is therefore detrimental to your company and any cost savings you make through waste minimisation go straight to your bottom line.

The costs of waste disposal are rising. European and UK legislation requires increased environmental protection at waste disposal sites, leading landfill operators to invest in highly engineered sites and to raise the cost of disposal to landfill accordingly.

The recently published *Waste Strategy* (DETR, 2000) sets out the Government's strategy for achieving more sustainable waste management and the role of business in achieving national targets. This document highlights the importance of the waste hierarchy of reduction, re-use, recovery and disposal. Waste reduction at source is always the best commercial and environmental option.

Costs savings from waste minimisation

Waste reduction is a growing area of business interest for many organisations. One of the principal driving forces for this trend is the realisation that waste is a commercial issue; the less waste you create, the less you pay to have it removed.

Savings in waste disposal costs can be particularly significant. The costs of waste disposal tend to be underestimated, despite their recent substantial increase with the introduction of the landfill tax. They are likely to continue to rise as the government discourages landfilling of waste. Efficient recycling and waste minimisation prog-rammes can significantly reduce your waste disposal costs by retrieving materi-als for recycling and improving resource usage. On average 70 per cent of office waste is recyclable, so there is significant potential for savings.

The Environmental Protection Act (Duty of Care) Regulations on waste already impose stringent controls on the disposal of waste, placing an additional burden on the busy facilities management team. The initiatives described in this manual can help reduce your liabilities under the Duty of Care and Special Waste Regulations.

Benefits of waste minimisation

❑ Significant environmental and commercial improvement
❑ Cost savings from reduction in waste disposal costs
❑ More efficient waste management practices to achieve reductions in waste produced and increase waste recycling
❑ Waste reduction measures which are cost effective and promote good housekeeping
❑ Increase in staff awareness of environmental issues

THE BUSINESS CASE

Environmental performance and sustainable development

Numerous studies have demonstrated a link between the environmental policies and performance of companies. The Ethical Investment Research Service (EIRIS) is used by a growing number of investors in the UK to research the environmental and ethical track records of leading British companies. Insurers have begun to charge higher premiums to those companies which cannot demonstrate effective environ-mental management strategies to reduce risks.

New indexes such as the US Dow Jones Sustainability Index will gauge a company's grasp of wider sustainability issues, and environmental and social performance will become more important to investors as government and public attitudes change in defining the 'sustainable business'.

Government position

The UK government has yet to introduce mandatory requirements for industry to communicate its environmental performance. However, the government strongly encourages companies to report on their environmental impacts voluntarily. The UK government is putting particular pressure on the FTSE 350 to produce environmental reports which demonstrate efforts to improve performance. Progress so far has been limited – whilst 65 per cent of the FTSE 350 report in some form, only 19 per cent produce more than two pages on their environmental impacts.

The popular view is that a regulatory approach by the government is being held in reserve, pending a failure of industry to take the voluntary approach. The government's approach has been characterised by a steady flow of specific guidance and a willingness to 'name and shame' laggard companies who are yet to move on reporting. The Environment Agency publishes an annual list of the UK's biggest polluters and Business in the Environment publishes annual league tables of engagement. The DETR has written to those non-reporting companies, some of whom have made promises to report as a result.

Central to sustainable development is that companies should seek to integrate themselves within the local community, yet be aware of the global impacts of their products or services in social, economic and environmental terms. These three aspects of a company's operations are sometimes referred to as the triple bottom line (TBL) and are reported on by a growing number of companies. *See Chapter 10, Contacts and Resources* ➘ Sustainable development has been described as 'development which meets the needs of present generations without compromising the ability of future generations to meet their own needs'. The concept arose after the UN Conference on Environment and Development (commonly known as the Earth Summit) in 1992, and has been a major principle guiding international and national environmental policy since.

Stakeholders

Campaigning and environmental groups

A growing culture of partnerships is emerging between industry and environmental groups. This is essential if the longer-term goals of sustainable business are to be achieved. The production of an environmental report is one way companies can demonstrate a commitment to improvement on a publicly stated performance level. Involving environmental groups in the compilation of environmental reports, for example, can in itself act as a conflict resolving exercise. *See Chapter 10, Contacts and Resources* ➘

Customers

Customers increasingly want to know more about the environmental implications of the products and services they buy. The environmental report is an effective way to communicate to customers. A company can answer any concerns its customers may have regarding the potential environmental consequences of buying its products or services, and can inform customers of its efforts for improvement. By publishing these efforts, informed customers are less likely to migrate to competing firms who have incorporated their 'environmentally friendly' operations in their marketing strategies.

Local community

Many companies now communicate their social or economic impact on the community – whether through local employment, or donations to local charities. This can serve as very good publicity and demonstrates that a company acknowledges the importance of responsible citizenship.

Financial services: Investors, banks, insurers

Potential investors are increasingly interested in a company's environmental performance. For instance The Co-operative Bank's ethical investment policy includes the pledge not to invest in companies that needlessly pollute the environment. This trend is being reinforced by the growth of ethical funds. Pressure groups and commercial companies have pledged to produce green ratings of companies as information for investors; this is likely to increase ethical investments among smaller lenders.

Insurance companies have been quick to realise the potential impact of large-scale future claims due to environmental problems and are increasingly including environmental criteria in their calculations of premiums. Organisations who have not fully assessed their risks and taken steps to manage them will find insurance companies will demand higher premiums or even refuse insurance altogether.

Low environmental risk is critical to commercial lenders whose loans are secured on the basis of the physical assets of a company. If the assets of a company default to a bank, that bank will be responsible for the environmental liabilities of the company. The cost of cleaning up contaminated land could end up far outweighing the value of the original loan. This is a risk few banks would be willing to take.

Staff

Employee awareness of environmental issues is on the increase; pressure to implement sound environmental practice, particularly recycling, often comes from staff rather than management. This enthusiasm needs to be tapped; it is a useful resource, providing motivation and creating awareness. The successful introduction of recycling schemes can have a very positive effect on staff morale and can improve communication, since it cuts across all business functions.

Graduate recruitment

Environmental issues are now included in the school syllabus. Graduates are increasingly aware of and concerned about the environmental credentials of the company they wish to work for. A company which is seen to be responding positively to environmental issues is perceived as acting responsibly.

Benchmarking initiatives

The growth in environmental reporting has led to a number of benchmarking initiatives that compare performance against a number of criteria. Companies are able to benchmark themselves against others in their sector – a process which highlights their strengths and weaknesses against general practice. This can be a useful way of improving their own practices and may give fresh input into their own procedures and the effectiveness of their current systems. Examples are the Business in the Environment Index and the PIRC survey of the reporting efforts of the FTSE 350.

Small businesses, local authorities and schools

Small businesses and the supply chain

Very few small companies have seen environmental issues as an immediate pressure. Small companies can, however, gain considerable benefits from environmental awareness. Energy efficiency and waste minimisation measures can be implemented with no capital investment and can produce surprising savings. A simple environmental policy and action programme can have marketing benefits and may well become essential for selling to some companies and local authorities.

Management standards

Supply chain pressure is being encouraged by the growth of environmental management standards. These are voluntary standards that aim to improve environmental management practice by ensuring that it is addressed as an integral part of the management process. The main standards are ISO 14001 and the European Eco-Management and Auditing Scheme (EMAS). Certification provides an internationally recognised, and externally verified, testament to your commitment to continuous improvement of environmental performance. Those registering to these standards have found it an effective way of gaining a competitive advantage.

Environmental reporting

Smaller firms have been slow to realise that the above factors are important to their business and to see any justification for reporting. However, many leading companies are beginning to assess their supply chains and the environmental performance of their suppliers and contractors. By collecting data and reporting in advance of this demand those proactive companies will retain or gain environmental performance-dependent business.

Schools

Schools are under increasing financial pressures, and simple cost-effective initiatives which save money and generate income are highly valued. Environmental education is now part of the curriculum, and there is tremendous potential to link sound environmental practice within the running of the school with curriculum activities. For example: the introduction of recycling and waste reduction measures helps to raise awareness of the value of resources, and setting up a wormery in the school grounds is both fun and educational! Encouraging participation from children helps produce environmentally responsible adults.

Local authorities

The success of Agenda 21's global action plan for achieving sustainable development ultimately depends on practical projects and local action. It has been estimated that over two-thirds of the statements in Agenda 21 – the most significant outcome of the 1992 Earth Summit – cannot be delivered without the cooperation and commitment of local government.

All local authorities should be developing a local strategy for achieving sustainability – a Local Agenda 21 – and involving the whole community in doing so. Achieving a sustainable community will mean each local authority taking a lead in education and the provision of information promoting individual lifestyle changes, as well as reviewing its own planning and policy functions.

As part of this commitment to Agenda 21, it is important that local authorities are demonstrating good practice within their own operations. For example, all local authorities are working towards achieving the target of recycling or composting 25 per cent of household waste by the year 2005. It is therefore important to introduce waste minimisation and recycling measures in-house.

An increasing number of local authorities are using the European Eco-Management and Auditing Scheme for local government (LA-EMAS) to structure their environmental programmes.

Best value

Best Value is a key mechanism by which central government is working with local governments to modernise the way in which services are provided. Legislation requires all principal local authorities to adopt the 'Best Value performance management framework'. This involves undertaking fundamental reviews of all their activities over a five-year period. Local authorities must analyse both the need for a service and existing approaches to delivering it. They have to consult the public about service standards and cost, and users and the wider community will be involved in reviewing current performance and setting 'demanding targets for efficiency and quality improvements' (DETR, 1998). Councils need to compare their services against those of the best local authorities and providers from the voluntary sectors. Competition remains 'an essential tool for securing involvement' (DETR, 1998) and there is a strong presumption in favour of voluntary competitive tendering, with authorities being encouraged to work closely with businesses, voluntary organisations and other service providers to establish a 'more mixed economy of service provision' (DETR, 1998). The aim is to take a broader view of competition. As part of Best Value, authorities have to publish detailed annual performance plans outlining past achievements. They need to measure their performance in terms of new national performance indicators devised by the Audit Commission (Audit Commission, 1998), to develop local performance indicators and to submit to regular Best Value inspections.

Case Study 1.1

SUBJECT: **Street Environment Services and Best Value**

ORGANISATION: **Camden Council**

LOCATION: **London**

STAFF: **487 (Environment Department)**

Background

Street Environment Services is part of the Street Management division in the Environment Department of the London Borough of Camden.

Action

Street Environment Services provide refuse collection and recycling and street cleaning services to everyone who lives, works in or visits Camden. The refuse collection and street cleaning services are provided on behalf of the Council by Serviceteam. The contract, which had a value in 1999/2000 of £8.15m, began in October 1996 and is due to expire in 2001. The Council provides recycling services, including a purpose-built recycling centre in Kentish Town, over 100 on-street mini-recycling sites and a glass collection service for businesses in Covent Garden.

Camden was chosen to pilot the government's Best Value initiative. Best Value is about meeting the needs of service users by delivering economic, efficient and effective services and having an overall commitment to continuous improvement. As part of Camden's year one programme in 1998, Street Environment Services carried out a fundamental service review against the four Cs of Best Value – challenge, compare, consult and compete.

Results and future action

Challenging the purpose of the service helped the Council to focus on minimising waste generation in Camden, as opposed to just providing an efficient refuse collection service. Street Environment Services are now working on implementing their Best Value Action Plan. Not only does this include cost and efficiency targets, but also challenging targets for waste reduction and recycling. They are also targeting key groups for consultation and involvement, for example, working in partnership with Wastebusters Ltd to set up Waste Alert Camden, with over 50 businesses signed up to reduce their waste. Street Environment Services are also managing their own environmental impact through their ISO 14001 environmental management system, certified in July 1999. This will help them to continuously improve and meet the principles of sustainable development, key requirements of Best Value. ∎

SUMMARY OF BENEFITS

- ❑ Legislative compliance
- ❑ Cost savings
- ❑ Competitive advantage
- ❑ Increased investment
- ❑ Improved staff morale
- ❑ Better graduate recruitment
- ❑ Improved management control

CHAPTER 2

Getting Started

HOW TO USE THIS MANUAL

The Green Office Manual will help you to reduce the environmental impacts of your office. Every office has activities that impact upon the environment, regardless of its size or activity. You can help to minimise these impacts by recognising where they occur, planning ways to avoid them and implementing your plans. Quantifying your current performance will help you to assess your environmental position, work out your own environmental footprint and monitor improvement. These results can be used to produce an Environment Report to communicate your environmental commitment to your stakeholders. We also help you to benchmark your performance in relation to industry standards.

The Manual is designed to do this in three ways according to the progress you have already made:

1 If you are just getting started on environmental improvements, the Manual sets out a structured approach to identifying and tackling the key environmental issues within a planned programme. The chapters on Environmental Management and Environmental Reporting explain how to achieve accreditation to an environmental management standard or how to produce an environment report.
2 If you have an established environmental programme but you need help with specific issues in the office, you can use this Manual as a reference book. Where you need guidance on specific issues go to the relevant chapter. Further information on legislation, useful contacts, publications and other sources of help are listed in Chapter 10, Resources.
3 Each of the main chapters covers a specific functional area, highlighting the key environmental issues, relevant legislation and the practical action you can take to reduce the environmental impact of your office. Chapters are further divided into subsections, each describing a specific issue. Each subsection ends with a summary of the points you should cover in your environmental programme. You can use these Summary Guidelines as a checklist to make sure you have covered all the important points.

In addition the Manual contains:

- Common pitfalls and how to avoid them!
- Case studies, covering a broad cross-section of industry sectors and organisation sizes, used to illustrate particular issues. (Case studies are based on Wastebusters' auditing work and on the experience of other organisations.)
- A Resources chapter with contact details of useful organisations and publications available. This includes details of relevant websites. All organisations mentioned in the text are listed.

Finding the information you need

To find information quickly on a particular subject, you can:

- ❑ look in the Contents at the beginning of the Manual;
- ❑ search for the subject in the index;
- ❑ look at the introductory overview at the beginning of each chapter;
- ❑ look at the Chapter Summary at the end of Chapters 3 to 9 for a list of essential conclusions on the key areas covered.

To find information about a supplier or service provider, refer to the Contacts and Resources chapter. Definitions of the common environmental terms used in the Manual are given in the Glossary at the end of the book. Acronyms and abbreviations are listed in full at the front.

HOW TO USE THIS MANUAL

A PLANNED APPROACH

If you are just starting, or have introduced one or two informal environmental initiatives, you need to take a planned approach to ensure long-term success. The challenge is to make environmental issues part of your company culture. *See Chapter 7, Communication*

☞ Practical action

This section outlines a simple process that you can follow to establish and maintain an environmental programme and quantify your environmental performance. References are made in the text to chapters in the Manual that provide information and support at each stage.

To implement a formal environmental management system, guidance is given in *Chapter 8, Environmental Management*. You can also refer to this chapter for more detail on the steps outlined below. To report publicly and benchmark your performance against industry standards. *See Chapter 9, Environmental Reporting*

Initial commitment

If you want to develop a meaningful environmental programme you need to accept that you will have to change the way you do things.

The first step is to get senior management commitment. Without this commitment you will be unable to overcome the barriers to change or tackle difficult issues such as transport and purchasing.

To convince top management to commit themselves to an environmental programme you will need to spell out the business benefits. Chapter 1 Why Green Your Office? sets out the business case for sound environmental practice.

Allocate time and resources

Organisations that rely on informal initiatives or depend on volunteers often find it difficult to maintain momentum. Volunteers have other calls upon their time and schemes that use the enthusiasm of a single individual can collapse if that person leaves. Maintaining good environmental practice in your company after the initial enthusiasm wears off presents a major stumbling block for organisations.

Setting up a project team

The next stage is to agree who is going to do the work! Appoint a project manager to establish a project team to coordinate the programme. Each key functional area should be represented on the team (in small organisations, a team member may be responsible for multiple areas). These key areas are set out in Chapters 3 to 6. The functional areas covered should include:

- Waste management
- Catering and cleaning
- Purchasing
- Information technology and reprographics
- Building and energy management
- Transport
- Sales and marketing.
- Press and PR and external affairs
- Personnel and training.

Don't forget to include your contractors, particularly for catering, cleaning and mechanical and electrical (M&E) staff. This is particularly important if facilities management and property services are contracted out. In a small office these may all come under one person!

Aims of the review

- ❏ Establish your current status in terms of environmental performance
- ❏ Identify potential for improvement
- ❏ Identify areas of weakness, particularly concerning legislative compliance
- ❏ Gauge staff awareness levels of environmental issues: an important consideration in planning an environmental launch programme
- ❏ Identify potential cost savings
- ❏ Quantify current performance

A PLANNED APPROACH

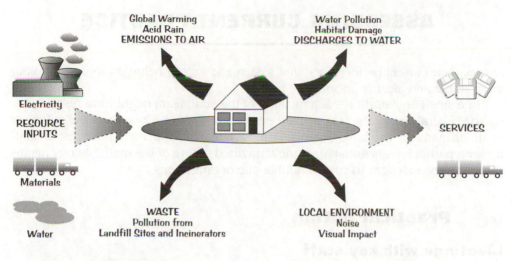

Figure 2.1 *Typical environmental effects of the office*

Reviewing your position

In starting any new initiative you need to establish your current performance. A review of current practice and how this affects the environment will provide a baseline from which you can improve and quantify current performance.

Gaining commitment

The key to the success of an environmental programme is to involve people in the process. This enables them to contribute their ideas and helps to gain their commitment to the introduction of the programme. Include keen staff whether or not they have any specific responsibility for any of the areas covered by the review.

Many organisations involve staff in the design of initiatives at an early stage and in our experience this is often a successful way of sustaining initiatives (Chapter 7 Communication gives you information on involving staff to generate ideas and action).

Summary guidelines

✔ Avoid the use of chemicals
✔ Enlist senior management commitment
✔ Develop your project team
✔ Ensure key departments are represented
✔ Allocate time and resources to the project
✔ Assess current performance
✔ Agree the aims of the review

A PLANNED APPROACH

ASSESSING CURRENT PRACTICE

Assess your current performance in a systematic way to help you to develop your programme and identify priorities.

In a small organisation, each member of the audit team might have responsibility for several areas; the 'team' may even consist of one person – the office or facilities manager. In a large organisation, each team member will have responsibility for a particular functional area; the structured nature of the methodology means that it can be extended to cover multiple-site organisations.

Practical action

Meetings with key staff

Hold meetings with relevant staff and management. In large organisations, each team member would discuss issues with their department. Some organisations, such as local authorities, will have regular team meetings at which the review can be held. In small organisations, the project team are likely to provide all the necessary information themselves. To make sure that you are identifying all the relevant information you can use the Summary Guidelines at the end of each chapter of the Manual as a checklist.

Identifying your effects

In order to help you to recognise the general effects that you have on the environment use Table 2.1. This identifies the typical environmental effects of an office. The table links the activity and effect to the chapter heading. Use the table to identify the issues relevant to your organisation.

Drawing up a policy

The review will assess your current position. The next stage is to decide what you can do to improve and how you can do it. A policy setting out your commitment to environmental improvements provides the framework for this process.

If the environment is to be integrated into normal business practice a commitment from senior management is essential. A formal policy signed by senior management adds this essential credibility. (Chapter 8, Environmental Management gives further information on designing policy statements.)

Developing environmental action plans

There is often a large gap between policy and action! Environmental policies need to be backed up with a realistic and achievable action plan. An action plan is simply an organised way of making sure that staff know what they can do, when and how (Table 2.2 gives an example of a simple action plan that can be used to structure your environmental initiatives).

Use the information contained in Chapters 3 to 8 to develop your action plan.

Table 2.1 *Typical environmental effects of the office*

Activity	Outputs	Environmental effect	Chapter
Emissions to atmosphere			
Energy use (heating, lighting, PCs etc)	CO_2	Global Warming	Building Management
Refrigeration, fire fighting, air conditioning	CFCs, HCFCs and Halons	Depletion of the ozone layer	Building Management
Transport	CO_2, NO_x, SO_2, particulates	Global warming Ill health	Transport
Discharges to water			
Cleaning and grounds maintenance	Various chemicals	Pollution of water courses	Purchasing
Natural resource use			
Water use	Water	Energy required to deliver to your office	Building Management
Paper purchasing	Paper	Reduction in diverse wildlife habitats	Purchasing
Furniture	Wood	Destruction of old growth forests	Purchasing
Waste			
All areas of the office	General waste	Wastes natural resources and causes air and water pollution	Office Waste
Use of IT equipment	IT waste	Wastes natural resources and contains toxic materials	Office Waste

Identify the practical action you can take, set improvement targets and allocate responsibilities.

Monitoring and review

Your action plan may look impressive but it is only effective if you monitor improvement over time. Reviews help you to find out what you have achieved, where your problems lie and what you can do about them. An annual review will help to define new objectives and targets to ensure continuous improvement.

Formal management systems

If, having developed a planned approach, you wish to go one step further into a formal environmental management system, Chapter 9, Environmental Management, gives you a full description of the necessary steps and certification schemes. The formal

Table 2.2 *Model action plan*

Objective and target	Target date	Project manager	Costs	Indicator	Key actions
Waste					
Recycle 90% of waste paper	January 2000	A Manager	Reduction in waste disposal cost	Amount of paper being recycled	Set up office paper recycling scheme Encourage staff to use scheme Donate savings on disposal costs to charity
Reduce total yearly waste production per person by 5%	January 2000	R Waste	Reduction in waste disposal cost	Total yearly waste per person	Use email for all internal memos Print and photocopy double sided where possible Ask suppliers to take back waste packing
Energy					
Building Management					
Transport					
Purchasing					

Summary guidelines

✔ Meetings with key staff
✔ Identify your effects
✔ Develop an environmental policy
✔ Prioritise initiatives
✔ Develop an action plan
✔ Monitor and review your position

ASSESSING CURRENT PRACTICE

route has a number of advantages; in particular it can be externally verified to give your environmental programme public credibility.

Environmental reporting

Environmental reporting can help you make the most of your efforts. Being open about your environmental position will promote responsible environmental management.

CHAPTER 3

Office Waste

INTRODUCTION

Efficient waste reduction, re-use and recycling measures will significantly reduce your waste disposal costs. Waste reduction at source – careful purchasing to prevent waste – is environmentally and commercially the best option. Accurate assessment of the raw materials required by your organisation and consideration of the whole life cycle of products will reduce waste and improve efficiency. Likewise, the introduction of preferred waste management options, such as donation of obsolete furniture to charity or recycling of all white paper, will reduce the volume of material going into your bins and, in doing so, significantly reduce disposal costs.

The practical actions described in this chapter will help you to reduce the environmental impact of your office by cutting the volume of waste going to landfill and reducing the amount of energy used to produce virgin materials through increased re-use and recycling. This chapter will also raise your awareness of relevant environmental legislation which is significantly affecting how waste is handled in the UK.

In small offices, the volume of waste produced can be quite low. In this case, it may be difficult to find a contractor willing to collect material for recycling; and storing the material for later collection can be a problem due to limited storage space. The answer is to reduce the waste at source, as described under Waste Reduction, later in this chapter. Offices in multi-tenanted buildings should approach other tenants and landlords to create joint recycling schemes.

Schools are under increasing financial pressures. The introduction of mixed paper recycling schemes in schools will reduce disposal costs and can also raise additional revenue for the school from recycling credits. Waste reduction measures improve use of resources and are also cost effective. Likewise, central government and local authorities are under increasing pressure to ensure that their in-house practices are consistent with the waste reduction and recycling messages they promote to the public. The government is committed to reducing its own waste and greening its operations. A new Cabinet Committee on the Environment has been established and a network of Green Ministers, one in each Whitehall department, are responsible for developing policies and targets which will enable their departments to manage buildings and buy goods and services in a sustainable way. Many government departments and local authorities are conducting office waste minimisation audits and implementing improvement plans in order to demonstrate good practice.

Waste Strategy 2000 for England and Wales

The government's White Paper on Waste, *Waste Strategy 2000 for England and Wales* (DETR, 2000), forms part of the UK's Sustainable Development Strategy, *A Better Quality of Life* (DETR, 1999),[1] and emphasises the need to reduce the amounts of industrial, commercial and domestic waste produced each year. This requires an urgent increase in minimisation of waste at source and increased rates of recycling and recovery (meaning recycling, composting and materials or energy recovery).

Industrial and commercial waste

The Waste Strategy sets a new target to reduce the amount of industrial and commercial waste landfilled to 85 per cent of 1998 levels by 2005. In 1998/1999, 42 million tonnes of commercial and industrial waste were landfilled. The government wants businesses to consider the waste hierarchy when making decisions on waste disposal, in particular that:

- incineration with energy recovery is only considered after opportunities for waste reduction, recycling and composting have been explored; and
- waste is disposed of as close to the place of production as possible – the 'proximity principle'.

The government also plans new Producer Responsibility targets for certain industrial sectors; an initiative to reduce junk mail (3.3. billion items were sent to UK consumers in 1999) is to be developed and there is an increased target for the recycled content of newspaper to 70 per cent by 2007. An aggregates levy is also to be introduced in 2002.

The strategy also looks to business to:

- Set targets for waste reduction, and for the FTSE 350[2] to report publicly on progress.
- Seek out new uses for waste products and recycled materials.
- Design products which can be recycled more easily.
- Devise schemes to inform consumers about recycled content of products.

Attention is drawn to the importance of waste for climate change through greenhouse gases released during transportation, landfill and incineration and the potential for displacing the burning of fossil fuels through energy from waste plants. There was also indication that fees for Special Waste consignment notes may be reduced where waste is being moved to recycling or recovery.

---

1 *Down to Earth* (Scottish Executive, 1999) outlines the major issues of sustainable development in Scotland. In Wales, the National Assembly is drawing up its proposal for the promotion of sustainable development. In Northern Ireland it is anticipated that many issues relating to sustainable development will be matters for the new Assembly, in line with the draft Regional Strategic Framework, *Shaping our Future* (Department of the Environment, NI, 1998).

2 The top 350 companies as listed on the UK's Financial Times Stock Exchange.

Central and local government

As well as introducing tradable permits for local authorities, to limit the landfill of biodegradable municipal waste, the strategy also includes two new sets of statutory targets for local authorities under the Best Value initiative. For management of municipal wastes these are:

- to recover value from 40 per cent of waste by 2005, 45 per cent by 2010 and 67 per cent by 2015. 'Recover' means to obtain value through recycling, composting, material recovery (such as anaerobic digestion) or energy recovery (through combustion or other fuel producing technologies).

An essential part of being able to meet these recovery targets is the achievement of the second set of statutory targets for recycling and composting of household waste:

- to recycle or compost at least 25 per cent of household waste by 2005, 30 per cent by 2010 and 33 per cent by 2015.

The Greening Government programme, working to improve the environmental performance of departments, will be boosted by a new pilot scheme which will require public procurement of recycled products, beginning with paper goods. This will be developed by the DETR and the Office of Government Commerce (which was established in April 2000 to bring together the Treasury's Procurement Group, The Buying Agency, Central Computers and Telecommunications Agency and Property Advisors to the Crown Estate). Guidance is already provided on green purchasing in *Environmental Issues in Purchasing* (DETR/Treasury note); however, the pilot project will go much further, putting in environmental policies which designate recycled-content products for purchasing.

The strategy also emphasises the importance of partnerships between public and private sector bodies in developing waste solutions, and gives recognition to the valuable role of community sector organisations and initiatives. The government plans a Waste and Resources Action Programme, to provide advice and guidance to industry and promote waste exchanges.

Incineration

All waste management options including the sending of waste to incineration, are discussed. The strategy suggests that incineration should only be considered after recycling and recovery options have been examined, but states that for cases where recycling or recovery are not worthwhile, it may well form a significant part of a sustainable waste strategy. In summary, businesses and local authorities need to take a harder look at the benefits of waste reduction and the environmental savings to be had from recycling in order to meet these new requirements.

Legislation

The legal definition of waste is 'any substance or object which the producer or the person in possession of it discards or intends or is required to discard'.

> 'Controlled waste' is any household, commercial or industrial waste such as waste from a house, shop, office, factory, building site or any other business premises.

There is a vast amount of legislation relating to the storage, handling and disposal of waste and it is often difficult for office managers to know what is relevant to them. The key pieces of legislation that your company must comply with are detailed below.

Waste policy in the UK is constantly developing, primarily in response to our international and European commitments. Many of the directives aim to harmonise measures concerning different waste streams to avoid obstacles to trade and distortion of competition within the European Community. The government also has an important role in the international aspects of waste; the importing and exporting of waste is tightly regulated. One of the most important drivers of UK waste legislation was the 1975 Framework Directive (amended in 1991) which established general rules for waste management. An important objective of the Directive is to ensure:

> 'that waste is recovered or disposed of without endangering human health and without using processes or methods which could harm the environment and in particular without:

> • Risk to water, air, soil, plants or animals.
> • Causing nuisance through noise or odours.
> • Adversely affecting the countryside or places of special interest'.

Emphasis is placed on the prevention, reduction, re-use and recycling of waste and on the use of waste as a source of energy. In the UK, the Directive has been largely implemented through the Environmental Protection Act (Part II) 1990 and the Waste Management Licensing Regulations 1994.

Environmental Protection Act (1990): Duty of Care

The Environmental Protection Act (EPA 1990) introduced the Duty of Care, which aims to curb illegal disposal of controlled waste. A legal duty of care is imposed on everyone involved in the waste chain, from producer, to transporter, to disposer, to take all reasonable steps to ensure that waste is handled responsibly and that each participant in the waste management chain is carrying out their obligations under the legislation. If a waste producer gives their waste to someone else to dispose of, for example a subcontractor, they are responsible for ensuring that the subcontractor is authorised to handle and transport that waste and recycles or disposes of it safely. Anyone breaking this law can be fined an unlimited amount.

The main implications of the Duty of Care are:

- A business must know how much waste it generates and what it consists of.
- A business must ensure that its waste is collected by a Registered Waste Carrier or Exempt Carrier.
- A waste transfer note containing a description of the waste for disposal or recycling must be raised.
- A business must satisfy itself that its waste is dealt with properly and legally through the disposal chain, to the extent that it can reasonably be expected to ensure safe disposal.
- Material collected for recycling is still classed as waste and its disposal or recycling is governed by waste regulations.

Further guidance on the application of the Duty of Care is available in a practical guidance note, *Waste Management: The Duty of Care – A Code of Practice* (DETR, 1996).

Waste storage

Proper storage of waste is required under the Duty of Care Regulations. Waste producers must ensure that waste is secure to prevent leakage and spillage. General office waste is usually relatively innocuous; however, hazardous and Special Wastes such as paints, solvents and large volumes of batteries or fluorescent tubes do arise and should be dealt with according to the relevant regulations.

Storage of wastes should at least comprise the following:

- A secure area for storage of skips holding general wastes. Access to skips by third parties could result in illegal deposit of hazardous or Special Wastes with general wastes. In the case of multi-tenanted premises, even where the company has little control over wastes from other tenants being mixed with their general wastes for disposal, you are responsible for checking that the storage facilities are satisfactory.
- Hazardous and Special Wastes should be stored in a secure and preferably contained area to control spills or leaks. Flammable wastes in sufficient quantity require specifically designed storage. Incompatible wastes must be segregated. *See Chapter 5, Building Management*↘

Contractors

Under the EPA - Duty of Care legislation, the duty to correctly dispose of waste lies with the original waste producer: you cannot delegate this legal responsibility to your contractors. However, failure to comply is not an offence of strict liability once the waste has been transferred to a carrier or disposal contractor – if the waste producer can prove that they took all reasonable measures to ensure that the waste was dealt with properly and legally. Since no precise definition of 'reasonable measures' is given in the Regulations or the Approved Code of Practice, it is essential to use reputable contractors who will comply with the Duty of Care on your behalf. Anyone found to be breaking this law can be fined an unlimited amount.

To verify a contractor's compliance, you should:

- Make sure that the contractor provides the necessary paperwork (see Documentation, below).
- Check that the waste carrier has a current certificate of registration or exemption and make sure you have a copy of it.
- Check that the disposal sites used are licensed to accept the wastes being taken to them: either check the waste disposal site licence or contact the Environment Agency. Check the exemptions of sites receiving waste for recycling.
- Find out what happens to the material when it leaves your premises. Visit the contractor's premises and disposal sites to make sure that what the contractor tells you actually does happen. Ensure that you are happy with the security of the contractor's operations. *See Case Study 4.5*↘

Documentation

When waste (including material for recycling) is passed from one person to another, a transfer note must be filled in and signed by both persons. Repeated transfers between the same parties can be covered by one transfer note for up to a year. Both people involved in the transfer must keep copies of the transfer note and description of waste on file for two years. The written description must provide as much information as someone else might need to handle the waste safely.

The transfer note must include:

- A description of what the waste is and how much there is.
- Type and size of containers it is in.
- Time and date the waste was transferred.
- Names and addresses of both persons involved in the transfer.
- Certificate number of the registered waste carrier (where applicable) and name of the Environment Agency which issued it.
- Licence number of the waste management licence (where applicable) and name of the Environment Agency which issued it.
- Reasons for any exemption from the requirement to register or have a licence.
- Name and address of any broker involved in the transfer of the waste.

Waste Management Licensing Regulations (1994)

A waste management licence is required by anyone wanting to deposit, recover or dispose of waste. Licences are issued by the Environment Agency or SEPA. The objective of the waste management licensing system is to comprehensively license waste management activities, including the competence of operators to ensure that they:

- do not cause pollution of the environment;
- do not cause harm to human health;
- do not become seriously detrimental to the amenities of the locality.

There are a number of waste management activities that do not require a licence, including sorting, shredding and baling wastes for recycling and storing waste ready for these operations. From 1 January 1995 it has been a legal requirement for such an establishment to register their exemption.

This legislation has further increased the cost of waste disposal as waste brokers must now pay for a waste management licence.

The Landfill Tax

In October 1996 the government introduced the Landfill Tax. The tax is levied according to the weight of waste disposed and is charged through the waste disposal contractor, back to the waste producer. Charging higher rates for disposal of waste is an incentive to reduce the quantities of waste produced as the tax is inevitably charged back to the waste producer. An organisation taking steps to reduce waste will therefore see immediate financial benefits. The Landfill Tax was increased to £11 per tonne on 1 April 2000 and is set to increase annually by £1 per tonne till 2004.

European and UK legislation also requires increased environmental protection at waste disposal sites, leading landfill operators to invest in highly engineered sites and to raise the cost of disposal to landfill accordingly.

The Landfill Tax is intended to reflect the indirect costs of disposing of waste to landfill which are not represented through the original disposal charge. The tax has become part of a gradual package of tax reform, moving taxation away from personal income and on to pollution and other environmental concerns. Revenue raised through the Landfill Tax can be used by newly established environmental trusts to minimise the effects of landfill and encourage waste minimisation at source.

Producer Responsibility Obligations

A key principle of the European Union's environment policy is that the cost of preventing pollution or of minimising environmental damage due to the pollution should be borne by those responsible for the pollution. Environmental 'taxes' are increasingly used as a mechanism for encouraging less polluting alternatives and practices.

Packaging waste

Packaging waste is the only element of the waste stream currently subject to producer responsibility legislation. Packaging makes up around 7–10 per cent of industrial, commercial and municipal waste and is currently estimated at around 10 million tonnes annually. The UK has implemented the EC Directive on Packaging and Packaging Waste (1994) through the **Producer Responsibility Obligations (Packaging Waste) Regulations 1997** and the **Packaging (Essential Requirements) Regulations 1998**. These regulations, which apply to England, Scotland and Wales (similar regulations are in place in Northern Ireland), aim to raise the level of recovery and recycling of packaging waste and ensure that packaging is manufactured to minimum requirements in terms of hazardous material content, durability and recyclability.

In 1999, the government announced several immediate and planned changes to the Regulations. Businesses that have an annual turnover in excess of £2 million in April 2000 and handle more than 50 tonnes of packaging or packaging materials in any one year are obligated under the regulations.

Note that 'handling' of packaging refers to packaging which you supply on to your customers, *not* packaging that is waste on your premises (ie packaging around goods that you use). This packaging is the obligation of your supplier, who may contact you for information regarding the disposal of this material. You may be able to use this opportunity to get suppliers to take back packaging when they deliver, thereby fulfilling their obligations and reducing your costs. Conversely, any packaging you make or use to distribute your products contributes to your own obligation. **Remember, envelopes and packaging containing your sales brochures and unsolicited mail are packaging.**

Obligated companies must:

- Register with an appropriate agency (EA or SEPA) or join a registered collective collection scheme.
- Recover and recycle a percentage of their packaging waste (specific percentages will depend on where the business is in the packaging chain, ie packaging manufacturer; converter; packer filler; retailer).
- Provide annual data on the amount of packaging handled, recycled or recovered.
- Inform customers about their role in increasing recovery and recycling (retailers only).

The government has set targets that 43 per cent of packaging waste should be recovered and 10 per cent recycled by the end of 1999 and 45 and 13 per cent respectively in the year 2000.

The Environment Agency has a duty to monitor compliance with the Regulations in England and Wales and, where appropriate, to take enforcement action. To date, three companies have been prosecuted for non-compliance.

Many offices do not handle enough packaging to be directly obligated; however, the Regulations may impact on your operations in a number of ways, in particular:

- If you supply goods to a business which is obligated, they may ask you to give details of the weight of the packaging which you supply to them.
- As the cost of packaging increases as a result of this and other waste-related legislation, it makes sense to look critically at the way you package your products. You should also investigate whether packaging can be economically recycled or even better avoided altogether through re-usable packaging or improvements in processes or distribution.

Packaging (Essential Requirements) Regulations 1998
These regulations came into full effect in January 1999 to cover the EC Directive on Packaging and Packaging Waste (1994) provisions on waste minimisation, avoidance of noxious and hazardous substances and the need for packaging to be re-usable or recoverable.

Proposed legislation

Waste from Electrical and Electronic Equipment Directive (WEEE)

This proposed Directive sets out measures that aim at:

- Preventing waste electrical and electronic equipment.
- Re-using, recycling and other forms of recovery of such wastes.
- Minimising the risks and impacts to the environment associated with the treatment and disposal of waste electrical and electronic equipment.

Estimates suggest that electrical and electronic equipment make up 2–3 per cent of the entire European waste stream and this figure is set to rise. This new Directive will have a large impact on both producers and users of electronic and electrical goods but it is not expected to be implemented until 2002–2003.

The Landfill Directive

The EC Directive on the Landfill of Waste came into force on 16 July 1999. The Directive aims to harmonise controls on the landfill of waste throughout the EU and its main focus is on common standards for design, operation and aftercare of landfill sites. It also aims to reduce the amount of methane, a powerful greenhouse gas, emitted from landfill sites. Municipal biodegradable waste has been targeted for reduction as it is the biodegradable element of waste which produces methane as it breaks down. This Directive will require substantial changes to the way we manage waste in the UK.

The main requirements of the Landfill Directive are:

- By 2016 to reduce biodegradable municipal waste to landfill to 35 per cent of the total produced in 1995.
- Banning co-disposal of hazardous and non-hazardous wastes and requiring separate landfills for hazardous, non-hazardous and inert wastes.
- Banning landfill of tyres (by 2003 for whole tyres, 2006 for shredded tyres).
- Banning landfilling of liquid wastes, infectious clinical waste and certain types of hazardous waste (eg explosive, highly flammable) all by 2001.
- Provisions on the control, monitoring, reporting and closure of sites.

Government and industry initiatives

The government's *Waste Strategy 2000 for England and Wales* (DETR, 2000), acknowledges that changes in the way we think about waste and resources are essential to achieving sustainable development. This document highlights the importance of the waste hierarchy of reduction, re-use, recovery and disposal.

The primary targets set out in *Waste Strategy 2000* are:

- to reduce industrial and commercial waste sent to landfill to 85 per cent of 1998 levels by 2005;
- to recover 45 per cent and recycle or compost 30 per cent of municipal waste by 2010.

Waste from industry and commerce receives a high profile within the draft strategy, which states, 'Where waste is created we must recognise waste as a resource and recover more value from it'.

The Landfill Tax and the regulations implementing the Landfill Directive are considered to be the main instruments for achieving these goals. The UK is also likely to see an increase in incineration as a means of disposing of its rising waste burden.

The waste hierarchy

The Waste Strategy reinforces the importance of the waste hierarchy of reduction, re-use, recovery and disposal. Waste reduction at source is always the best commercial and environmental option. Reducing waste at source through careful purchasing and better utilisation of materials is the best way to make dramatic savings on your waste costs and reduce your impact on the environment. (Consider the recyclability and ultimate disposal of a product when making purchasing decisions, see Chapter 4, Purchasing.) Following this you should aim to re-use and recycle as much of the waste generated in your office as possible. Disposal of waste to landfill or incineration should be a last resort after all the above options have been considered.

National Waste Awareness Initiative (NWAI)

The NWAI is the largest dedicated waste awareness campaign ever launched in the UK. The campaign targets the general public and aims to achieve a measurable

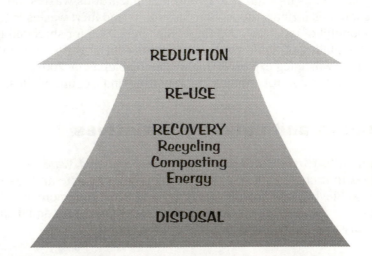

Figure 3.1 *The waste hierarchy*

change in awareness, attitudes and behaviour towards waste throughout the UK. Its objectives are: to improve the public's understanding of waste issues and recognition of the need for waste management facilities of all kinds; increase the level of personal ownership and responsibility for waste; and to promote reduction, re-use and recycling.

The initiative has been developed with the support of a wide range of sectors including non-governmental organisations, waste management companies, community recycling groups, regulators and central government and was officially launched in April 2000. The campaign is recognised by the government in its Waste Strategy and will produce a nationally recognised branding for waste awareness initiatives with the flexibility to adapt to local campaigns.

Tidy Britain Group

Tidy Britain Group is an independent charity campaigning for the improvement of local environments. It has a specific brief as the national anti-litter organisation.

Local awards schemes

Several local authorities now run business environment awards or tidy business schemes. An example of this is the Clean City Awards Scheme. Launched in 1994, the Clean City Awards Scheme is an initiative by the Corporation of London designed to develop a partnership with City businesses to achieve a cleaner environment through improved waste management.

The scheme aims to:

* Promote good waste management practices.
* Reduce waste stored on the highway.
* Ensure compliance with the Duty of Care regulations.
* Improve security.
* Encourage City organisations to take pride in their surroundings.

Entry into the award is free and there are now 450 premises registered on the Scheme. They represent 288 companies and 57 per cent of the 66,000 tonnes of commercial waste collected in the City over the past year by the Corporation's waste collection contractor.

Annual awards are given to businesses that meet a range of criteria following regular monitoring of their premises. Premier Awards are given to the two most outstanding sites each year.

WASTE DISPOSAL

Commercial waste in the UK is estimated at 21–29 million tonnes per annum (DETR, 1999a). The majority of waste from offices is disposed to landfill (85 per cent), 7.5 per cent to incineration and just 7.5 per cent is recycled or re-used.

🍁 Environmental issues

There is significant pressure to increase the amount of waste that is recycled or re-used as a result of the negative impacts of the UK's increasing waste burden.

The disposal of general waste has a significant environmental impact:

- Landfill sites can emit landfill gases (primarily methane and carbon dioxide). Both are significant greenhouse gases.
- Leachates from landfill sites can cause groundwater contamination.
- Landfill is unsightly and an inefficient use of land.
- There is a shortage of landfill sites: some of London's waste is transported to Oxfordshire for disposal.
- There is concern over the control of emissions from incinerators.

Landfill gas can be harnessed as a valuable source of energy. Methane capture is currently practised at over 150 landfill sites in the UK and in 1996 generated 136 MW of electricity.

In the UK, incineration is expected to have an increasing role in sustainable waste management strategies. Incineration is the burning of waste at high temperatures; this reduces the weight of the waste by about two-thirds and its volume by 90 per cent. Uncontrolled burning of waste can give off poisonous gases such as hydrochloric acid, dioxins and furans, and heavy metals. This often gives rise to concerns regarding the local impacts of incineration. However, very tough emission standards, stricter than those which apply to fossil fuel combustion, now apply to energy from waste plants.

Energy can be recovered from waste through direct waste incineration, through its use as a fuel substitute, through material recovery where energy is released as part of the process and through recovery of fuel (primarily methane) from landfill. There are currently 10 energy-from-waste plants in the UK generating some 200 megawatts (MW), enough electricity for a quarter of a million homes. Others are being constructed and planned. The potential for EfW is at least 1000 MW of renewable energy by 2010–2015.

In addition to generating electricity, there is the opportunity for combined heat and power plants which can provide heating for neighbouring homes and businesses. The government is promoting the uptake of combined heat and power (CHP) plants as they will also be a key factor in meeting our greenhouse gas emission targets.

Waste incineration with energy recovery combined with CHP plant and community heating systems has the potential to provide an integrated, sustainable and cost effective means of managing waste locally, particularly in urban areas. Incineration without energy recovery is categorised as waste disposal alongside landfill and is not seen as a favourable option in most cases.

☞ **Practical action**

Assess current arrangements

To assess the potential for reduced waste disposal costs for your company, you need to first investigate your current waste disposal arrangements. Some companies carry out a waste audit to establish a baseline against which progress can be measured. Larger organisations may find it cost effective to employ consultants to undertake their waste audit and prepare an action plan.

A waste audit should:

- Assess compliance with Duty of Care on the handling, storage and disposal of all wastes.
- Identify all points at which waste is produced.
- Establish methods for accurately measuring waste.
- Identify any hazardous wastes and consider how they can be eliminated or separated.
- Establish priorities for waste minimisation schemes.
- Look at opportunities to reduce, re-use or recycle wastes.
- Set quantified targets for waste reduction.
- Set responsibilities and timescales for achieving these targets.

Waste disposal costs

Establish the current costs of waste disposal. Charges are usually based on the size and number of containers and the frequency of collection. It is essential to find out exactly how charges are calculated as you may be overcharged, particularly if your waste minimisation and recycling efforts are successful in reducing the waste to be collected.

Remember that the true cost of waste includes the value of the paper, stationery, furniture and other equipment that you are throwing away. Check your bins and see if there is anything that should not be there. Could any wastes be avoided, re-used or recycled?

Additional disposal costs that should be included in your waste costs may be: clinical or sanitary waste; confidential waste (see below); special wastes (solvents and paints); ad hoc building and maintenance waste skips and recycling collection charges.

Reducing waste at source or retrieving materials for recycling will enable you to reduce the size and frequency of collection and therefore reduce costs.

Use Table 3.1 to calculate your total annual waste disposal cost.

Table 3.1 *General waste disposal costs*

Number of bins collected per year		Cost of collection of one bin		Rental charges or fees pa		General waste disposal cost (£)
	X		+		=	?

Table 3.2 *Additional waste disposal costs*

Ad hoc skips/ collections		Recycling collection charges		Special and sanitary waste collection charges		Additional waste disposal cost (£)
	X		+		=	?

Table 3.3 *Total annual waste disposal costs*

General waste disposal cost (£)		Additional waste disposal cost (£)		Total annual waste disposal cost (£)
	+		=	? + ?

Size of containers and frequency of collection

Identify the size and type of waste containers currently used. Contact your waste contractor to establish the maximum volume of material that they will take at each collection. You may be able to make substantial savings by reducing the number of bins, their size or frequency of collection. If a significant proportion of your waste is paper or cardboard (that cannot be reduced at source or recycled), investigate the cost effectiveness of investing in a compactor.

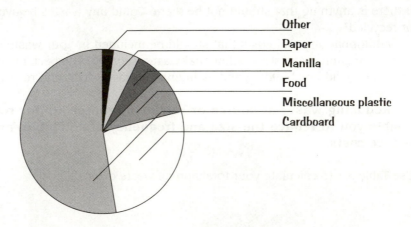

Other
Paper
Manilla
Food
Miscellaneous plastic
Cardboard

Figure 3.2 *Waste stream analysis for Wastebusters Ltd: An example of a good practice office*

Table 3.4 *Standard capacities of waste bins based on Landfill Tax calculations (HM Customs & Excise)*

Container size (litres)	Approximate weight of general waste contained (kg)
A black sack	10–15
1100 (Euro bin)	220
950 (paladin)	190
660	132
360	72
240	48
120	24

Table 3.5 *Weight of common waste products*

Waste type and quantity	Weight
4000 glass wine bottles	1 tonne (0.25 kg each)
50,000 drinks cans	1 tonne (0.02 kg each)
250,000 plastic vending cups	1 tonne
One laser printer toner cartridge	2 kg
One ream (500 sheets) of A4 paper (80 gsm)	2.5 kg

Storage areas

Identify storage restraints and potential areas for additional short-term storage. Storage areas should be assessed for fire risk. Ensure storage areas are adequately secure and well signposted to prevent them becoming a dumping ground!

Assessing materials

A waste audit should identify re-usable and recyclable products entering the waste stream and highlight where avoidable wastage may be occurring. Every office produces varying quantities of waste; however, the proportion of waste types is surprisingly consistent across all offices.

The proportions of plastic and cardboard are high in this office (Figure 3.2) because an effective recycling programme for paper and glass removes these materials from the waste stream. Wastebusters are currently unable to recycle cardboard and plastic effectively, and have therefore made a specific target of reducing these

Table 3.6 *Ready-reckoner: Total waste produced*

Number of waste bins used and their capacity	Approximate weight of general waste contained	Frequency of collection pa	Total waste produced pa
4 x 660 litre bins	4 x 60 kg = 240 kg	50 collections pa	50 x 240 kg = 12,000 kg

Table 3.7 *Ready-reckoner: Waste stream analysis*

Waste type	Percentage of total waste	Total weight of waste produced pa	Estimated weight of waste type produced pa
White paper	57	12,000 kg	6840 kg

wastes through waste minimisation, liaison with suppliers and re-use where possible. Produce a pie chart of your office waste stream, and compare with Figure 3.2.

Contact your waste management contractor for a guide to the average weight of your bins. Waste contractors are legally bound to weigh every load they receive but it is often difficult to get specific figures as waste is collected from several premises during a round. If you are unable to determine the actual weight of your bins, use the conversion figures in Tables 3.4 and 3.5 as a guide.

Use the calculation in Table 3.6 to translate the volume of your waste bins into weight in kilograms. This figure should **include waste that is recycled**. Calculate the weight of waste you recycle using the figures in Tables 3.4 and 3.5. Remember to add the volumes of any ad hoc collections of bulk wastes identified above.

Use the ready-reckoner in Table 3.7 to estimate the percentages of the main waste types in your waste stream. For example, if your company produces a total of 12,000 kg of waste per annum and you have estimated that 1320 kg of this is paper, you can calculate that 11 per cent of your total waste is paper. Paper is easily recyclable and diverting it from your general waste to landfill can significantly reduce your waste disposal costs.

Using Tables 3.8 and 3.9 you can calculate the weight of waste you dispose of per person every year. If your bins are not full when collected you will need to take this into account. If your bins are cubic yard containers use 0.15 instead of 0.2 as the conversion factor.

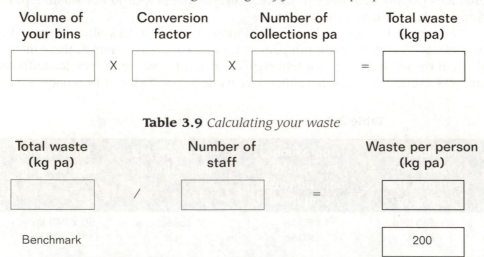

Table 3.8 *Calculating the weight of your waste per person*

Volume of your bins		Conversion factor		Number of collections pa		Total waste (kg pa)
	X		X		=	

Table 3.9 *Calculating your waste*

Total waste (kg pa)		Number of staff		Waste per person (kg pa)
	/		=	
Benchmark				200

Table 3.10 *Main office waste arisings and recommended disposal routes*

Waste	Waste classification	Preferred method of disposal
Highly confidential paper	General, commercial	Shred in house (or use specialist contractor) and recycle
Non-confidential white paper	General, commercial	Segregate and recycle
Cardboard	General, commercial	Flatten and recycle
Glass bottles: wine, mineral water and mixers	General, commercial	Segregate by colour and recycle
Aluminium and steel cans	General, commercial	Segregate (steel sticks to a magnet) and recycle
Plastic vending cups	General, commercial	Collect and recycle
Disposable items: hand towels, napkins, paper plates, plastic dishes and bottles, sandwich wrappings	General, commercial	General waste disposal
Toner cartridges	General, commercial	Return to supplier for recycling
Building waste from reorganisations and refurbishment	Difficult	Re-use within building or donate to local group for recycling
Electrical waste eg obsolete computers, printers and associated parts	Difficult	Return to supplier for recycling or donate to local refurbishment organisation
Used cooking oil	Difficult	Recycle
Food	Organic	Compost
Feminine hygiene products	Clinical	Disposal by specialist contractor
Fluorescent light tubes and bulbs (containing mercury)	Difficult	Store and recycle through specialist contractor
Fluorescent light tubes and bulbs (containing sodium)	Difficult	Disposal by specialist waste contractor
Chemical wastes from cleaning and building and grounds maintenance	Hazardous	Responsibility of contractor undertaking work, ensure they dispose of as special waste

Use this data to produce a pie chart of your waste stream, compare with Figure 3.2 and set targets for reduction in specific materials. Use Table 3.10 to ensure that you are maximising reduction and recycling opportunities.

SELECTING WASTE MANAGEMENT/RECYCLING CONTRACTORS

Recent developments

The major waste management companies are responding positively to the pressures on industry to implement waste reduction and recycling measures, and many are expanding their services to include recovery and recycling. Equally, several recycling companies are developing their services to include waste management.

There is also a growth in materials recovery facilities (MRFs) and waste-to-energy plants. An MRF is an operation which processes mixed wastes to recover materials for recycling. There are two main types, dirty or mixed waste MRFs and clean MRFs.

Grundon's Waste Management Park at Colnbrook sites a dirty MRF. The plant can take general household and commercial waste and requires no pre-sorting of materials. However, these systems have been criticised for reducing the need for active public participation and for producing greater quantities of less desirable materials and achieving recycling rates of no more than 20 per cent. In source-separated or 'clean' MRFs the recycling rate and revenue received on materials is much higher. There are often higher collection charges for waste processed through MRFs.

However, many local authorities are considering plans for MRFs and waste-to-energy plants in response to the Landfill Tax and the need to respond to the government's recycling targets.

There are considerable regional variations in the recycling facilities provided. It may be more difficult to find recycling contractors in rural areas but you should be able to substantially reduce your waste costs through reduction and re-use and focusing on only buying products that can be easily recycled in the local vicinity.

☞ Practical action

Choose the right contractor

Consider both specialist recycling companies and waste management companies. There may be benefits to your company of using one contractor for both services! Smaller specialist recycling companies often provide additional flexibility and are generally well placed to handle smaller organisations on a local basis. Whatever contractor you choose, ensure that they are equipped to deal with all of your waste requirements and can collect at times to suit you.

Clarify costs

Clarify exactly how costs are calculated. Costs can fluctuate due to materials markets. If the contractor is handling waste and recycling, is the revenue on paper off-set against the collection charges for waste? Are you paying for air?! Make sure you receive a breakdown of costs and any revenue you receive and get quotes from competing contractors. Make sure you take into account increases in landfill tax and price fluctuations within the recycling market.

Investigate!

Find out what happens to the material once it leaves your site. Is all material collected for recycling actually recycled? What happens to contaminated material?

Go out to tender

If you are a large organisation, go out to tender, preferably to a minimum of three companies. The market is highly competitive; ensure you are offered a competitive deal! Use the information collected in the waste stream analysis to give an indication of the potential volume of material. Combine the potential volume of recyclables from all offices in a large organisation. This often helps to ensure small offices are included in the collection round and larger volumes will attract a more competitive rate from contractors.

Contract terms

For larger organisations, make sure the terms for collection times and frequencies, equipment type and costs agreed are written into a contract. State the time period for which these terms apply. Stipulate how you wish to receive regular reports on waste volumes and recycling performance and make provisions (with financial benefits in your favour) for reductions in your waste volumes when your minimisation programme is a huge success! Ensure that the people responsible for environmental reporting in your company are involved in tender meetings. *See Case Study 4.5*↘

Environmental standards

Make sure the contractor is working in line with your own environmental policy. Check their environmental policy and report and ensure they have a clean safety and environment record over the past five years. Are they working towards an environmental management system such as ISO 14001? Do they have a commitment to maximise recycling and reduce the volume of material sent to landfill? If they are a landfill operator, do they take part in the Landfill Tax Credit Scheme and are they investing to improve their environmental performance?

⚠ Common problems

Increase in costs/drop in revenue

Less reputable companies will initially offer a low collection charge or even revenue, particularly on white office paper, in order to secure your business, only to increase the charges once the scheme is in operation. Ensure you agree terms in writing, preferably with a formal contract.

Summary guidelines

✔ Assess the volume and type of waste materials
✔ Identify storage restraints.
✔ Clarify how disposal and recycling costs are calculated
✔ Ensure specific details and costs are written in to contract documentation
✔ Check environmental credentials of contractors.
✔ Monitor your contractor's performance

SELECTING WASTE MANAGEMENT/RECYCLING CONTRACTORS

Fluctuations in materials markets

There are genuine fluctuations in the paper market and therefore it is difficult to guarantee revenue. Use a fixed price contract or monitor prices as quoted in the trade press such as *Material Recycling Week* as a guide.

Contamination

Promote the scheme effectively to avoid contamination. Make it clear what materials can and cannot be recycled, for example white paper is in, white paper envelopes with plastic windows are out! Agree an acceptable level of contamination with the contractor, otherwise you may find that your charges are suddenly increased or your waste is not collected!

Beware of cowboy operators!

Make sure your waste/recyclables are sent to landfill/recycling. Check the final destination of your waste.

Paying too much for waste disposal

If you use one contractor for recycling and waste, check that they are charging you competitively and monitor closely.

WASTE REDUCTION

Waste reduction is at the top of the waste hierarchy and is the most environmentally and commercially beneficial option. Remember that all waste is originally brought in as an asset and the true cost of waste includes the value of the products discarded. Waste minimisation should therefore be a priority and be promoted prior to recycling. Always follow the waste hierarchy; **reduce, re-use, recycle!** Avoid producing waste in the first place, then re-use and recycle what you have left.

☞ Practical action

There are a number of areas of potential waste reduction in the office, the most obvious being paper. Paper is considered here, but the principle of reduction, re-use and recycling can be applied to almost all office wastes.

Promote re-use

Smaller offices can re-use paper in-house very effectively. For example, paper that has only been used on one side can be fed back through the printer or fax machine. Obsolete letterhead paper can be turned into scrap pads.

Promote double-sided printing and copying

Make double-siding easy and make it the norm in your office. Set printers and photocopiers to double-side as default. Staff will then have to disable this mechanism to print or copy single-sided. An explanatory poster above the copier will help. Double-sided printing and copying also saves money on paper, postage and storage requirements.

Control office copying

Specify the use of print room facilities for high volume copying. This enables greater control over large runs and minimises wastage. Copy counters can calculate charges to different cost centres and raise awareness of wastage. The print room's policy should be to print double-sided unless otherwise specified.

Reprographics

If printing or marketing work is contracted out, build policies to minimise wastage and double-side unless otherwise specified into the contract.

Better use of technology

Make the use of email and electronic fax facilities standard in computer training. Ensure training for presentation packages such as 'PowerPoint' is available to those who need it. Electronic diaries and voice mail are becoming increasingly common and can considerably reduce paper consumption whilst improving efficiency.

Avoid unnecessary paper waste

Avoid wasteful header sheets for routine faxes; use fax tabs where possible. Make sure machines are not set to print out a transmission report for every fax. Discourage the printing of hard copies or documents, unless absolutely necessary. Storing documents electronically, password protected, also removes some of the problems around secure storage of confidential documents. A specific area for potential reduction in local authorities is to reduce circulation of Committee Papers. Discuss circulation with members and officers to identify areas of reduction. Members are often grateful to have more targeted information to read!

Marketing materials

Decisions made at the design stage can significantly reduce paper usage. Consider the size of the print used, page layout and the weight of paper. This is particularly important in the case of documents with a large circulation such as your annual report or corporate brochure. Control the number of copies printed and use electronic communication where possible to view drafts and revisions. Resist the temptation to over-order marketing materials or designing them to be robust, particularly if the information is likely to date quickly.

Case Study 3.1

SUBJECT: **Waste Minimisation**

ORGANISATION: **Wilkin and Sons Limited**

LOCATION: **Tiptree, Essex**

STAFF: **180**

Background
Wilkin and Sons of Tiptree are an internationally renowned jam and marmalade manufacturer with 180 staff. They have 70 product lines including a new organic range and produce 100,000 jars of product per day.

Action
The company has always been concerned for the environment and has taken considerable steps to address water and energy consumption, reduce waste and recycle materials. The company adopted a coordinated approach to waste minimisation starting with a comprehensive scoping audit carried out by the Environment Agency. As a result of this, an in-house waste and energy team was established and a range of waste minimisation and management improvement measures have been implemented. Senior level commitment has been central to the success of Wilkin and Sons' improvements, accompanied by keen staff and good communication of the benefits of good practice both internally and with other local businesses.

Results
Savings to date include:

- 50 tonnes reduction in waste to landfill saving £2500 per year.
- Over 250 tonnes of waste recycled including 80 tonnes of cardboard, 40 tonnes of glass and 25 tonnes of metal.

Other achievements:

- Office paper and plastic cup recycling schemes set up (free of charge).
- Segregation of waste at source to ensure maximum recycling rates.
- Raw materials and cleaning/maintenance chemicals purchased in returnable containers.

And every company has its own unique areas for potential savings…

- 108 tonnes of process fruit waste for composting and animal feed.
- 177,000 litres of liquor used to cook oranges re-used, saving £4000!

Wilkin and Sons are actively involved in the Essex and Colchester waste minimisation clubs and have close ties with the Environment Agency.

'A few years ago what thoughts we had on waste minimisation were tinged with scepticism. Since then we have become converts. Waste minimisation does incur costs, certainly, as well as requiring a good measure of commitment and consensus, but these are more than rewarded. Not only are there direct financial benefits for the Company, but I am convinced there are also intangible, psychological benefits that spring from the knowledge that we are doing something which also benefits the wider community.'

Peter Wilkin, Chairman of Wilkin and Sons Ltd ∎

Barclays produces a quarterly video that provides its staff with an update on the business worldwide. Some 10,000 videos are distributed annually. A video re-use scheme was introduced for the December 1999 edition. A return address is printed on the video sleeve; the returned videos are then collected by the reproduction company which erases the old edition and records the new. A green dot is applied as evidence of re-use as it is considered feasible to re-use each video three times.

Reduce waste in meetings and presentations

Avoid the use of A3 flip charts in meeting rooms where possible. Use white boards and recorders where available. Use computer-based presentation packages whereby information can be projected directly from a PC screen, avoiding the need for non-recyclable acetate slides. Provide paper recycling bins for scrap paper and circulate minutes by email.

Stationery

Hold a stationery amnesty to retrieve all those stray pens, pencils, etc. Office moves can be seen as an opportunity to order new stationery. Make sure departments take their stationery with them!

For example, AEA Technology Environment recovered over £62,000 in unused stationery and computer equipment, and saved some £8,000 in not having to order new items, following a recent office 'Spring Clean' initiative. The idea to encourage staff to return unused stationery and computer equipment to stationery cupboards for reuse was raised by an employee. A project manager was appointed to take the initiative forward. Posters and a newsletter were produced to highlight the benefits, the role employees could play, and the items they could consider for reuse. As a result, over 13,000 items of stationery and in excess of 150 items of computer equipment were recovered.

Case Study 3.2

SUBJECT: **Glass Recycling and Catering**

ORGANISATION: **Crofton Halls**

LOCATION: **Orpington, Kent**

STAFF: **10**

Background
The Crofton Halls are community halls providing meeting facilities for the local community and operated by Bromley Council. The facilities comprise meeting rooms and halls with a total capacity of 600 people.

The halls are used by a wide range of community groups including: playgroups, fitness classes, disability groups, social functions, weddings and fundraisers. The halls have about 155,000 visitors a year.

Action
Crofton Halls recycle around 1 tonne of glass per month with Cleanaway and have distributed information material on recycling throughout the premises. Aluminium cans are collected by the Oakfield Recycling Project. Toner cartridges and office paper are recycled. The management is currently developing environmental recommendations to be distributed to caterers on how they can minimise their environmental impact through such measures as the use of cutlery and porcelain plates rather than disposable materials. The Halls are also looking to purchase environmentally sensitive cleaning and sanitary products in the upcoming financial year.

Results
By implementing relatively simple recycling schemes and involving all staff, the Crofton Halls can expect to see sizeable savings on a yearly basis. These will be increased by ongoing environmental improvements and an educational approach towards engaging visitors, caterers and suppliers alike to follow by their example.

- 15 tonnes of glass diverted from landfill per annum.
- £100 of disposal costs saved per annum. ■

Cleaning and catering
For waste reduction initiatives in cleaning and catering *see Chapter 4, Purchasing*

Case Study 3.3

SUBJECT: **Waste Alert Club Network**

ORGANISATION: **Wastebusters Ltd**

LOCATION: **London and Surrey**

STAFF: **4**

Background

Waste Alert is a project created and managed by Wastebusters Ltd. It is a network of waste minimisation clubs helping small businesses to reduce costs and increase efficiency through improved waste management and exchange of materials. Larger organisations are encouraged to act as mentors, by providing good practice case studies and support to smaller companies through the supply chain. Waste Alert is unique in being the first waste minimisation club to focus specifically on small businesses and waste exchange and to replicate in the UK.

The network covers the boroughs of Bromley and Bexley, Camden, Haringey, Islington and Harrow. This network provides significant potential to exchange information and best practice and is supported by a large network of contacts and resources. Wastebusters act as facilitators to encourage good practice and disseminate the benefits of waste minimisation without re-inventing the wheel in each new area. The network is the result of building successful partnerships with a range of organisations including local authorities, the Environment Agency, Thames Water, Shanks Waste Solutions, Cory Environmental and the corporate sector including Glaxo Wellcome.

Action

Club members receive ongoing support and advice for waste minimisation initiatives, which are tailored to their individual needs. Services offered include a free consultancy visit and information packs, the Waste Exchange, a dedicated helpline service, a quarterly newsletter, regular free events, opportunities to network with other local businesses, updates about important changes to legislation and recycling discounts.

Waste Alert South Thames was the first club in the network to be established and was launched in May 1998. In the first year, members re-used and recycled 200 tonnes of waste and saved over £50,000, an average of £1000 per member. The Waste Exchange service is one of the most popular aspects of the Club. Members' exchanges have included 700 bike frames, which were sent to Botswana and South Africa, 1000 CDs from London Weekend Television's music library were sent to Aylesbury Recycling (part of the Aylesbury Day Centre in Lambeth) who are distributing them free to local schools, and everything from office furniture, textile off-cuts, computers, books and carpets. Nine Transit vans of clothing were sent to Kosovo, Croatia and Belarus and even sawdust has been exchanged! Other materials such as specialist silver bubble-wrap used to deliver computers to Wastebusters office, made great astronaut costumes for a local school! Scrap stores are a useful outlet for clean commercial waste such as paper and card, which would otherwise be consigned to landfill. Scrap stores are used by schools, playgroups, theatre groups and artists and give a second useful life to just about any materials.

Results
- 3 Waste Alert Clubs across London.
- 270 business members.
- 834 tonnes of waste diverted from landfill.
- £233,000 savings in waste disposal and purchasing costs for members. ∎

⚠ Common problems

Paperless office?

Many staff are not confident about storing correspondence and emails on their computer system and prefer to print them out for filing. Ensure staff are fully trained in electronic communication and storage and amend procedures where necessary to avoid unnecessary printing, circulation and storage of documents.

Summary guidelines

- ✔ Do you need it?!
- ✔ Investigate opportunities to use less
- ✔ Investigate re-usable or recyclable alternatives
- ✔ Increase use of technology to reduce paper usage
- ✔ Encourage staff to come up with ideas on waste reduction
- ✔ Promote waste reduction initiatives before recycling
- ✔ Find out about waste minimisation and exchange in your area. Contact the ETBPP for your nearest club

WASTE REDUCTION

Printers and photocopiers

Printers and photocopiers are often accused of having a mind of their own! Ensure all staff are trained to operate printers and copiers and put posters above to explain double-siding and other specific operations. Arrange a regular maintenance programme to reduce paper jams.

Waste exchange

The concept is simple, one man's waste is another man's gold. First invented in the UK and made famous by the salvage and recycling operations of World War II, materials and waste exchanges offer a vital link between business and local communities and are enjoying a resurgence in the UK.

Waste exchanges provide a 'matching' service, a kind of dating agency for waste!

For example: 679 unwanted sound effect CDs from London Weekend Television's music library were given to the Aylesbury

Case Study 3.4

SUBJECT: **Waste Exchange: Waste Alert Clubs**

ORGANISATION: **Reclign**

LOCATION: **Sydenham, London**

STAFF: **2**

Background

Reclign design and create fine hand-made furniture and artefacts. All of their unique pieces are crafted from reclaimed timber that gives the items their own history. Reclign was established in 1997 by John Turner and became a member of Waste Alert South Thames in March of this year. Some of the work completed by John has been made from wood that was retrieved from the old veranda at the 'Ham Polo Club' in Richmond, as well as the site of the new 'Vinopolis - City of Wine' attraction in Southwark. Reclign also stocks pieces by other artists who are working in reclaimed materials, including cards, wrought iron beds, stained glass and ceramics.

Action

Reclign has used the Waste Alert monthly Waste Exchange listing on several occasions and has made a number of beneficial contacts through the Waste Alert club network in London.

The London Wood Bank (LWB), another Waste Alert South Thames member, reclaims wood from various construction sites around London. The LWB supplied Reclign with a van of re-usable wood and Reclign now sells recycled greeting cards supplied by the LWB. Furthermore, LWB now display Reclign's work at trade events, forming a valuable partnership between two small businesses.

Reclign benefited from another exchange, this time from Waste Alert Bromley and Bexley when Langley Park School for Girls renovated their science laboratories. As the labs were demolished, Reclign picked up three vanloads of high quality wood, including some mahogany. As a result of this exchange, 2 tonnes of waste were diverted from landfill.

Waste Alert has also put Reclign in touch with other members of Waste Alert; Blue Mountain Café in Forest Hill now display Reclign's work and Fortress Antiques in Dulwich are currently planning to work with Reclign for an exhibition. Reclign's partnership with Waste Alert has received publicity in *Materials Recycling Weekly*, a National trade magazine, as well as in the local press. This promotion has led to offers of waste timber and display space in other outlets.

Results

This best practice example proves that there are useful alternatives to landfilling or burning old wood. It also shows that networking, made possible through business clubs like Waste Alert, can have positive impacts on the local business community by increasing communication and trade between SMEs.

- £200 in purchasing costs saved.
- £800 in extra sales generated.
- More than 3 tonnes of wood diverted from landfill.

'Waste Alert epitomises the strong ethical values I believe in and are the foundation of Reclign. I get extremely excited by their enthusiasm and I'm overwhelmed by the help they've given and the work, against the odds, that they are doing. Everyone in the world should join.'

John Turner, Reclign ■

Day Centre, which runs a re-use and recycling facility. The CDs have been distributed free to local schools. It is estimated that these specialised CDs will save the eventual users over £8700 in purchasing costs.

Similarly, approximately 400 books cleared from Arcturus Publishing in London Bridge were 're-housed' at the Voluntary Day Centre in Forest Hill, which put together Christmas packages for underprivileged families. This diverted one-third of a tonne of waste from landfill and saved the Care Centre £3150 in purchasing costs.

Waste exchange is the ideal waste management option for bulky wastes such as furniture and IT equipment where the savings through both disposal costs and purchasing costs for the recipient can be substantial. In addition, waste exchanges can often re-use things that cannot be recycled.

RECYCLING

Following your efforts to reduce and re-use, recycle as much of your remaining waste as possible. On average 60–70 per cent of office waste is recyclable.

Recycling is not without its own environmental impact; however, it generally has clear environmental benefits over disposal to landfill. Recycling waste materials provides a valuable supply of recyclate for product manufacturers and diverts waste from landfill. Using more recycled materials in everyday products means that less virgin raw materials need to be extracted and in turn more waste is diverted from landfill or incineration. Buying recycled products also stimulates the recycling market. *See Chapter 4, Purchasing* ↘

Case Study 3.5

SUBJECT: **Recycling**

ORGANISATION: **Kodak Ltd**

LOCATION: **Harrow**

STAFF: **2000**

Background

The Kodak site in Harrow has 2000 employees. It manufactures a wide range of film materials for the printing and publishing industry and for photographers and photo processing companies across Europe, Africa and the Middle East. It is the only Kodak manufacturer of these products in the UK.

Action

Kodak started their recycling practices over 30 years ago with the reclamation of silver from manufacturing processes. This economic prudence is being extrapolated into other waste management areas and this materials re-use and recycling will help Kodak reach its goal of world-class manufacturer of photographic products. Kodak (Harrow) gained ISO 14001 status in 1998 and numerous steps have been taken to increase re-use and recycling and improve the environmental performance of the whole site. In 1999:

- 2200 gallons of oil were collected and recycled.
- 156 tonnes of polythene was collected and re-used to make low grade plastic materials such as rubbish bags.
- 233 tonnes of excess molten polythene was collected into troughs and solidified into polythene logs. These were then sold on to make screwdriver handles.
- Around 2500 tonnes of waste coated paper was sold to Fibre Fuels in Slough to make fuel briquettes.
- 222 tonnes of cardboard was collected and returned to the suppliers, who pulp it for re-use.
- Chemical containers (metal and plastic) were returned to suppliers for washing and re-use.
- £700 was donated to the Children's Ward of Northwick Park Hospital as a result of toner cartridge remanufacturing.
- Office furniture was donated to schools and charities and computers were either re-used or recycled.

Results

- The recycling rate of all materials at Kodak (Harrow) increased from 64 per cent at the start of 1999 to 80 per cent by the end of the year.
- Material going to landfill was reduced by 60 per cent in 1999.
- Annual cost saving from re-use and recycling practices is £40,000 per year.

Kodak's recycling target has now been raised to 85 per cent in 2000. ∎

☞ Practical action

To investigate the feasibility of recycling schemes in your office establish the following:

Potential volume of material

Recycling contractors will need to know the anticipated volume of waste you wish to recycle in order to assess feasibility of collection. It is not environmentally sound to make a long journey to collect half a sack of paper!

Contractor to be used

Recycling facilities vary considerably depending on the area of the country. Before you collect materials for recycling, find a local contractor who can meet your requirements cost effectively. Larger organisations may benefit from setting up a national contract to cover all offices. *See Selecting Waste Management/Recycling Contractors, page 34* ✦ If you work in a smaller office, or waste volumes are low, contact your local authority Recycling Officer, who should know what services are available for different materials in your area.

Collection arrangements

Collection charges and/or potential revenue are linked to volume. For example, a contractor may charge to collect a small quantity of paper (especially if it is mixed and of poor quality). However, you may be able to negotiate payment for high-quality white paper if the volume is sufficient. Note that the price can be affected by fluctuations in the paper market.

Storage restraints

If storage is limited, it may be impractical to store material for several weeks to reach the minimum volume required by the contractor. Ensure that safety and fire risks are fully considered when assessing suitable storage areas.

Establish your recycling rate

Use the figures for total waste generation (page 31) to establish your potential recycling rate. On average, 60–70 per cent of office waste is recyclable.

Table 3.11 *Recycling rate*

Annual waste recycled (kg)		Total annual waste disposal (kg)				Recycling rate (%)
	÷		X	100	=	

Compare your recycling rates with industry averages. *See Chapter 9, Environmental Reporting* ➘

Type of material

Establish exactly what the contractor will and won't accept and at what rates, prior to setting up a contract. For example: most toner cartridges are recyclable, but not all; some contractors demand segregated materials, others will accept mixed for a charge.

Communication and promotion

It has to be easy for staff to recycle, otherwise it will not happen! Staff need to know what can and cannot go in collection bins to avoid contamination. Dispel the myths! *See Chapter 7, Communication*

PAPER

 ## Environmental issues

Paper, which accounts for over a third of our waste, is often still disposed of in landfill sites or by incineration.

Recycling paper has many environmental benefits and has a high profile:

- High-quality recycled paper can be made without re-bleaching, if it is correctly sorted.
- Recycling paper helps to reduce the pressure on biodiversity resulting from intensive forestry. The paper industry plants more trees than it chops down, but natural habitats are often destroyed to make way for intensive tree farming.
- Recycling paper is more energy-efficient than making virgin paper from wood.
- Paper – a biodegradable resource – is diverted from landfill; this helps reduce methane emissions.

For more detail on the environmental issues associated with paper. *See Chapter 4, Purchasing*

Changes in the paper market

The paper market is renowned for fluctuations. This has affected the feasibility of some recycling services in the past and has led to increased costs for collection of mixed paper. The construction of two de-inking plants in the UK at Aylesford (SCA) and Kemsley (UK Paper) has successfully increased the demand for paper collected for recycling; however, paper recycling rarely raises the revenue it did in the past, and in some cases you will have to pay for collection. In spite of the fluctuations in the paper market, paper recycling schemes are still cost effective because they reduce waste to landfill and therefore waste disposal costs.

There are now many more opportunities for sourcing high-quality recycled business papers; for example, UK Paper produces the high-quality 'Evolve Business' paper from the Kemsley plant which provides an excellent opportunity for all offices to close the recycling loop. *See Chapter 4, Purchasing* �‚

☞ Practical action

High-quality office paper and computer paper can be recycled very efficiently to make more office papers and tissue paper. Mixed waste paper and the lower grades are generally used for low-grade paper products and packaging material.

There is an expansion of recycling schemes for mixed paper, which helps reduce some of the traditional problems of contamination. Mixed paper schemes minimise the total volume of material sent to landfill. However, separation of white paper where volume is sufficient will give a higher revenue.

When considering the viability of paper recycling schemes, consider the generic points made earlier in the chapter and the specific points below.

Assessment

Volume and type of material
Collection charges and/or potential revenue are linked to volume and quality of material. Mixing white paper with cardboard and newspapers will probably ensure that the paper merchant leaves your load behind!

Some merchants will collect mixed coloured and white paper, which will mean less effort at your end. However, it is financially and environmentally preferable to separate white office paper from mixed, since it can be used to make high-quality office paper. Mixed paper can usually only be used to make low grades of paper.

Recycling low-grade waste
Cardboard, newspapers, brochures and magazines are potentially recyclable, but are all low-grade waste. These have a low market value, so paper merchants will often make a charge to collect them. Charges vary considerably and it is often easier to find a willing contractor if they are also collecting your higher-grade waste. A more practical alternative for cardboard is to ensure that suppliers retrieve packaging materials when they deliver.

Revenue and collection charges
The paper market is fairly volatile: prices paid for recycled paper do fluctuate. This may mean that the costs of recycling are not constant. Revenue for paper is generally based on quantities of half a tonne upwards. For smaller quantities, you are very unlikely to receive revenue, but should be able to have segregated white office paper collected for a nominal charge. Small organisations may be able to find other waste exchange opportunities for used paper.

Confidential waste
If the contractor chosen for paper recycling operates to good levels of security, it should be possible to reduce the volume of material sent for confidential shredding.

Obviously some material is highly sensitive, but there is often room for more discrimination. Staff must realise that there is a cost to the company. Are internal memos really confidential? If the remaining material is highly sensitive, be extremely vigilant regarding the level of security provided by the contractor. It may be more cost effective to combine security waste with non-confidential paper and therefore find a contractor to handle both. Establish how charges are calculated: per collection of a minimum volume or per sack.

Follow these guidelines:

- Ensure confidential waste bins are clearly labelled and locked. Security risks can be of concern in-house as well as externally.
- Ensure the contractor provides tagged security sacks and certificates of destruction.
- Verify the level of security provided by the contractor. They must have a system of security clearance for waste handlers and their security procedure must extend to the transit of the materials. Vehicles should be kept locked and transit time minimised.
- Give clear instructions to the contractor regarding subcontractors: subcontracting should not be allowed without clearance from yourselves. Regular monitoring of the contractor's performance is important.
- Clarify: the cost per tonne of security shredding, minimum quantities for collection and the amount of material to be shredded.
- Visit the contractor's site to check the security of their premises and operations.

Collection systems

It has to be easy for staff to recycle paper, otherwise it will not happen. However, you must create a balance between having enough containers (so that staff do not have to go far to use them) and having too many (making it too easy encourages contamination and many bins will cost more to empty!). Most recycling companies can provide you with suitable containers in a wide range of colours and sizes. They can even be printed with your company logo.

- Use medium-sized bins (holding about 10 kg of paper) distributed evenly around the office, allowing one container per 7–10 staff. This means that staff need to think before they throw paper away, but don't have to do a route march to reach the bins! Put extra bins in key areas such as copier and print rooms.
- Add individual desktop trays to supplement the above scheme. Make staff responsible for emptying their own desktop trays into the larger bins. Purchase desktop trays from your recycling contractor or use the lids from paper boxes. The lids of Evolve Business recycled paper produced by UK Paper are designed for use as paper trays.
- As an alternative, make all individual bins paper only and have a centralised bin for all other general waste (one per office or six people). This will reduce costs as cleaners will only have to empty the single centralised bin instead of many smaller bins and will make people think about the paper they discard.

Case Study 3.6

SUBJECT: **Paper Recycling**

ORGANISATION: **Broomleigh Housing Association**

LOCATION: **Kent [three sites]**

STAFF: **250 [office]**

Background
The Broomleigh Housing Association is one of the UK's largest housing associations with over 14,000 units. They have four offices in Bromley and the majority of their housing stock is concentrated in the borough.

Action
Following an ETBPP Helpline visit, the Broomleigh Housing Association now recycles office paper at its three Bromley offices. They are also looking at environmental management systems through a project with the Housing Foundation. They have a committee dedicated to environmental issues within the organisation and are aiming for certification in environmental management.

Broomleigh has also incorporated environmental criteria into the development of housing stock. They have worked with Architype Architects (members of Waste Alert South Thames) to develop self-build housing that focuses on energy efficiency and the use of recycled materials.

Results
Initiatives such as paper recycling and the monitoring of energy usage are expected to save Broomleigh over 100 tonnes of waste per year and nearly £4000 in disposal costs. With further improvements the organisation can expect to save significantly more whilst continuing to strengthen their environmental profile.

- 100 tonnes of paper waste saved per annum.
- £4000 saved in disposal costs per annum. ∎

Cleaning contractors
Cleaning contractors play an important role in the success of recycling schemes and they should be involved in the planning stage. It is very frustrating, if you have been collecting paper for recycling, to find that your cleaning staff have thrown it out! One of Wastebusters' clients thought they had been recycling for three years, when in fact the cleaning staff had been putting the green bags in the skip! There need not be any additional work for the cleaners as the amount of waste you are discarding will be identical – well, hopefully less! If you have problems with your

cleaning contractor, use the re-negotiation of their contract as an ideal time to raise the issue. For example: a change of cleaning contractor at Lehmans, to Lancaster Cleaning, has had a significant impact on the success of the paper recycling scheme. Lancasters were enthusiastic and also recognised the opportunity to improve waste handling arrangements by the introduction of a more efficient recycling scheme. They monitored the scheme daily and allocated a specific member of staff to managing the recycling.

Cleaning staff need to know what the arrangements are and what is expected from them. Follow these guidelines:

- Collection of recyclables needs to be coordinated with the cleaning schedule. The cleaners will need to retrieve the recycling sacks to meet collection times.
- Establish contact points for cleaners and recycling contractors to handle any problems on a day-to-day basis.
- Find out if there is an additional charge for handling recycling schemes. Most cleaning companies appreciate that they need to be receptive to recycling. After all, they are not handling any extra waste.
- Find a short-term storage area for recyclables prior to collection.
- Make sure that the cleaners retrieve and replace recycling sacks when the bins are full.
- Hold regular feedback sessions with cleaners to resolve issues before they become problems.

⚠ Common problems

Contamination

Many companies introduce a dual-bin system, whereby a bin for paper recycling is placed under each desk alongside the general waste bin. This system obviously encourages staff to recycle, but it also encourages contamination. A frequent problem is that everything goes into the paper recycling bin including plastic cups, sandwich wrappers, etc. If paper recycling schemes are heavily contaminated, paper merchants will not collect or will charge for collection. This is where most schemes fail.

Manilla envelopes, newspaper and anything with a lot of glue or a plastic laminated finish should be avoided. Check with your contractor what they will not take. Make it clear to staff what can and cannot be recycled. Reduce the use of laminates in your publicity material.

> ### Summary guidelines
>
> ✔ Assess the potential volume and type of material
> ✔ Find a market for the material
> ✔ Investigate collection arrangements
> ✔ Consider storage restraints
> ✔ Decide on the method of collection
> ✔ Launch the scheme: refer to Chapter 7 for details
>
> **PAPER**

Case Study 3.7

SUBJECT: **Recycling**

ORGANISATION: **British Hospitality Association**

LOCATION: **London**

STAFF: **11**

Background

The British Hospitality Association (BHA) is the National Trade Association for the hotel, restaurant and catering industry. It has been the industry's principal driving force to lobby government since it was formed over 90 years ago. The British Hospitality Association represents 25,000 hotels, restaurants and contract caterers.

As well as promoting the benefits of environmental action to members, the BHA in 1999 started to devise an environmental strategy for implementation at the Head Office in London.

Action

After a consultation visit from Waste Alert Camden (who helped the BHA to identify the key areas of the environmental impact of their activities) a nine-point action plan was drawn up which included the subject of waste management.

It was decided that facilities should be provided for the recycling of paper (including magazines, glossy brochures, etc); glass; cardboard and toner cartridges. A spare office was set aside as a dedicated recycling area. Containers were provided for the sorting of waste and unused furniture was removed by the council for recycling. It was decided that waste paper should be collected by Pulp Faction Recycling, based in North London, for a small fee. Toner cartridges are refilled twice and subsequently collected for recycling by the stationery supplier, PADS, free of charge. Glass is recycled at a local bottle bank.

Results

The recycling initiatives are proving to be very popular with the BHA team. Over 30 bags of waste paper have been collected so far – approximately 1.5 tonnes of waste. The small cost of removal should be offset by savings made by implementation of other areas of the action plan; for example, using a lighter weight recycled paper for letterhead paper and an energy management campaign.

The initiatives have been noticed and implemented by other companies that the BHA works with; for example, toner recycling is now run as a joint initiative with the Periodical Publishers Association (based in the same building). They will be working together again in 2000 to implement a recycling scheme for fluorescent tubes. ■

Storage restraints

Your storage restraints will determine the frequency of collection required. For example, in Central London, storage is generally very tight, since space costs money! The fire risk also needs to be considered when assessing suitable storage areas. If you have storage space, you may be able to store half a tonne of paper and therefore receive revenue. Work with neighbouring businesses to combine collections or storage facilities.

Communication

The key to the successful introduction of recycling programmes is effective communication. Without the commitment of individuals, the programme will never be successful and achieve the potential cost savings identified. See Chapter 7, Communication, for effective launch programmes.

ORGANIC WASTE

Environmental issues

The UK currently landfills around 27 million tonnes of municipal waste each year. Approximately 60 per cent of this is biodegradable – waste that is capable of undergoing anaerobic or aerobic decomposition, such as food and garden waste, paper and paperboard. The environmental and economic impact of using landfill sites is discussed under Waste Disposal in this chapter.

The importance of composting has been highlighted in the Waste Strategy as essential to meeting the proposed targets set in the recently adopted EC Landfill Directive. These targets have strong implications for local authorities and the public but will also affect the way businesses handle their organic waste.

- By 2020, reduce biodegradable municipal waste landfilled to 35 per cent of the total produced in 1995.
- Intermediate targets of 75 per cent by 2010 and 50 per cent by 2013 are also imposed.

For further details on grounds maintenance and green waste, see Chapter 4 Purchasing.

Practical action

Donate waste food

In the past, it has been possible to dispose of food waste (from company restaurants, for example) as pig swill. However, food hygiene regulations have been tightened up and it now has to be sterilised first, which is generally prohibitively expensive.

However, Crisis, the national charity for single homeless people, have set up Crisis Fareshare. They will collect quality surplus fresh food and redistribute to hostels and day centres providing meals to homeless people in London, Southampton, Birmingham, South Yorkshire, Huddersfield and Manchester. They have strict controls over food handling and ensure that all sites are adhering to the food hygiene regulations and ensure correct food storage and preparation at all times.

They ask that donated food is of good quality and within its use by date. It needs to be stored and prepared according to current legislation. If it is pre-prepared it needs to be kept chilled and covered.

Introduce composting

If your food waste is unsuitable, or this facility is not available in your area, consider introducing a composting system, to cope with both food and, if your company has its own grounds, garden waste. Composting is the biological decomposition of organic waste under controlled conditions.

There are three main methods of composting: wormeries, traditional composting and large-scale composting.

Wormeries

A wormery uses tiger worms to digest waste and can reduce its contents by as much as 80 per cent. They need more attention than the aerobic system (compost heap). It can be kept indoors or outdoors and is suited to small volumes of material. A 50:50 split between garden and food waste is preferable. Wormeries produce good quality compost and liquid fertiliser. The compost produced is richer than that produced by traditional methods and can be used to refine compost from traditional heaps. Wormeries are ideal for use by smaller offices in rural locations.

Shot in the Dark, an environmental media company in West Yorkshire, has an innovative recycling scheme. Cardboard boxes and packing materials are re-used where possible and if not re-usable are sent to a local community farm where they are shredded and used for animal bedding. This is then put into a wormery where it is decomposed and then sold as compost!

Traditional composting

Traditional composting is suited to a large volume of material and can cope with a higher garden waste content than a wormery can, since compost heaps generate enough heat to kill weed seeds. They must be outdoors with good drainage to cope with run-off. Traditional compost heaps do not break waste down as finely as wormeries. An additional outlet may be needed for excess compost: local schools, nurseries, allotment growers and your own staff may be grateful recipients! Your local council may be a good source of information.

Large-scale composting

Where the volume of compost is sufficient, it may be more practical to take organic waste to a composting plant. Some local authorities have developed composting facilities for household waste. However, there is normally a charge for this, so it is only viable if there is a substantial volume of material.

Case Study 3.8

SUBJECT: **Composting**

ORGANISATION: **Horniman Museum and Gardens**

LOCATION: **Lewisham, London**

STAFF: **12**

Background
The gardens consist of 16 acres of park with a Victorian conservatory that is used for private functions. The gardens also include the CUE (Centre for Understanding the Environment) which is an ecologically designed building surrounded by ponds and a bed of reeds with a grass roof. The Museum and Gardens have over 250,000 visitors a year.

Action
Since October 1997 the gardens have introduced a composting scheme for all green waste. This includes grass cuttings, leaves and wood trimmings. Material is processed through a chipper and a substance called 'garota' added to speed up the composting process. The gardens are keen to publicise the scheme to visitors and the general public to raise environmental awareness and demonstrate good practice.

Other wastes
The remaining wastes are litter, mixed metals, and glass from functions in the Conservatory. Cleanaway provide 2 x 1100 litre Eurobins for litter. The gardens are also intending to introduce a glass recycling scheme through Cleanaway, which is cheaper than the charges for general waste.

A small quantity of mixed metal is produced annually which is currently now taken, free of charge, to a scrap dealer to be recycled.

Plants are grown by the gardens and plant pots are re-used. Compost no longer needs to be purchased from an external supplier.

Results
The scheme has been very successful and has reduced the demand for skips from 50 per annum to 10. Charges were £120 per skip, giving cost savings of £4800 per annum. In addition, the gardens are no longer buying in compost – this was costing £68 per tonne and the quality produced by the gardens is better. The gardens estimate that the scheme is saving £35 per cubic metre of compost produced. The estimated annual savings are over £10,000, with approximately 20 tonnes of waste diverted from landfill. In total, by minimising waste in its gardens, the Horniman expects to save over £12,000 per annum. ∎

Assess your options

Potential volume and type of material

This will determine the most suitable composting option. Wormeries are not capable of handling large volumes of waste, unlike traditional compost heaps. Wormeries cope better with a 50:50 split between garden and kitchen waste. If the volume of garden waste is greater than kitchen waste, then a traditional compost heap is more suitable.

Collection systems

If you introduce an in-house system, you can easily retrieve materials from your restaurant and grounds. However, if the volume is substantial, you will need to arrange transportation of the material to the nearest site. The assessment of volume will determine financial viability.

Summary guidelines

- ✔ Donate quality excess food to Crisis or similar local charity
- ✔ Install a wormery if the volume of material is small with a high proportion of kitchen waste (particularly useful for small companies with their own kitchen facilities)
- ✔ If the majority of the material is garden waste, use a traditional compost heap
- ✔ Take material to a municipal site where volume ensures it is cost effective
- ✔ Find additional outlets for the compost, if necessary, for example, schools and nurseries
- ✔ Monitor the quality of material going into the composting system
- ✔ Buy back compost and close the loop

ORGANIC WASTE

Close the loop

In addition to composting it is important to buy compost made from organic waste or to use your compost made on site and in so doing close the recycling loop. For example, Dorset County Council has a policy to compost all green waste. They use the local composting plant, Eco-Composting at Christchurch, to compost their green waste and buy the compost back for use in their grounds maintenance. *See grounds maintenance in Chapter 4, Purchasing* ↱

Schools

Schools have good potential to introduce traditional composting and wormeries as part of the curriculum as well as encouraging waste reduction. Composting schemes, particularly wormeries, are popular with children, and can be linked to environmental education through the Science Curriculum.

Henry Doubleday Research Association (HDRA) is a national organic gardening organisation and aims to encourage composting in households, schools and local authorities. They are an excellent source of advice and provide leaflets on composting as well as information on the wide range of composters on the market. They work with a number of local authorities to help them develop composting programmes.

HDRA are also very active with schools and run a number of activities including the Schools Recycling Week. Recycling and composting can be linked to at least seven curriculum subjects: science, mathematics, English, art, design and technology, geography, and history. *See Chapter 10, Contacts and Resources* ↴

⚠ Common problems

- Do not include meat and fish in compost material: they attract vermin.
- Keep wormeries out of direct sunlight to prevent destruction of the worms.
- Do not put grass in any quantity into wormeries: it heats up and gives off ammonia, which will kill worms.
- Do not put weeds with seeds into a wormery: the wormery does not produce enough heat to break down the seeds, which will germinate when the compost is used.
- Traditional heaps tend to need more looking after than wormeries. Ensure sufficient manpower is available.

GLASS

🍁 Environmental issues

The raw materials used to make glass are not expensive or rare, but silica (sand) is extensively quarried and causes unsightly damage to the landscape. Glass is also relatively heavy and bulky, constituting a large percentage of waste by weight. Glass can be recycled very efficiently, with an energy saving of 25 per cent. One tonne of recycled glass saves 30 gallons of oil.

The glass industry is committed to achieving a 58 per cent recycling rate by 2000.

The companies that are most likely to have glass for recycling are those with staff restaurants and client function rooms.

☞ Practical action

Assess the current usage
Assess current usage to find out the potential volume for recycling. Note that contractors often need glass to be separated by colour.

Establish a collection system
Glass can often be retrieved directly by the catering contractors when trays are cleared from the staff restaurant and hospitality suites cleared after functions. Glass is often already separated from general waste for health and safety reasons.

Case Study 3.9

SUBJECT: **Glass Recycling and Energy Efficiency**

ORGANISATION: **Joanna's Restaurant**

LOCATION: **Crystal Palace, London**

STAFF: **20**

Background
Joanna's Restaurant joined Waste Alert in June 1999 and was interested in reducing the amount of glass sent to landfill.

Action
Waste Alert put Joanna's in touch with Cleanaway, who run the Bottleback glass recycling programme. Joanna's shares a glass bottle recycling depot with neighbouring restaurant Tamag Thai, saving 13 tonnes of glass waste from landfill and over £100 in disposal costs.

Joanna's will also be looking to minimise cardboard waste and have reduced their waste by using sugar pots and salt and peppershakers, rather than using disposable sachets.

Results
- 13 tonnes of waste diverted from landfill.
- £400 in disposal cost saved per annum. ∎

Find a contractor
Some local authorities offer glass collections and there are a number of organisations throughout the country offering this service. For smaller organisations, and where volume is low, it will be difficult to find a contractor to collect the glass: you can take small amounts to the local bottle bank.

An alternative to using bottled water is to introduce an in-house water purification system, which means that bottles can be re-used. *See Chapter 4, Purchasing* ➤

VENDING CUPS

🍁 Environmental issues

Plastics use oil for production, which is a finite raw material and in most cases does not biodegrade.

☞ Practical action

Single-walled polystyrene (that is, plastic) cups can easily be recycled. Following collection, the polystyrene is formed into pellets. The material is used for a variety of non-food applications, including video cassettes, office equipment and industrial reels.

Assessment
There are at least three different types of vending cup on the market, but collection systems are only established for one, single walled plastic, so you must identify the type you are using:

Waxed paper cups
Facilities for recycling waxed paper cups are not currently available. The wax coating requires chemicals to break it down for recycling, which rather defeats the object!

Expanded polystyrene cups
Expanded polystyrene cups are theoretically recyclable, but collection facilities are not widely available.

Polystyrene (single-walled) cups
Facilities to recycle single-walled polystyrene cups are widely available.

Using mugs
Using mugs is environmentally and economically preferable. However, this can be difficult for hygiene reasons. The replacement of vending cups with mugs is usually reliant on staff having (and using) washing-up facilities. This is generally more practical in smaller offices.

You could issue staff with their own mugs overprinted with your company logo and a message; this provides a good opportunity to promote an environmental message. Some vending machines have sensors that enable them to detect that there is a mug in the dispenser: in this case the machine does not issue a cup. Statistics about the percentage vend of cups and mugs can usually be provided by the vending company. These statistics can be used to monitor relative usage and to feed back results to staff.

Summary guidelines

✔ Use vending machines with sensors that allow mugs to be used. Using mugs is preferable to increasing the number of plastic cups being recycled!

✔ Where vending machines are used, ensure that single-walled polystyrene (plastic) cups are used, rather than expanded polystyrene or waxed paper

✔ Check that Save-A-Cup provide collection facilities in your area

✔ Eliminate vending machines in smaller offices where storage of used cups is impractical. Use mugs instead

✔ Feedback the results of recycling, to maintain motivation. Use Save-A-Cup publicity material and stationery products made from vending cups

✔ Place Beca bins by each vending machine

Collection Systems

Save-A-Cup provide a collection service for single-walled polystyrene (plastic) cups. They provide Beca storage bins, flaking machines and labelled sacks. Beca bins are specifically designed to stack cups, which substantially reduces the space they occupy. Cleaning staff must put the cups into the labelled sacks for collection. Flaking machines are more expensive but significantly reduce on-site storage requirements. In the collection of unflaked cups, 30 per cent of the gross weight is liquid.

Save-A-Cup provide back-up publicity to encourage staff to recycle and have developed a range of office stationery products made from recycled vending cups. These are useful and functional promotional tools. Did you know it takes seven vending cups to make one ruler?

METAL: DRINKS CANS

 Environmental issues

The raw materials used to manufacture cans are iron ore, tin and bauxite. This involves mining operations in developing countries which can be very destructive to the environment. Following extraction, the raw material is transported to smelting plants: the smelting of all metals is very energy intensive. Once filled and transported, cans have a relatively short shelf-life before they are disposed of in the waste stream. In the UK, cans are made from tinplate and/or aluminium and can be recycled many times into new cans.

Recycling aluminium drinks cans not only saves natural resources, reduces litter and waste to landfill but also saves up to 95 per cent of the energy needed to produce aluminium from virgin raw materials. Recycling aluminium cans is an excellent way to raise money for charity. Over 4 billion cans will be sold this year, worth over £30 million to collectors.

☞ Practical action

Assessment

Separating materials
Seventy per cent of drinks cans are aluminium, the remainder are steel. Aluminium and steel can be separated using a magnet (steel sticks to a magnet, aluminium does not) or look for the recycling symbol on the side of the can. Aluminium cans have shiny bases. Some contractors will collect aluminium only and some contractors will pay for aluminium cans, so if practical it is better to separate steel from aluminium in-house.

Using can crushers
Can crushers will reduce the space the cans occupy. Wall-mounted can crushers and bins with can crushing devices that sort steel and aluminium are available.

Choosing a collection system
The restaurant is generally a good location for a can bank, relying on staff retrieving cans from their trays. This scheme can easily be extended if successful. Assessment of current usage will help identify potential volumes.

Find contractors
British Alcan or ACRA will provide details of regional collection arrangements. Some paper recycling companies will also collect cans. Contact your local 'Cash for Cans' Recycling Centre for support materials and information about local services. These contacts will also be able to provide you with storage containers. *See Chapter 10, Contacts and Resources* ↴

Summary guidelines

✔ Obtain containers and publicity material from ACRA and British Alcan
✔ Find a local contractor and establish what they will collect prior to setting up the scheme
✔ Install can crushers if the volume of cans used is high
✔ Find out whether you will receive revenue on aluminium cans
✔ Nominate a charity to donate any revenue to
✔ If the volume of cans is too small to make collection viable, take the cans to your nearest recycling facility

METAL: DRINKS CANS

Promote the scheme

Can recycling is a highly visible way to promote recycling and used aluminium drinks cans are valuable; collecting them for recycling is a great way to raise funds. If all the aluminium cans sold in the UK this year were to be recycled, over £30 million could be paid to the collectors.

Decide what charity you want to collect for. Survey staff if you do not have a nominated charity and promote the chosen charity on notice-boards and near the can bins. Give staff regular feedback on the amount of money raised and encourage them to bring cans from home.

IT EQUIPMENT

More than one hundred tonnes of obsolete computers are dumped in landfill each year in the UK. There are a number of characteristics which make them a priority waste stream. Firstly, it is an increasing waste stream. The number of items disposed of will increase significantly as products bought during the consumer electronics boom of the 1980s and year 2000 non-compliant computers and equipment enter the waste stream. Technological changes are speeding up obsolescence and reducing the average lifetime of equipment. Small amounts of hazardous materials are often integral to electrical goods; they may also include valuable and scarce raw materials. Their physical durability means that once discarded, they do not decompose and take up space in landfill for many years to come.

The scrap value of this waste could be as much as £50 million annually. Rising landfill costs and mounting pressure for producer responsibility legislation (see Waste from Electrical and Electronic Equipment, page 25) has led to an increasing number of companies who specialise in electronics refurbishment and recycling. An increasing number of computer manufacturers are developing equipment which is designed for ease of disassembly and recycling. *See Chapter 4, Purchasing* ➤

☞ Practical action

Upgrade existing equipment

Avoid purchasing new equipment by upgrading existing equipment where possible. Don't over-specify. Not all staff need high specification machines.

Return to manufacturer

Return equipment to the manufacturer for refurbishment. Computers can be broken down into component parts for re-use and recycling. Copper and silver from cables can be recycled, as can plastic and metal casings.

Re-use equipment in-house

Encourage exchange of equipment within your organisation. Another department

Case Study 3.10

SUBJECT: **Computer Re-Use**

ORGANISATION: **Prospects Career Services**

LOCATION: **Bromley, Kent**

STAFF: **80 in Bromley; 500 total [London and the Black Country]**

Background
Prospects Career Services is a not-for-profit company, committed to helping young people achieve success through their choices in education, training and employment. The company provides careers information, advice and guidance services for young people in Bromley, Bexley, Croydon, Sutton, North London and the Black Country.

Action
Prospects' offices in Bromley and Bexley joined Waste Alert, keen on minimising the amount of office waste they produced. They are in the process of establishing an office paper recycling scheme.

Due to a recent upgrade of their computer system, Prospects had a number of redundant computers on hand and were keen to put them to good use. They contacted Waste Alert, who put them in contact with Convoy of Hope who arranged the pick-up from their Croydon depot. Convoy arranged for the transport of the computers to Kosovo, where they will be installed in a local school.

In total, approximately 70 computers will be passed-on to teach children basic computing skills. One PC system will also be going to a hospice in Chernobyl and another to an old persons' home in Croatia.

Ray Auvray, Chief Executive for Prospects, said: 'We're grateful to Waste Alert, who have enabled us to protect the environment and help these young people at the same time.'

Prospects also held a 'Black Bag Day' where all unused paper, rubbish and furniture was cleared out. With the help of Waste Alert, nearly three tonnes of paper was recycled and unused furniture will be re-used internally or through the Waste Exchange. The prize for the oldest item discovered went to the person who found *The Problem Career*, a book dated 1926!

Results
- 4 tonnes of waste and 70 computers re-used.
- £375 saved on disposal costs. ∎

Summary guidelines

✔ Do not put computers in the skip!
✔ Upgrade equipment where possible
✔ Work with manufacturers/suppliers to set up return and refurbish contracts
✔ Use specialist recycling companies to handle obsolete equipment
✔ Offer to staff or donate to schools or local charities

IT EQUIPMENT

may have a use for what you are throwing out! A lower specification computer could be used as a print server or by someone who uses packages with lower requirements such as word processing-only programmes.

Sell or offer to staff

Staff will often be pleased to purchase equipment. Offer to staff at reduced rates.

Give to local charities or schools

Charities will often be glad of your obsolete equipment. In the case of local authorities, equipment can often be passed on to schools. Your local waste minimisation club may offer an exchange service.

Find specialist recycling company

There are a number of specialist recycling companies who offer a range of refurbish and recover services. Revenue is available for equipment in working order, of a maximum age. Charges for collection are dependent on location, quantity and type of equipment. Producing an inventory of equipment as it is discarded will ensure you receive maximum revenue from it. *See Chapter 10, Contacts and Resources*

OTHER OFFICE WASTES

Toner cartridges and inkjets

Over 6 million toner cartridges are used in UK offices every year and this figure is rising by 15 per cent per year. Around half of these are disposed of to landfill. Cartridges are very bulky waste which will not degrade for thousands of years. In addition, the ink powder they contain is potentially hazardous and should be treated accordingly.

There is a multitude of types of laser and inkjet cartridges on the market but the majority of them are now able to be remanufactured, a process which saves a significant amount of non-renewable resources.

You may be able to earn revenue from your obsolete cartridges. Newly introduced cartridges can be worth up to £4 each, most others are worth £1 or £2. Some collectors will pay you directly, others will arrange for this revenue to be donated to

Case Study 3.11

SUBJECT: **Furniture Re-Use**

ORGANISATION: **Castle Homes Limited**

LOCATION: **Hadlow Road, Sidcup, Bexley, Kent**

STAFF: **8**

Background

Castle Homes of Sidcup is a privately managed temporary residency for troubled youths. They experience a high turnover of tenants from a range of backgrounds, thus requiring the facilities to not only accommodate their tenants, but entertain them as well. Castle Homes of Sidcup joined Waste Alert in July of this year and has made significant costs savings, notably through the Waste Exchange.

Action

Castle's first savings were achieved by purchasing two used wardrobes through Respond, a furniture charity operating in the Thamesmead area. This saved the organisation over £80 in purchasing costs. They have also arranged for Bexley Council to collect their paper-based materials for recycling at no cost. This eliminates the need for a wheeled rubbish container, saving £85 in yearly disposal costs and 1 tonne of rubbish.

Castle Homes has received a snooker table complete with cues and balls, three armchairs, two overhead projectors, a TV, video and cabinet and 50 plastic and metal chairs through the Waste Alert waste exchange.

Results

Castle Homes illustrates how a series of small changes can lead to large cost savings:

- 2 tonnes of waste diverted from landfill.
- £1380 in purchasing costs saved.
- £85 per annum disposal costs saved. ∎

your chosen charity. It is usually necessary to collect at least 10 cartridges in order to earn revenue.

New cartridges cost up to £100 each. High quality remanufactured cartridges are now widely available which could save you up to 40 per cent of your costs. *See Chapter 4, Purchasing* ↘

Mobile phones

There are currently over 14 million mobile phone users in the UK and it has been predicted that half of the population will own a mobile phone by 2002. Currently old, disused or broken handsets are likely to end up in landfill.

A new initiative launched in May 1999 aims to ensure that mobile phones are collected and recycled. Ten industry partners including all of the major manufacturers and ECTEL (the European Telecommunications and Professional Electronics Industries Association) have joined forces to run a national take-back scheme called Returnable Telephony. Phones, batteries and accessories regardless of manufacturer or network can be returned to any Vodaphone, Cellnet, BT or One 2 One shop nation-wide. The plastic housing of the phone is separated and then passed on to a plastics recovery company. The circuit boards are also separated and the gold and other metals are recovered. The only part of the phone that is not currently recoverable is the display screen, as it contains heavy metals.

☞ Practical action

Assessment
Find out how many mobile phones are in use in your organisation and what happens to them when they are replaced.

Collection systems
* Establish a collection system for obsolete mobile phones and accessories.
* Locate your nearest collection point by contacting your network operator or through the ECTEL website.

Batteries

Every year we throw away over 400 million batteries into landfill sites. Batteries contain heavy metals such as lead, mercury and cadmium, with smaller amounts of lithium, cobalt, zinc, silver and other chemicals. Cadmium does not degrade and cannot be destroyed. Since 1994, all general purpose batteries (as sold by members of the European Portable Batteries Association, EPBA) in Europe are mercury free; however, some batteries containing small amounts of mercury continue to be imported into Europe and the remaining pre-1994 batteries will still be entering the waste stream.

There are three main types of batteries that are used commonly in offices: general purpose batteries (Dictaphones, pagers), button cells (watches, cameras, calculators) and rechargeables (laptop computers, video recorders).

Use of rechargeable (nickel cadmium) batteries is increasing. They are most suitable in high drain appliances such as mobile phones, camcorders and laptop computers. Rechargeable batteries differ from conventional batteries in that they discharge at a uniform rate throughout their life rather than fading slowly. This rapid 'cut out' means they are not suitable for smoke or burglar alarms or electronic data storage devices and personal organisers. Nickel cadmium rechargeable batteries should not be disposed of with normal waste.

Up to 65 per cent of a general purpose battery is recyclable. Facilities for recycling batteries in the UK are minimal; however, proposed legislation going through the European Commission would require the collection and recycling of all portable batteries. The main battery manufacturers have set up recovery schemes for their own rechargeable batteries which are then sent to the continent for recycling and recovery.

REBAT is an initiative managed by the British Battery Manufacturers Association to encourage collection of portable nickel cadmium batteries in the UK, as required under European legislation. When future European legislation requires the collection of all portable batteries, REBAT will extend its remit to manage all types and may develop a labelling scheme to indicate recyclable batteries, which incorporates the REBAT logo.

Of the main battery types commonly used in the office, only NiCd batteries can currently be recycled. *See Chapter 10, Contacts and Resources* �’

Practical action

- Use the mains wherever possible when you have the choice.
- Use rechargeable batteries and a battery charger. The energy needed to make batteries is 50 times greater than the energy they give out.
- Ensure you are using non-mercury batteries (from an EPBA manufacturer).
- Take used batteries to a recycling centre if they have collection boxes. If not, ring your local council's Recycling Officer and ask for advice.
- Send batteries back to manufacturers, where such a scheme is available, or set up a scheme with your local supplier if possible. *See the Office Waste section of Chapter 10, Contacts and Resources* �’

Packaging

Packaging makes up around 7–10 per cent of industrial, commercial and municipal waste and an estimated 10 million tonnes are disposed of annually.

Packaging, generally made of cardboard, wood and plastics is a bulky waste that is not always easy to recycle. Packaging made from different materials (eg different types of plastic or polystyrene and cardboard), needs to be separated prior to recycling. Composite materials such as foiled plastics and Tetrapack, are almost impossible to recycle. Waste cardboard has a very low value and therefore it is not always cost effective to arrange for it to be recycled. The Producer Responsibility Regulations (page 23) will influence the market for waste packaging in the future as more companies are obligated to recover and recycle. However, while small amounts of packaging may currently be difficult to recycle, they are ideal for re-use.

Some manufacturers will collect packaging for re-use or recycling; increasingly suppliers are delivering products in re-usable packaging. Wooden packaging is less common in offices but is still used for pallets and crates for distribution and import of products and is included in the Producer Responsibility Obligations (Packaging Waste) Regulations 1997.

☞ Practical action

- Arrange for your supplier to take back packaging when they deliver, especially on regular or standard items.
- Specify minimum packaging when you order goods. Complain if they come overpackaged!
- Compact or flatten cardboard boxes to reduce the space they take up in your bins.
- Contact your local waste minimisation club; they may know of an outlet for your packaging.

Fluorescent tubes

There are approximately 80,000,000 fluorescent tubes disposed of annually in the UK. Fluorescent lighting tubes contain mercury (as much as 30 mg), cadmium and lead. Crushing used tubes produces dust and vapour emissions that present a health hazard. Disused sodium lamps are a potential fire risk until they are correctly broken and the sodium neutralised.

Fluorescent tubes do not currently come under the Special Waste Regulations. They are categorised as Difficult Waste under the Environmental Protection Act 1990. However, the hazardous nature of the mercury they contain means that particular care should be taken over waste fluorescent tubes.

☞ Practical action

Introduce a relamping programme
All bulbs should be replaced together, at a fixed time, to maintain consistent lighting levels. This will also reduce your maintenance costs. The tubes can be disposed of by a hazardous waste contractor or recycled in bulk and you will maintain consistent lighting levels throughout your building(s).

Recycle fluorescent tubes
Recently facilities have been developed to enable fluorescent tubes to be recycled. These are competitively priced with specialist disposal facilities. Lamps are crushed and sieved in a closed dry recycling process. Mercury can be extracted from the fluorescent powder once separated from the glass and metals. All the materials can be recycled, including the mercury, which is used in new lamps. Details are available from Mercury Recycling.

Check the contractors' and the intended waste site licences to make sure that they are licensed to handle fluorescent tubes and that they are being recycled.

It will help to know how many tubes you dispose of when considering the feasibility of recycling. Use the following to estimate the number of tubes generated:

- One tube per 9 m² of office space.
- Each tube lasts about two years.

Dispose of fluorescent tubes safely

The DETR recommend that special arrangements should be made if more than one tube is disposed of to six bags of general waste. If quantities of 20 or 30 tubes are to be disposed of at any one time, a waste contractor with appropriate disposal facilities should be identified. The contractors' and the intended waste site licences should be checked to make sure that they are licensed to handle such waste. *See Chapters 5, Building Management and 10, Contacts and Resources* ⬎

Furniture

Furniture is a bulky, high value waste which often has substantial opportunities for re-use. *See Chapter 4, Purchasing* ⬎

 Practical action

Re-use

Could obsolete furniture be used elsewhere in the building? Executive chairs from a conference suite could be used in other meeting rooms or the entrance lobby.

Refurbish

Always consider refurbishment prior to disposal, often furniture is thrown out because it doesn't match the new décor. Re-upholstering or renovation can give the necessary facelift to existing furniture.

Exchange

Contact your local waste minimisation club or local authority for details of local refurbishment charities in your area. They will refurbish furniture and either sell it or use it in community projects.

CHAPTER SUMMARY

❏ Ensure contractors are licensed and comply with the Duty of Care on your behalf
❏ Assess the potential for reductions in waste disposal costs
❏ Introduce waste minimisation and recycling schemes where practical and monitor them
❏ Have a publicised 'launch' for recycling and waste reduction programmes and feedback progress to staff
❏ Re-negotiate waste disposal arrangements when schemes are established

CHAPTER 4

Purchasing

INTRODUCTION

It is important to recognise that you 'buy in' environmental impacts through your supply chain. Therefore, the performance of the products and services that you buy directly affects your own environmental position. In the service sector, the most significant environmental effects of an organisation may be those that are bought in.

Dealing with suppliers who are committed to sound environmental performance can make your job easier and help you to achieve your purchasing objectives. Equally, poor performance from your suppliers weakens your own environmental position. This is particularly important where you are buying in products with a high environmental impact/profile. Suppliers and contractors can represent significant risks where they are conducting an activity which is covered by environmental legislation. For instance, you may be relying on your cleaning contractors to comply with the Environmental Protection (Duty of Care) Regulations 1991 on your behalf; in such circumstances both you and your contractor have responsibilities under the Act. *See Chapter 3, Office Waste, for further details* 🔾

Many organisations see green purchasing as having an inevitable cost premium attached, but this does not have to be the case. Considering environmental criteria in purchasing decisions provides a change in focus away from purely cost-based decisions. The first question you should ask is: do you need it in the first place? The best environmental and commercial option is not to buy it!

We outline standard purchasing principles and the environmental issues associated with a number of common office products with guidance on how to select the most environmentally preferable. We also cover the common services such as cleaning and catering which are often contracted out.

Including environmental criteria into tender and contract documentation formalises this commitment. For small organisations a simple policy statement supported by guidelines can be sufficient. *See Wastebusters' Purchasing Questionnaire on page 87* 🔾

The chapter also contains an overview of purchasing structures in different organisations and the points to remember when purchasing services.

Guest Article

The Environmental Supply Chain Forum

by Barbara Morton, UMIST

Organisations in both the private and public sectors are increasingly having to deal with the environmental consequences of the products and services they purchase. This has implications for those purchasing these products and services and, increasingly, for their suppliers. In many respects, 'the environment' has become a factor in purchasing decision-making, alongside traditional criteria such as price, quality, delivery, technical capacity and financial stability of the supplier.

The pressures on organisations to address their own environmental performance (and that of their suppliers) can be seen to come from a number of sources, many of which are common to the public and private sectors. They include the concerns of the local community, regulators and legislators, investors and insurers, customers and suppliers.

Public sector organisations have particular duties and responsibilities connected with the environment, including those relating to the types of goods and services they purchase. For many organisations in the public sector, this has resulted in the development of purchasing policies which themselves may form part of a wider environmental management system, such as ISO 14001 or EMAS. In the public sector, concern for Best Value is a major influence on purchasing, and environmental improvement must be seen to be consistent with this requirement.

Minimising business risk

In the private sector, purchasing is being recognised as a means of delivering on environmental commitments and as a means of minimising risk to the business.

This can be seen from two perspectives: that of the customer and that of the supplier.

From the customer's point of view, there is a need for the company to secure supplies of products in the future, particularly where the item is critical to the business. Where environmental regulation or other pressures threaten the survival of a supplier of critical items, it is in the customer's interests to act. The customer may either seek an alternative, more environmentally sound supplier or the company may decide to encourage its existing supplier to adopt environmental improvement measures. In either case, long-term security of supply is the goal.

For the supplier, there are a number of priorities associated with environmental performance improvement. To retain business and to achieve competitive advantage, they need to be able to demonstrate their commitment to environmental improvement and, increasingly, to produce evidence to support this.

Many companies are beginning to look for appropriate measures of environmental improvement 'on the ground', whereas in the past they might have been satisfied with an environmental policy statement from suppliers.

Suppliers are also concerned, to a greater or lesser extent, with the impact of environmental regulation on their business. In industrial sectors subject to particular scrutiny, they need systems and procedures in place which will ensure that their operations are compliant with legislation. Suppliers also need to attend to the needs of their shareholders and investors, who increasingly want to see evidence of good environmental performance. The impact of Business in the Environment's Index of Corporate Environmental Engagement (surveying major UK companies) has illustrated the potential for environmental activity within companies to be driven by external influences. Comparisons between companies and benchmarking systems are powerful tools for driving improvement, not least because of their public relations aspects.

In order to minimise risk, it is clear that those responsible for purchasing need to look beyond the boundaries of their own organisation. The impact of products and services extends all the way from the extraction of raw materials, through many stages of production and assembly, to use, re-use, recycling, and ultimately to disposal (if necessary). Under increasingly stringent environmental regulation, companies have been encouraged to look for more and more innovative ways not only to minimise the impact of their products, but also to take them back for re-use. Examples of this can be found in the electronic and electrical goods market and in the automotive sector. This trend will increase as environmental regulations on waste are tightened.

The reasons for this tightening of regulation can in many cases be traced to the need in large parts of Europe to reduce the quantities of waste going to landfill. As charges for waste disposal continue to rise in the UK, organisations will put pressure on suppliers to take back products at the end of their useful life and to take back much of the packaging associated with the products purchased. Extending this process even further results in companies moving away from offering 'products' as such, towards offering to supply the 'function' provided by a product.

Using the model of the office photocopier, there has been a trend away from buying the piece of equipment towards 'leasing' it and having the supplier provide a range of associated services during the life of the photocopier in any particular organisation. The supplier would be responsible for taking away the machine at some stage, and usually replacing it with a newer model. This concept has been extended to new areas, for example in floor coverings, where instead of buying a carpet the organisation effectively 'leases' the floor covering for a period of time, leaving the supplier responsible for maintenance and removal. In this case, the purpose of the exercise is to minimise waste in the whole supply chain by putting the 'redundant' floor covering back into the production process for manufacture of new product.

Such innovations have implications for both the design/specification process and for accounting.

Whole life costing

In making purchasing decisions, organisations are now looking more closely at the total cost of products and services across their whole life, including waste disposal charges. When all of the costs associated with a product / service are taken into account, a product which appears to be more expensive (based on purchase price alone) will be shown to be a more cost-effective solution. The concept of 'whole life costing' has been well used in the purchase of fleet vehicles, for example.

Unfortunately, for most organisations, it is still very difficult to trace costs back to the products and services with which they are associated. Waste management costs are often 'hidden' in overheads, for example, and cannot be attributed to particular purchases. Another difficulty lies in the fact that a number of budgets may be associated with products and services during their purchase, use and disposal, making the tracking of costs all but impossible under current arrangements. Only when the 'true' costs of products and services become visible will 'environmental purchasing' become acceptable and indeed routine.

Product design and specification

Organisations are also examining more closely the design and specification of their purchases, in order to identify opportunities for savings. This is often done most effectively in association with suppliers. Innovative approaches to products aimed at reducing fuel consumption, energy consumption, amount of packaging material required and volume of waste generated can result in both a direct cost saving to the organisation and reduced environmental impact. This is the sort of 'win-win' approach favoured by many organisations.

Environmental improvement along supply chains

'Win-win' is more likely to result from a recognition on the part of customer and supplier that they have common interests when it comes to environmental improvement in the supply chain; that no one organisation operating alone can address all of its environmental impacts. 'Environment' therefore becomes part of the commercial relationship between the customer and the supplier. As modern procurement practice drives organisations towards closer relationships with fewer suppliers, it is clear that the ability to satisfy a customer's require-ments on environmental performance will be critical to the supplier's long-term survival (and growth, potentially).

How have organisations addressed environmental improvement in the supply chain?

One of the most popular, but badly used, tools for driving environmental improvement along the supply chain has been the supplier environmental questionnaire. Where such questionnaires are used appropriately and integrated into existing systems, they can result in real benefits to both customers and suppliers. Indiscriminate and inappropriate use of questionnaires is confusing and potentially counter-productive, however.

Some organisations have adopted systems requiring their suppliers to gain, or commit themselves to gaining, certification to environmental management systems. Others allow suppliers to implement a system without necessarily going for certification, while the customer often requires the system to be audited as part of supplier assessment. Public sector organisations must ensure that the approach they adopt complies with public procurement rules, however. Organisations can be expected to focus on indicators of environmental performance in the coming years, which is likely to involve the development of more relevant 'questions' or indicators for assessing supplier performance. ■

Industry initiatives and purchasing tools

The Buy Recycled Campaign

To maximise the benefits of recycling, the materials that you collect need to be turned into a new product. By buying recycled you are increasing the demand for these products, encouraging the recycling industry and reducing the amount of waste going to landfill. Collecting materials for recycling is only the beginning of the chain. If you're not buying recycled, you're not recycling! This national campaign aims to encourage recycling activity and the purchase of recycled products and packaging by the public, thereby stimulating markets for recycled materials. Launched in November 1998, the campaign is promoted by Waste Watch, the national organisation working on raising awareness of waste issues and the '3Rs' (Reduce, Re-use, Recycle), and the Local Authority Recycling Advisory Committee (LARAC). WasteWatch also produce the UK Recycled Products Guide, a comprehensive listing of over 1000 products containing recycled materials. *See Chapter 10, Contacts and Resources* ↘ A Buy Recycled logo is a central feature of the Campaign, and it is used to communicate its aims. These are:

- to achieve an environmental 'closed loop system' by means of its Buy Recycled logo;
- to close the recycling loop using a campaign slogan: 'BUY IT, RECYCLE IT, BUY RECYCLED';
- to encourage increased public participation and support for recycling schemes;
- to raise public awareness of recycled products and packaging with recycled content;
- to inform the public of the availability and quality of such products and packaging, thus stimulating recycling markets.

The Campaign is coordinated by local authority Recycling Officers, and is aimed at the public through local authority contacts and buildings, in association with supermarkets and other retail outlets. Most recently, Sainsbury's has become the first retailer to join, and it has persuaded suppliers of some of its own-brand products to apply for the Campaign's logo.

Case Study 4.1

SUBJECT: **The Environmental Supply Chain Forum**

ORGANISATION: **UMIST**

LOCATION: **Manchester**

Background

The Environmental Supply Chain Forum established at Manchester School of Management at UMIST (University of Manchester Institute of Science and Technology) provides regular opportunities for participants to share experiences and determine good practice in environmental supply chain management.

The Forum was launched in December 1996 as part of a research project funded by the Global Environmental Change Programme of the Economic and Social Research Council. Forum participants include:

- environmental managers
- health and safety managers
- purchasing, procurement and supply chain managers
- academics with experience in the field
- representatives of business support groups
- representatives of non-profit organisations
- government officials
- representatives of NGOs.

Participants come from both business and industry and from the public sector.

A wide range of industry and commerce is represented at the Forum, including:

- electricity and water companies (including United Utilities as founder members of the Forum);
- construction companies;
- telecommunications companies;
- office equipment manufacturers;
- pharmaceuticals companies;
- high street retailers;
- banks.

Public sector participants include representatives of government agencies, local authorities and the NHS, for example. Some meetings take place at UMIST, while others are hosted by participating companies and organisations.

Action

The Forum has built a network of participants who are willing to share experiences and determine 'best practice' in the integration of environmental criteria into purchasing and supply chain management. In their 1997 Environment Report, United Utilities PLC commented

'We have become a founder member of UMIST's Environmental Supply Chain Forum, established with the aim of exploring and disseminating environmental procurement best practice through formal meetings and informal networks as there appear to be many benefits from sharing experiences.'

Meetings of the Forum have addressed issues identified by participants themselves as being of particular interest, including:

- supplier assessment
- developing green specifications
- appropriate environmental criteria for tenders and contracts
- integration with environmental management systems
- how to respond to customer demands for environmental information.

Sector-specific meetings have also been arranged, for example the April 1999 meeting focused on the construction industry.

Results

The innovative approach adopted by the Environmental Supply Chain Forum is designed to deliver practical benefits to its participants. A number of tools and techniques have been demonstrated by invited speakers, aimed at assisting companies to meet their environmental supply chain objectives. Networking has led to work being commissioned by Forum participants.

Since April 1999, the Forum has become a partner in a two-year project funded by the European Regional Development Fund, aimed at assisting SMEs in the north-west of England. The *Supply Chain Environmental Management Programme* involves the Forum as a network of lead purchasing companies. The Programme aims to encourage SME suppliers to adopt clean technologies and good environmental practice, and to assist them to develop eco-products related to the environmentally sustainable strategies of their key customers.

Future projects

Development plans for the Forum include the creation of a website to serve as part of a 'Virtual Forum' for Environmental Supply Chain Management. The proposed website will include access to the following:

- environmental supply chain 'best practice' material;
- hyperlinks to other websites;

- on-line discussion groups;
- publications resulting from Forum meetings and academic research output;
- regularly updated information on current issues in environmental supply chain management;
- news about future events of particular relevance, including conferences and workshops.

Plans for the website reflect the growth in the number of enquiries on the subject being received through the network. In recent months, good contacts have been established worldwide, including the Philippines and Hong Kong where a similar network is being established with input from the UMIST coordinator. ∎

The ISO 14000 series and the Mobius loop

The International Standards Organisation has recently made moves to harmonise standards for eco-labelling schemes and ISO 14024 has been approved to cover environmental labelling.

ISO 14021, which relates to environmental claims, is likely to be promoted by the government as the main source of guidance on implementing the voluntary UK Code of practice on green claims. If a claim is made that a product or packaging is recyclable, the use of a symbol will probably remain optional, but if one is used it may well be the Mobius loop, which if used to indicate recycled content should have a percentage value next to it.

The Mobius Loop is an internationally recognised recycling symbol of three arrows, representing each aspect of a recycling programme: collection, remanufacturing/reprocessing into a new product, and finally purchase by the consumer. The symbol is only supposed to be used on goods that are 'recyclable' or include 'recycled content'.

European Union ecolabelling scheme

The Ecolabel is designed to reduce confusion by providing an authoritative and independent label to identify those goods with the lowest environmental impact in specific categories. The scheme is intended to promote products which have a reduced environmental impact along their life cycle, and provide consumers with a way of identifying products which have less environmental impact than others. The scheme focuses on the domestic market and to date the market response has been poor.

The scheme is administered domestically by the UK Ecolabelling Board. Conditions for awarding an ecolabel are defined by product group and include a range of environmental and technical criteria. Companies whose brands qualify for the label can apply for permission to display it on their products. The scheme has had a slow start but is steadily expanding, with the following office product groups now covered: copying paper, indoor paints and varnishes, single and double ended light bulbs, personal computers and portable computers, printed matter. Criteria are also under consideration for batteries, converted paper products and a host of other product groups.

Cyclic, solar, safe

Case Study 4.2

SUBJECT: **Purchasing for Sustainability**

ORGANISATION: **BioThinking International**

LOCATION: **London [virtual office]**

Background

Edwin Datschefski has developed a radical but simple framework for sustainability. Based on the principles of materials and energy flow in nature, **cyclic|solar|safe** is an easy to understand protocol for understanding products and how they can become more sustainable.

Focusing on product systems and mimicking nature

It is very achievable to undertake mass production using the basic protocols followed by natural systems. There are five design requirements for sustainable products. The first three mimic the principles used by plant and animal ecosystems:

1 *Cyclic:* The product is made from organic materials, and is recyclable or compostable, or is made from minerals that are continuously cycled in a closed loop.
2 *Solar:* The product uses solar energy or other forms of renewable energy that are cyclic and safe, both during use and manufacture.
3 *Safe:* The product is non-toxic in use and disposal, and its manufacture does not involve toxic releases or the disruption of ecosystems.

The fourth requirement is based on the need to maximise the utility of resources in a finite world:

4 *Efficient:* The product's efficiency in manufacture and use is improved by a factor of ten, requiring 90 per cent less materials, energy and water than products providing equivalent utility did in 1990.

And the fifth recognises that all companies have an impact on the people who work for them and the communities within which they operate:

5 *Social:* The product and its components and raw materials are manufactured under fair and just operating conditions for the workers involved and the local communities.

For a given product, it is possible to score each of these requirements out of 100, and this information can be expressed in a simple logo, or it can be presented in text as a vital statistics-style index: 50|30|90|40|10.

Action

Buying sustainable products and services

Most environmental purchasing programmes concentrate on assessing the management performance of existing suppliers rather than focusing on product performance. But the whole point of better buying is to locate and purchase better products! By analysing the products and services it buys and changing which ones it buys accordingly, any organisation can make a significant difference to its upstream and downstream environmental impacts. Taking it a step further, an environmental sustainability plan can be mapped out.

The first step is data collection, finding out how many tonnes of each type of material flow through the organisation. Then comes an assessment process that ranks these materials flows by the amount of ecological space they take up, showing which ones are the most important. From this an 80:20 plan can be drawn up. This takes the products that cause 80 per cent of the impacts (there are usually 20 or less), and then makes a plan for them to be 80 per cent sustainable by the year 2020.

For a service organisation, these will typically include the old chestnuts like fuel and paper, but the list will often surprise as well.

Once the priority products have been identified, set up a team for each product area, and have them do a thorough cyclic|solar|safe score on each one. Once a product has been assessed, the direction for improvement is usually obvious. As with 80:20 sustainability for manufacturing, the challenge can require two approaches: an immediate, 'low-hanging fruit' approach and a more strategic long-term plan.

For example, using the 80:20 principle on environmental audit data collected from nine London offices, it was found that 80 per cent of office impacts come from:

- Business travel and commuting.
- Building energy.
- New build and refurbishment.
- Paper and print.
- PCs.
- Water.
- Waste.

This means that only 20 per cent of impacts arise from other areas such as: catering, electrical, lamps, batteries and other electronic waste, stationery and PC consumables, furniture and carpet, refrigerants, clothing, post and couriers.

Don't ignore these, but recognise that they should take up a smaller amount of your time than the 80 per cent impact areas.

Results

Once the direction is clear, the solutions will present themselves – and so will the barriers! Changing which products are bought or the purchase specifications themselves is a balancing act between price, performance and user perceptions. With care and dedication, these factors can be navigated through, but most of all there needs to be commitment from the top.

The beauty of an 80:20 Product Plan is that it is clear and simple, so that senior executives can understand it and it can be communicated clearly and incorporated into the organisation's overall business strategy. By moving away from the 'how can we be less bad?' mentality to the 'how can we be more good?' mindset, we can make sourcing products that are cyclic, solar and safe an engaging and satisfying challenge.

Edwin Datschefski is a Director of BioThinking International. For more information, call 020 7628 0992 or see www.biothinking.com ∎

The Total Cost Approach and life cycle analysis

The Total Cost Approach is a methodology which helps you to look beyond the purchase price of a product. There is a strong link between purchasing and waste management, but this is often not recognised, there being little communication between those responsible for each function. It often costs more to dispose of a product than it does to buy it in the first place but you should not wait until you have to dispose of a product before you find this out. The true costs of waste disposal are often underestimated. *See Chapter 3, Office Waste, for further information* ↱ Substantial reductions in waste disposal costs and therefore Landfill Tax liability can be achieved by the consideration of recyclability and disposal in purchasing decisions (eg toner cartridges).

Using the Total Cost Approach will highlight the cost effectiveness of investing in an initially more expensive product to reduce costs in the long run. For example, efficient light bulbs are more expensive to buy than regular bulbs but use approximately one-fifth of the power and last up to eight times longer.

Life cycle analysis (LCA) is another purchasing tool which takes into account all stages of a product life cycle from the sourcing of the raw material to end-of-life disposal. The key issues are sourcing of raw materials, manufacturing processes, packaging, distribution, usage, re-use, recyclability and disposal. The area of highest impact varies considerably from product to product; some, such as furniture, can have a high environmental impact in several stages of the life cycle.

Standard principles

Before you buy any product ask the following questions:

1. Do you need to buy this product?

The best environmental option is to purchase less. Before purchasing a product or service consider whether you could mend or repair existing equipment or use products more efficiently.

2. Can you use a lower specification brand?

Some products can be made from a lower specification material which uses less resources without compromising quality. For instance, low-grade paper can be sufficient for use in internal note pads.

3. Does the product contain re-used or recycled materials?

Purchasing a product which is manufactured using re-used or recycled raw materials encourages the re-use or recycling of waste. Many office products, such as paper and toner cartridges, are now available with a recycled content.

4. Which product is cheapest over its whole life?

Look for the lowest whole life cost, not just the lowest capital cost. Relatively expensive products, such as energy efficient light bulbs, may last longer and create less waste, leading to overall savings. Try to make an estimate of the running costs of the product over its lifetime.

5. Does the product contain chemicals requiring Safety Data Sheets?

If the product, such as a cleaning chemical, is potentially harmful it will be supplied with a COSHH Safety Data Sheet detailing how to handle it. Try to replace these products with alternatives that do not require such precautions.

6. Can the product be re-used or recycled once obsolete?

Try to purchase products that can be re-used or recycled at the end of their useful life. For instance, thermal roll fax paper cannot be recycled and so purchasing this type of fax rather than plain paper models will mean all faxes received must be thrown away.

7. Will the product require special disposal arrangements?

Some potentially hazardous products such as paints, solvents and oils can cause particular environmental damage and incur significant financial costs upon disposal. Try to find an alternative that is safer and cheaper to dispose of, for instance water-based rather than solvent-based products.

IT-based requisition procedures and e-commerce

Direct computer links with suppliers, possibly controlled through the office supplies department, can save time and money and give you improved management control; for example, suppliers can provide you with detailed printouts for improved control.

Schroders London Group has a centralised contract for general stationery. The supplier was selected as a result of their innovative intranet-based ordering system and flexibility. This has resulted in improved efficiency and a considerable reduction in administration. The aim is to reduce the range of products prior to promoting environmentally preferable products. This will improve control and facilitate monitoring.

E-commerce or Electronic-commerce (the purchasing of goods through the Internet) has arisen alongside the massive growth in Internet-based companies and the increased accessibility to Internet facilities. However, none of these Internet-based companies has environmental policies or systems in place. Therefore, whilst there is general acceptance that e-commerce will be the second industrial revolution, there is also a growing concern that lack of regulation will cause environmental damage. One prediction made has been that shares in white vans will soar as home delivery services become more popular!

Despite these concerns, e-commerce has a number of potentially positive sustainability impacts:

- eco-efficiency aspects – reduced paperwork, administration, communication
- easier collection of environmental performance information (where it exists)
- easier access to markets for sustainable products. Smaller traders are able to advertise and market their products directly to an international market.

The amount of products and services bought over the Internet is likely to increase in the future; it is important that you apply the same environmental criteria to e-commerce purchasing decisions as you would to any others.

Small business and the supply chain

Large organisations with well-established environmental programmes are increasingly looking to green their supply chain. Many small businesses are still unconvinced of the business case of improving environmental performance, which can leave them unprepared if a company they supply sends them an environmental questionnaire or requests specific environmental information. Responsible environmental management is therefore an important competitive issue for small businesses.

Ethics and the environment

The environment has become, along with other issues such as child labour and working conditions, an ethical issue. Consumers in the UK are becoming more concerned about the links that their purchasing has with environmental destruction and wider issues of social conditions in developing countries. This has been demonstrated by the public response to genetically modified food and an increase in organic and fair traded goods, particularly tea, coffee and chocolate! Examples are Café Direct, Clipper and Ridgeway, Green & Black and Desire.

Effective environmental purchasing can reduce your liabilities, promote the sustainability of your organisation, reduce costs, improve control and reduce the impacts that you have on the environment.

Local authorities and schools

Purchasing structures in local authorities

Best Value has replaced Compulsory Competitive Tendering (CCT) for local authorities (see Introduction). Purchasing within local authorities falls broadly into three groups: departmental purchasing, central purchasing and purchasing consortia. In any specific local authority all three may be in use at any one time.

Departmental purchasing

Many local authorities have devolved purchasing within departments where 70–80 per cent of officers have some purchasing responsibilities. Control over purchasing decisions can be weak in these circumstances without strong management and effective communication of environmental policies.

Central purchasing

Many local authorities have central purchasing units which act within the authority as trading units. These can coordinate purchasing and allow a point of focus for enquiries. Central purchasing units can advise and educate staff on environmentally preferable purchases but they cannot enforce choices. Central purchasing units can also act as an aid to bulk purchasing, with the following benefits:

- Control over items stocked in line with environmental purchasing policy.
- Stock control – enhanced management and use control.
- Monitoring – provides information on purchasing within different departments.
- Ensures the best deals – allows bulk discounts.

Purchasing consortia

Purchasing consortia are groups of local authorities that have decided to combine their central purchasing units in order to consolidate their purchasing power. Consortia can use their buying power to promote environmental alternatives and to establish good deals from suppliers. The Central Buying Consortium, a group of nine local authorities, has a collective annual spend of £3/4 billion (Groundwork, 1996).

Planning your purchasing strategy

This chapter is mainly concerned with the specific environmental issues associated with purchasing a range of products and services to help you make informed individual decisions. However, our experience has shown that a systematic approach to environmental purchasing is necessary if real progress is to be made.

Establish an environmental purchasing policy

Environmental purchasing should be rooted in an official policy decision endorsed by senior management. An environmental purchasing policy, which commits your organisation to buying goods and services with a reduced environmental impact

Case Study 4.3

SUBJECT: **Departmental Purchasing**

ORGANISATION: **CBS Supplies**

LOCATION: **Cheshire**

STAFF: **26,000 [Cheshire County Council]**

Background

CBS Supplies is the major provider of office supplies to Cheshire County Council. The Environmental Policy for Cheshire County Council includes a commitment to integrating environmental considerations into purchasing decisions. The policy states: 'As a major purchaser of goods and services the County Council will endeavour to select and promote those which are least damaging to the environment and will work with its suppliers to address such issues'. CBS Supplies support this policy commitment and have included a selection of environmentally friendly products in the catalogue. The aim of this was to make it easy for individual purchasers to identify environmentally preferable products. The requirement to purchase the items was supported by the authority's Environment and Policy Committees.

Action

In 1997 Cheshire County Council commissioned Wastebusters to develop the range of environmentally preferable products and establish minimum environmental performance criteria for these products to ensure correct labelling. The aim of the project was to provide clear guidance to the authority in the selection and labelling of environmentally preferable products by establishing minimum performance criteria. This also provided guidance to CBS Supplies to identify specific brands which meet some or all of the criteria.

This will ensure that individual purchasers have confidence in the labelling system and use it effectively to reduce the impact of their purchasing.

Results

Minimum environmental performance criteria were established for the main product groups: paper stationery, pens, pencils and markers, office and desk accessories, filing, presentation and storage, office equipment, computing, cleaning and maintenance, domestic and electrical, audiovisual, art and craft.

An environmental labelling scheme was introduced into the 1998/1999 catalogue supported by an explanation of the scheme to promote the Environmental Policy.

The new catalogue has been very successful in changing people's purchasing decisions in favour of green products.

For 1999/2000 a separate Green Office Products Catalogue has been produced with the endorsement of the Chair of the internal Green Group and carries Member endorsement.

The Council has introduced a policy to use Evolve Office for all their photocopier paper and business papers, which has a high recycled content. Cheshire Supplies now stock only Evolve.

Cheshire Supplies include the minimum environmental performance criteria in their tenders.

Cheshire County Council is now looking to extend the range of green products.

For further information contact John Pearson, Environmental Officer, Cheshire County Council (email pearsonjr@cheshire.gov.uk). The work can be viewed in further detail on the authority's website www.cheshire.gov.uk/eco/perform/home.htm ■

and sets out objectives by which this will be achieved, should be circulated widely. *See Chapter 8, Environmental Management for more details on policy formulation* ➘

Identify areas of maximum impact

Concentrate your efforts on the goods and services which have the greatest environmental impact. As a rule of thumb, environmental impacts can be associated with purchasing spend; identify your ten most expensive items/areas of highest expenditure and start there. However, be careful, there may also be items of lower expenditure with a high environmental impact.

Plan what to tackle first

Use your review of maximum impacts to prioritise the areas that you will tackle first. Go for the easy wins! For instance, paper has a high profile; a decision to purchase recycled paper can be an effective and relatively easy first achievement.

Communicate to staff

Communicate your policy to all relevant staff. See Chapter 7, Communication for further details. The implementation of an environmental purchasing policy may require specialist training. Provide staff with the environmental information and support.

Partnership sourcing

The principle of partnership sourcing is to work with your suppliers to jointly develop environmental performance towards a goal of continuous improvement. This approach can be very successful. Request environmental statements from your suppliers.

Integrate into your purchasing structure

Design minimum environmental standards for target areas and integrate these into tender documentation. Your environmental policy and minimum environmental standards must be included in pre-tender or briefing documents as well as final tender and contract documentation.

Supplier assessment questionnaires

Supplier Assessment Questionnaires are a widely used method of gathering information about the environmental performance of suppliers. Their use by several large companies in the UK such as British Airports Authority, B&Q and the Body Shop has led to their adoption by a number of smaller organisations.

Questionnaires can work on two levels: firstly by asking general questions about the environmental management practice of a supplier and secondly by asking specific questions about the environmental performance of products and services. Questionnaires can also serve to send a strong message to your suppliers as to the value of the environment to your organisation and can be used to promote improved environmental performance.

Organisations with a formal environmental management systems such as ISO 14001 or EMAS are committed to assessing their suppliers (see Chapter 8, Environmental Management). Integrate environmental criteria into the normal supplier assessment process so that environmental information can be held on a database along with general supplier information. This information can then be used to evaluate the relative environmental performance of suppliers in order to inform the tender process outlined above. Include environmental criteria in the tender evaluation matrix.

Wastebusters Ltd: purchasing questionnaire

Wastebusters are committed to a policy of responsible business management which seeks to minimise the impact of our operations on the environment. An integral part of our environmental policy is the improvement of our performance through our supply chain. We are committed to running our own activities in an environmentally responsible manner and using our purchasing power to improve environmental standards and encourage best practice.

We have developed a set of purchasing criteria to give clear direction to our suppliers and enable them to demonstrate how they can help us achieve our objectives. We have also found that suppliers respond well, and often promptly, to this form of communication. *See list on page 88* ↘ Before we buy any product we ask the following questions:

1   Do we need to buy this product?
2   Can we use a lower specification brand?
3   Does the product contain re-used or recycled materials?
4   Which product is cheapest over its whole life?
5   Does the product contain chemicals requiring Safety Data Sheets?
6   Can the product be re-used or recycled once obsolete?
7   Will the product require special disposal arrangements?

Do your products meet our criteria?

Please complete this short questionnaire.

Product Supplier Questionnaire

Your own offices	YES	NO
Are you involved in any environmental, waste or energy saving projects? Please give details in **Supporting Information.**	☐	☐
If London-based, are you a member of Waste Alert?	☐	☐
Do you reduce, re-use and recycle wherever possible?	☐	☐

Your products and suppliers		
Do you include any environmental criteria in your purchasing decisions? Please give details in **Supporting Information.**	☐	☐
Do you assess your suppliers on their environmental performance?	☐	☐
Have your products been designed to reduce their environmental impact?	☐	☐
Do you have a policy on the use of virgin materials, PVC, GMO, Fair Trade and organic food products (where applicable)?	☐	☐

Use of raw materials		
Are your products and packaging easily re-usable ie are they refillable or refurbishable?	☐	☐
Do your products and packaging have a recycled content?	☐	☐
Are your products and packaging recyclable? ie are they made from easily separable materials which can be recycled locally?	☐	☐
Are your products packaged with a view to minimising waste?	☐	☐
Are any of your products accredited to a recognised standard? eg NAPM, FSC, Eco-label.	☐	☐
Are your products and packaging marked for ease of recycling?	☐	☐
Will you collect the packaging of your goods once they have been delivered?	☐	☐

Use of resources: Energy and water	YES	NO
Are your products water and/or energy efficient?	☐	☐
Do you know how much energy your products consume when in use and in standby mode?	☐	☐

Transport and distribution

Are your products stored within Greater London?

What modes of transport do you use for deliveries?

Do you operate a journey planning system – logistics/fuel management

Do you carry out driver training?

Communication: Internal and external

Do you have a publicly available environmental policy, statement or report?

Are you accredited to or working towards an environmental management system? Please list in **Supporting information.**

Do you carry out any staff environmental awareness training?

Does your organisation work with the local community? ie do you employ local people or make donations to local charities?

Supporting information

Please list any environmental, waste or energy saving projects that you are involved in:

....

Please list any environmental criteria you include in your purchasing decisions:

....

Are you accredited to an EMS standard, or working towards an internal EMS?

....

Please attach any supporting material that would help you answer any of the above questions.

Please return by fax to Wastebusters on 020 7207 2051

Name .... Position ....

Company Name .... Business Area ....

Address ....

Who is responsible for environmental issues? ....

Would you like help with improving the environmental performance of your company? ....

Case Study 4.4

SUBJECT: **Purchasing Strategies**

ORGANISATION: **Barclays plc**

LOCATION: **National**

STAFF: **50,000 (UK)**

Background
Barclays banking group have a nationwide network of branches and have made a number of positive environmental initiatives in order to improve their environmental performance. They have also set up the Barclays Environmental Management Unit to coordinate Barclays' own environmental management system, a key part of which involves supply chain management.

Action
Barclays have over 20,000 suppliers across a significant number of spend areas. They have therefore adopted a Four Stage approach to incorporating environmental considerations into their procurement process.

1 *Policy:* An updated and practical policy was developed, together with a set of governing principles. The policy was then integrated into the Group Governance Manual.
2 *Risk ranking:* Looking at the environmental impacts of goods or services bought in throughout their life cycle, Barclays have built up an initial environmental risk-ranking model for all products and services procured.
3 *Standardisation:* Using the output from the risk-ranking model, a workflow priority has been established. Tools were developed to ensure relevant environmental information was gathered during the tender process. Information included: existence of environmental management systems, legal compliance, environmentally beneficial products and whether the company was willing to develop a partnership approach to improving environmental performance.
4 *Development of relationships:* For key suppliers relationships will be fostered for discussing issues including: environmental performance, products supplied, packaging, and waste. In addition, relationships will be developed with providers of environmental training for SMEs, and SMEs will be encouraged to utilise the services provided.

Results
The risk-ranking process will eventually cover 100 per cent of Barclays' suppliers and will allow Barclays to prioritise areas most crucial to the overall supply chain environmental impacts. With such a large number of suppliers, it is essential that Barclays assign rankings to products and services so as to improve performance. Barclays will continue to look at ways of working with their suppliers, in particular working with SMEs on improving performance.

Submitted by Barclays Environmental Management Unit. *See Chapter 10, Contacts and Resources* ⬎ ∎

Case Study 4.5

SUBJECT: **Waste Management Strategy**

ORGANISATION: **National Grid Company plc**

LOCATION: **UK**

STAFF: **3600**

Background

National Grid's primary business is the high voltage transmission of electricity from power stations to regional electricity companies and large industrial users. The business is structured into operating units with key responsibilities for the development and maintenance of an efficient, coordinated and economical transmission system.

An Environmental Performance Report is produced annually and verified externally to monitor performance against the Group Environmental Policy. The 1996/1997 report highlighted the need to improve quantification of current waste management practices, set improvement targets, and develop a Waste Management Strategy. As a result, a Waste Management Strategy Group was established with representation from the operating units to deliver a corporate waste strategy. This group found that there were a large number of waste management companies providing services to NGC and the company was keen to rationalise this by developing a National Contract for waste disposal.

Action

The Strategy Group commissioned Wastebusters to conduct pilot waste audits across representative sites from each operating division to assess current waste management practices and identify improvements which are cost effective and result in improved environmental performance. The audits focused on compliance with legislation, competitiveness of current waste disposal arrangements and quantification of waste streams. This information provided the basis from which to develop the waste strategy and negotiate the national contract. The strategy will then be communicated to staff for effective implementation.

Results

- Negotiation of a national waste contract with environmental performance criteria to ensure consistency across all sites and contribute to environmental reporting requirements.
- Development of a waste strategy to support the new contract.
- Significantly reduced administrative costs as a result of rationalising arrangements.
- Production of a National Grid Waste Classification List. This gives a list of common waste types at National Grid with good practice advice on disposal.
- Planned communication programme with specific objectives for improved waste management practice and waste minimisation measures.
- Improved quantified waste management information. ∎

Contract specification

Another method of integrating environmental information into purchasing structures is to determine minimum environmental standards and write these in to contract documentation. This approach involves less commitment but does not generate supplier information. If you integrate environmental criteria into your contracts you have a binding legal agreement that commits suppliers to meeting your environmental standards.

Encouraging suppliers to adopt recognised environmental management systems during the course of a contract can be another way of promoting good practice. *See Chapter 8, Environmental Management* ➘

⚠ Common problems

Information overload!

Questionnaires can produce large quantities of information which needs to be managed and integrated into existing purchasing structures.

Processing the information you gather can represent a significant cost in terms of staff commitment which should be recognised when deciding on your approach.

Don't ask for information you don't need!

Summary guidelines

✔ Recognise the importance of purchasing to your environmental performance

✔ Identify areas of purchasing with high environmental impacts

✔ Plan your purchasing strategy to fit within existing structures

✔ Identify the approach that will be most effective for you

✔ Use purchasing tools to help identify environmentally preferable alternatives

PURCHASING

Using and managing information

Many companies spend time and money gathering information with questionnaires but are then not sure how to use that information. Once the process has started, information needs to be managed, updated and used to inform decision making on an ongoing basis. Before you decide to use questionnaires, think how your purchasing decision making will be affected by the results. If you will not use the information you gather, do not gather it!

OFFICE STATIONERY

General office stationery can be one of the most overlooked areas of office purchasing. Items such as filing products, pads, pens, batteries and scissors are relatively small purchases but can represent a significant purchasing spend.

Environmental issues

Whilst viable alternatives are now available, many stationery products still use virgin materials and solvents. For example, writing instruments use raw materials and chemicals during manufacture, causing waste problems. Highlighter and marker pens can contain solvents, copy paper may use virgin pulp from unsustainable forestry practices. Most general stationery items are used in-house and there is little justification to use products made from virgin materials where recycled alternatives exist. Filing products can be made from low-grade paper waste which helps to create a demand for the raw material. PVC is used in some stationery products. It does not break down naturally and alternatives such as polypropylene should be sought wherever possible.

This section includes batteries, of which the UK used 634 million tonnes in 1998 (excluding rechargeables). Batteries are inefficient in their use of energy when compared to mains power, and may contain heavy metals, which contribute to air pollution if burned in a refuse incinerator and present a potential threat of water pollution if landfilled.

The Batteries and Accumulators Containing Dangerous Substances Regulations 1994 aim to reduce the quantities of heavy metals (mercury, cadmium and lead) entering the environment from spent batteries. Further legislation is due in late 2000, which will extend the labelling and collection requirements of the current directive.

Practical action

Demand accurate, detailed information

General stationery provides the opportunity to use recycled products. Most stationery catalogues include a range of products labelled 'environmentally friendly' but it is important to establish the criteria behind this label. Some suppliers' labelling systems can be misleading.

Work with suppliers

Work with your stationery company to increase the number of environmentally sound products in the catalogue. Bars can be put on the purchase of certain products, to ensure that the environmentally sound options are used. Most stationery companies will source specific products on your behalf if they do not feature in the catalogue. *See CBS Supplies case study, page 85*

Case Study 4.6

SUBJECT: **Recycled Stationery Products**

ORGANISATION: **Paperback**

LOCATION: **London**

STAFF: **15**

Background

Paperback was established in 1983 by two green activists with a mission to bring concern for the environment into the office world and the world of print and design, and as an employee-owned business it combines this environmental mission with a strong ethical stance. Initially the company sold mostly copier paper, envelopes and toilet rolls – there was little else available at the time – but it now stocks over a hundred product lines, including many environmentally friendly non-paper products.

In its first ten years of trading the company spent a lot of time sourcing new recycled printing papers and developing a market for them. Customers have included not only environmental organisations like Friends of the Earth and Greenpeace, but also such mainstream operations as the BBC, NatWest, The Body Shop and Sainsbury's. In the early 1990s Paperback also began looking at ways to develop the concept of the green office.

Action

It became clear that greening the office shouldn't begin and end with recycled paper, and Paperback has tracked down an impressive range of green non-paper products, including solar powered calculators; scissors made from recycled steel; A4 folders and pockets from recycled polypropylene; remanufactured laser toner cartridges and inkjet refills. The company also offers customers solvent-free recyclable ecotape; black sacks made from recycled degradable plastic; marbled pens made from recycled plastic; pencils made out of recycled vending cups; bins for recycling waste paper; solvent-free cleaners and water filter jugs.

Paperback's portfolio of office papers now includes not only three different recycled copier papers and several letterhead papers, but also Context FSC, Europe's first Forest Stewardship Council-approved watermarked letterhead paper made from 50 per cent post-consumer waste and 50 per cent FSC pulp (the Forest Stewardship Council is an international body that sets stringent environmental, economic and social criteria for sustainable forest management). The company has also recently introduced a range of bespoke ring binders and folders which offers attractive paper and board alternatives to environmentally damaging products like PVC.

Results

The company has produced an environmental statement outlining its policy on such things as the sourcing of products (suppliers must complete a detailed environmental questionnaire), the publication of environmental information to customers and the greening of its own office and distribution practices. Staff recycle waste paper, glass and other materials, and internal photocopying is frequently done on reject paper. Heaters have thermostatic controls and are fitted with timers. Computers come with energy star rating, and when Paperback had to upgrade its computers, the old ones were donated to a company which refurbishes and sells IT equipment at low prices to charities, local community groups and schools. And it goes without saying that recycled paper is used for all letterheads and promotional material! ■

Use specialist suppliers where possible

There are a number of specialist suppliers dealing only with recycled products. Specialist suppliers can be especially useful for small organisations which can have problems sourcing small quantities of recycled products at a competitive price.

Investigate waste reduction

There is often potential to reduce the cost of office supplies by improving control and making more efficient use of your resources. For example, box files can be re-labelled and re-used and a number of products are not strictly necessary. Office moves can often be used as an opportunity to order new stationery!

Buy recycled

Filing products made from recycled paper and board include binders and dividers, files, record cards, folders, memo and shorthand pads and removable self-adhesive notes (commonly referred to by the brand name Post-it). Recycled cardboard is used in some products instead of the traditional plastic casing for pens and pencils.

When choosing writing instruments, consider the type of plastic used in component parts and assess recyclability. There are currently very few schemes for recycling plastic due largely to the variety of plastic types used both singly and in combination. Thermoplastics can be re-melted and reshaped. Some of those which are currently recycled include polypropylene, polystyrene and polyethylene terephthalate (PET). Recycled plastic products available include pens, paperclip holders, mug stands, rulers and scissors.

Avoid solvents

Solvents are used to dissolve colour pigments. They are major ozone depleters and may give rise to volatile organic compounds, or VOCs. *See Catering and Cleaning, Environmental Issues, page 117*. Solvents such as toluene and xylene are mild carcinogens and are commonly found in markers specially formulated for writing on problem surfaces, such as glass, foil and oily metals. These solvents should be avoided unless absolutely necessary. Environmentally acceptable alternatives to solvents are water-based products.

Beeswax is an environmentally sound alternative to solvent-based varnishes which protects the wood in pencils from moisture and prevents it from swelling up and the lead being damaged. Alternatively, non-varnished pencils are widely available. Graphite is used in conjunction with clay as an alternative for the 'lead' in pencils. Some have a solid wooden end and shorter lead, since pencils are often thrown away before they are completely used up.

Batteries

Avoid using batteries and use mains electricity wherever possible or, better still, go for solar powered options, for instance, calculators. The energy needed to make batteries is 50 times greater than the energy they give out. Rechargeable batteries are more efficient in resource use and give savings in energy and cost. In smaller offices, using rechargeable batteries is often very practical, since it is easier to control.

Durability and disposal

The longer the life-span of a product, the greater the benefit to the environment. Ask if the product is designed to be re-used or discarded; are the materials used such that they can be recycled or made from recycled material to begin with? Replacements for durable products are needed less often so raw materials are not required as quickly to make a replacement. One significant development in this area is long lasting polymer leads for pencils.

Packaging should be kept to a bare minimum and be made of recycled or recyclable material such as cardboard or tin. Plastic wallets should be made from recycled polypropylene. Consider whether the manufacturer takes any action in recovering used packaging for recycling.

The options available for disposal of writing instruments are either landfill or incineration. But by far the most acceptable options in environmental terms are re-use and recycling. Manufacturers of writing instruments have made progress in devising ways of making their products recyclable and/or re-usable, and these types of products are stocked by a wide range of suppliers.

Refillability promotes re-use. Refillable writing instruments are now available in the form of pencils, highlighters, permanent markers, rollerball and fountain pens. This reduces the amount of casing (plastics, metals) going to landfill.

Hints for small organisations

Small organisations obviously do not have the buying power of larger ones, but environmentally preferable products are widely available, so shop around! If your office is small, but is part of a larger organisation, make use of national agreements. Improvements to the way resources are used, for instance if paper is re-used internally, can substantially reduce total usage.

Guest Article

You and Your Stationery Supplier

by Justin Keeble, Sustainable Business Adviser, Dudley UK Limited

Two people are responsible for the impact your office has on the environment; you and your office products supplier.

The UK has seen a recent growth in one-stop-shop stationers seeking to capture the market for all the demands of the office environment. Increasingly, these retailers are playing larger roles in influencing how the office environment functions and as a result the extent to which the office environment impacts upon the natural environment.

The past ten years have seen a significant shift within the office supplies industry from a focus on selling products to providing a service. Retailers have placed customer relationship management at the forefront of their sales strategy. As customers' needs have become more diverse and informed, new kinds of relationships are being defined. The challenge for those working in the office sector who care about the environment is to exploit the opportunities that this shift opens.

Cost has been the most significant factor in stalling the enthusiasm consumers have to procure products or services that carry a specified environmental performance. The willingness to pay rarely matches the intention to buy. However, cost may not be an issue in the years to come.

All office suppliers know that they can maximise their profits by seeking to reduce the bottom line without compromising the service provided. Forward thinking office suppliers know that their profits can be maximised by seeking to provide the same level of service but selling less product.

How are these forward thinking companies achieving this? They are developing added value services to:

- Encourage efficient, effective and prudent use of products in the office environment.
- Develop innovative ways of recycling and re-use of these products.
- Encourage sufficiency in the design of products, to provide the same level of service with reduced use of resources.
- Provide leasing functions to shift ownership of the product from the customer to the supplier.

In addition to these measures, many office supplies companies are developing a strong Internet presence. Tailored on-line product catalogues, remote ordering systems and e-commerce features complemented by improved and more efficient ordering processes are reducing the number of deliveries needed, at the same time as reducing the time spent on placing the original order.

If you want to reduce your bills and protect the environment, why not get a bit closer to your stationery company? They want to do the same!

Contact: environment@dudley.co.uk ■

⚠ Common problems

Cost

Some environmentally preferable office supplies are more expensive. However, cost is generally linked to volume. If your supplier is aware that you are serious about using these products and you guarantee the volume, you should be able to negotiate improved rates on this range. Some recycled products are cheaper than virgin equivalents. Increased market demand will also help to reduce costs.

Summary guidelines

✔ Encourage re-use and waste reduction (see Chapter 3)
✔ Use recycled products where they are fit for the purpose
✔ Work with your supplier to increase the range of environmentally preferable products
✔ Avoid using batteries where you can use solar power or mains electricity or use rechargeable batteries
✔ Use refillable and solvent-free products wherever possible
✔ Buy products with minimal packaging

OFFICE STATIONERY

Labelling

The labelling of environmentally preferable products varies considerably between different stationery catalogues. Some are confusing and you have to search pretty hard to find them. Names of products can be very misleading.

Quality

As with any purchase, it is possible to find some green products that do not work! It is therefore important to test them before distributing them throughout your offices (as you should do with any product). For example, while some correction fluids work well, others do not. Some recycled Post-it-type notes stick, whereas others don't! Product performance varies from brand to brand. Be selective about the products you introduce to ensure they are fit for the purpose.

Perception

Perception of recycled products can be poor. However, in recent years quality has substantially improved. Good quality recycled alternatives are available to most products.

PRINTERS, PHOTOCOPIERS AND PCs

🍁 Environmental issues

Electronic equipment currently uses a greater percentage of total office energy than it did in the early 1990s. As a major area of growth in energy consumption, the environmental impacts of office equipment are growing. *See Chapter 5, Building Management* �‚ for further information on environmental issues and energy use. Studies of the average power demands of computers and other office equipment show substantial differences between similar models by the same manufacturer.

Heavy metals, solvents and CFCs are used during the manufacturing process. CFCs were used for washing circuit boards, but since the Montreal Protocol work has been conducted to phase them out (see Furniture Purchasing section for more information). Some manufacturers have replaced CFCs with water and alcohol-based solvent cleaners although solvents give rise to VOCs.

Environmental issues associated with photocopiers are dealt with in Chapter 5, Building Management. This section deals with establishing performance standards.

Six million laser and desk-jet toner cartridges are used in the UK every year; 50 per cent of these end up in landfill sites. The bulk of this material will not degrade for thousands of years and represents a significant waste of non-renewable resources. *Disposal of equipment is covered in Chapter 3, Office Waste* ⤴

Most manufacturers now use packaging material with a recycled content. The Producer Responsibility Obligations (Packaging Waste) Regulations make manufacturers more responsible for the packaging they produce and will increase the number of return schemes.

Legislation

Electronic equipment is covered by the proposed Waste Electrical and Electronic Equipment Directive and the Packaging Directive. *See Chapter 3, Office Waste* ⤴ There are also health and safety standards relating to photocopiers and laser printers, particularly around indoor air quality.

Industry initiatives

Industry Council for Electronic Equipment Recycling (ICER)

The Industry Council for Electronic Equipment Recycling (ICER) has been created to push for legislation on electronics recycling. ICER draws together suppliers, manufacturers, retailers, recyclers, waste management companies, local authorities and bulk users. It is developing as a centre of expertise, establishing how much is recyclable and looking at product design, methods of recycling, collection and markets for recycled material. It seeks to ensure that any legislation is sensible and practical and that consumers are aware of what responsible companies are doing.

US-EPA 'Energy Star'

Energy Star is perhaps the most common energy saving standard currently in use world-wide. The standard is promoted by the US Environmental Protection Agency and awarded to units which meet or use less than 30 watt energy consumption when on stand-by mode and which restart quickly from stand-by. An Energy Star can be awarded to monitors and computer equipment.

Not all Energy Star equipment has the same energy rating; on stand-by mode some use less energy than others.

☞ Practical action

Remanufactured cartridges

Collect used laser printer toner cartridges for recycling and buy back remanufactured cartridges. Toner cartridges can be refilled or remanufactured, saving on average 25 per cent of normal purchase costs and 50 per cent on inkjets. There are many companies offering this facility, though quality varies considerably. The use of recycled toner cartridges should not affect the printer warranty. Reputable companies guarantee to cover the cost of the repair of your printer if damage is caused by a faulty cartridge.

Used cartridges have a market value of between £1 and £5 each, and a number of charities have fund-raising schemes (eg ActionAid, St Thomas' Hospital). If volume is low, use a supplier that provides pre-paid return envelopes.

Check suppliers' environmental policy

Obtain a copy of the manufacturer's policy and make sure that they have made a continuing commitment to real environmental action. *See Chapter 8, Environmental Management* ➘ for information about environmental policy. Look for a commitment to reducing chemical use: for example eliminating ozone depleting chemicals from the production processes and an active programme of solvent reduction.

Ozone levels

Low level ozone is produced by photocopiers, which can cause or exacerbate respiratory illness. Clarify the ozone levels set for equipment, these can vary considerably. *See Chapter 10, Contacts and Resources* ➘ Also check the frequency of filter changes built in to your service contract.

Look for specific environmental features

Most electronic equipment has an energy-save facility; some are manual and some automatic. This facility is most effective if it operates automatically. In practice staff will not use a manual energy-save button. Ensure acceptability of recycled papers and efficient double-sided copying facility. Most machines now have a double-sided (duplex) copying facility, although some cope better with double-siding recycled papers than others. For example Oce machines have a short paper path which reduces problems with paper jams.

Design for recyclability

Machines can be designed for ease of disassembly to facilitate recycling. Clear identification of different plastics makes recycling more viable. Refurbished parts and sub-assemblies can be re-used and equipment can be returned for refurbishment or updating.

Consider energy costs

Equipment that generates less heat will require less air conditioning, saving money in the long term, even if it is more expensive to buy initially. The government-funded Building Research Energy Conservation Support Unit (BRECSU) has produced guidance for purchasers of office equipment which aims to minimise energy consumption. For equipment purchases, ask your supplier or manufacturer to provide detailed specification information; means of setting stand-by mode and recovery times.

End-of-life disposal

Equipment can be returned to the manufacturer for refurbishment. Computers can be broken down into component parts for re-use and recycling. Copper and silver from cables can be recycled, as can plastic and metal casings. The latter are shredded and broken down into ferrous and non-ferrous metals. The manufacturer can recover precious metals such as copper, gold, silver and palladium on printed circuit boards. Hard disks, printed circuit boards and power supplies can be re-used by the manufacturer internally. Floppy disk drives and various chips can be re-sold to other manufacturers.

Reduce the impact of packaging

Manufactures should be adopting reduction, re-use, recycling and return schemes. Most manufacturers now use cardboard packaging which is made from 100 per cent recycled material. However, some manufacturers go further and promote the collection of the packaging material for recycling and re-use. Rank Xerox has reduced the amount of disposable packaging used for its equipment; unwanted packaging is sent back to parts suppliers for re-use. Reductions in the amount of packaging waste left on your premises will reduce your waste disposal costs.

Servicing arrangements

Ensure that the environmental performance and servicing standards provided by

Summary guidelines

- ✔ Check the manufacturers' Environmental Policy and ability to demonstrate real environmental improvements
- ✔ Buy remanufactured toner cartridges
- ✔ Consider ozone emission levels specified on photocopiers and printers and the frequency of filter replacement
- ✔ Look for positive environmental features: automatic stand-by, compatibility with recycled paper and double-sided copying facility
- ✔ Check that the manufacturer has a programme of reducing solvent and harmful chemical use in the manufacturing process
- ✔ Check that the equipment has been designed for energy efficiency such as US Energy Star
- ✔ Check that the manufacturer designs for ease of disassembly to aid recycling
- ✔ Check that the manufacturer uses re-usable or recycled packaging

PRINTERS, PHOTOCOPIERS AND PCs

a third party service contractor match up with those of the equipment manufacturer. Make sure you can use your own choice of consumables and paper. Many companies lose flexibility by being tied into a servicing contract which includes paper.

⚠ Common problems

- Some manufacturers use recycled paper as a scapegoat for any problems with equipment, which can cause problems with warranty agreements. Make sure that this is resolved before you start.
- Servicing companies are often not fully aware of environmental performance of manufacturers. This can lead to problems with the use of recycled paper. However, in a tender situation, most service companies will offer to test recycled papers for suitability.
- Some servicing contractors do not recommend the use of recycled papers in photocopiers even when the equipment manufacturer has their own brand or endorses a specific brand.
- Preventative maintenance is not carried out, therefore parts will not be running at full efficiency at all times.
- Ozone filters are not changed according to the manufacturer's recommendations (also dependent on size, usage and location).
- Servicing contractors should not charge call-out rates for difficulties arising from the use of recycled paper. Make sure this issue is clarified before contracts are signed.
- Consumables are generally included in your contract: if you are purchasing your own consumables, make sure you are not paying for something you do not receive or would rather provide yourselves.

OFFICE FURNITURE

🍁 Environmental issues

The destruction of the world's tropical rainforests in order to supply the timber trade is recognised as a major environmental concern. More than 12 million acres of tropical rainforest are destroyed each year. Particular areas of concern are South East Asia and West Africa. At the current rate of destruction, most tropical forests will have disappeared within 40 years.

The international timber trade plays a major role in tropical deforestation and the loss of old growth rainforests in temperate and boreal areas. Careless extraction of timber from forests can cause soil erosion, nutrient loss and the extinction of plant and animal species (reduced biodiversity). Logging also threatens the existence of indigenous forest peoples and communities dependent on the forest.

Less publicised concerns include the use of chemicals in the manufacturing process and the final disposal both of the packaging material and the furniture.

Forestry practice

The main issues in the commercial logging of tropical timbers are the destruction of the biodiversity of rainforests. Tropical rainforests represent valuable resources and are becoming one of the major sources of new medicines, but deforestation is causing the extinction of over 50 different species every day. Forestry practices can also be very wasteful; for every cubic metre of timber removed, another cubic metre of useful wood is left to rot. Tree respiration acts to fix carbon dioxide (the most significant greenhouse gas) from the atmosphere, so widespread logging results in higher CO_2 levels and an increased threat of global warming and climate change.

The environmental and economic effects of commercial logging on indigenous peoples are often not taken into account. Increases in landlessness and dispossession lead to social problems such as malnutrition and social and economic exploitation.

Claims about forestry practices can be misleading; terms such as 'sustainably managed' may have no independent verification and can therefore be meaningless. A sustainably managed forest is one where a comprehensive programme of land planning and reforestation is implemented with careful control of the amount of timber removed from the forest, and minimal forest disturbance. Less than 1 per cent of tropical timber comes from truly sustainable sources.

Conservation organisations have identified serious shortcomings in management systems in some countries, such as unlicensed felling and failures to observe minimum girths and minimum regeneration periods.

The Forest Stewardship Council (FSC)

Founded by representatives of the timber trade and NGOs, the FSC aims to support environmentally appropriate, socially beneficial, and economically viable management of the world's forests. To achieve this, the FSC accredits and monitors certifiers who audit the quality of forest management against agreed principles. Consumers can then use the FSC trademark as a guarantee that their wood comes from sustainably managed forests. The FSC group of members now includes major retailers such as B&Q, Do it All and Homebase, and in 1999 had certified over 150 forests in 28 countries.

WWF 95 Plus Group

The WWF 95 Plus Group is a group of companies representing over 20 per cent of the wood and wood products market in the UK who have made the following commitments:

- Members are committed to supporting credible independent systems of forest certification, based upon standards which take full account of environmental, ecological, biodiversity, social and economic needs, such as those promoted by

the pioneering work of the Forest Stewardship Council.
- Members are committed to buying increasing proportions of their wood products from independently certified sources. Certifiers include SCS, Rainforest Alliance, SGS, Soil Association and other independent certifiers when appropriate.

WWF 95 Plus Group members have a combined annual turnover in wood products alone of £3.5bn and over 20 million customers per week. Signatories include B&Q, Sainsbury's, Jewsons, BBC magazines, Railtrack and The Co-op.

The work of the WWF 95 Plus Group has raised awareness within the timber and timber products industries that large-scale consumers of products are not prepared to accept unsubstantiated claims about wood and that they want a credible guarantee that their timber and paper come from credible forests. The Group is raising standards of information, performance and management for all wood uses.

 Practical action

Refurbish furniture where possible
In comparison with purchasing new office furniture, refurbishment of worn out items can cost about half the price. Renovation can provide an environmentally preferable alternative to purchasing new products as it avoids the disposal of non-renewable resources and reduces costs. Business Seating (Renovations) Ltd provides a refurbishment service for all types of office furniture including chairs, desks and partitions. OFFERS and Furniture Recycling Network operate limited but expanding recycling schemes for office furniture. Contact details are at the end of this chapter. As the schemes are expanding all the time, get in touch with them to find out if they can provide a service in your area. *See Chapter 10, Contacts and Resources* ➘ for FSC accredited furniture suppliers.

Support the Forest Stewardship Council/WWF 95 Plus Group initiative
Demand information from your supplier about the country of origin and forestry practices, and contact FSC for a list of member organisations.

Use chipboard
Chipboard can be used as an alternative to solid wood in sheet form. Made from the top four feet of softwood timber trees which would otherwise go to waste, it is sometimes faced with melamine or laminate (paper-based and derived from softwoods) and edged in plastic. Low-grade paper waste is also made into chipboard. Second quality temperate veneers can be substituted for mahogany on chipboard panels.

Use non-timber alternatives
Non-timber alternatives such as sheets produced from recycled fibres and agricultural waste are becoming more widely available. Vending cups can be recycled into wood substitutes and are currently used in the manufacture of garden furniture and

office stationery. It is not possible to make a blanket judgement over the relative environmental performance of plastic, metal or wooden products, as sufficient life cycle analysis has not been conducted. However, the use of waste products for new materials closes the recycling loop and reduces disposal to landfill.

Recycled textiles

Synthetic materials and low-grade textiles can be used in the manufacture of 'flock', a filling material for upholstery in furniture. Textile collection points, textile banks, are becoming a common sight alongside glass and paper banks at public recycling sites. The use of textiles such as flock reduces the amount of post-consumer waste disposed of to landfill.

Durawood

Save Wood Products manufacture a wood substitute made from expanded polystyrene packaging. Packaging is compressed and recycled into a hardwood substitute. It can be used in the same applications as wood but it does not rot, is impervious to water and insect attack and does not require varnishing or oiling. McDonald's is using their polystyrene packaging to make garden furniture for use in picnic areas.

Manufacturing

There are a number of chemicals used in the manufacture of furniture which have significant environmental impacts. However, these can be avoided by choosing a manufacturer who uses environmentally preferable alternatives.

Plastic foams

CFCs were used in the past as a blowing agent in upholstery foams but have been phased out as a result of the Montreal Protocol. Intermediary replacement chemicals such as HFCs and HCFCs, also ozone depleting substances, are used to blow foam but will themselves be phased out over the next 30 years. Carbon dioxide and air are among the possible replacements for such environmentally damaging chemicals. An alternative to plastic foam is CMHR (Combustion Modified High Resilient) foam. CMHR foam has a better feel than conventional polyether foam and is generally more ignition resistant. It is manufactured using steam instead of freon gases and is therefore environmentally preferable.

Wood preservatives

Wood is often treated with preservatives such as pentachlorophenol and lindane, which give rise to toxic VOCs (for more information see Catering and Cleaning section). The use of non-toxic water-based preservatives is preferable.

Formaldehyde

Resin glue used in chipboard furniture contains formaldehyde, a toxic organic compound which is an irritant to tissue, causing eye, skin and throat irritation, nausea and allergic reactions. At high levels, it is believed to be carcinogenic. It is emitted as a vapour and is harmful during both production and use. Some types of board have low formaldehyde levels and are an acceptable alternative.

Case Study 4.7

SUBJECT: **Suppliers**

ORGANISATION: **B&Q**

LOCATION: **UK**

STAFF: **22,000 (in nearly 300 stores throughout the UK)**

Background

In 1998 B&Q merged with the French number one DIY retailer Castorama, and together B&Q and Castorama boast sales of £4 billion. The combined business has now moved up the ranks to be the world's number three in the DIY market.

B&Q recognises that every product it sells and business operation it undertakes has an impact on the environment. It is impossible to eliminate that impact, but it is possible to reduce it by modifying the way the business is run and considering the range offered. B&Q is, therefore, committed to the continuous reduction of the environmental damage caused by the day to day running of the business and the securing of raw materials, production, packaging and disposal of its entire product range.

B&Q acknowledges the catalytic role it can play in many industrial sectors and supply chains to motivate change. Customers cannot buy a greener product if it is not offered or they do not understand or believe the message. They cannot use or dispose of a product in a safe way if they are not told how to do so.

Action

B&Q itself is only one link in the chain to reduce the company's environmental impact, but being the country's biggest home improvement retailer, B&Q has the power to encourage its 600 suppliers to be committed to improving their environmental performance.

The first programme to increase the environmental awareness of our suppliers was called the Supplier Environmental Audit (SEA). Targets set for 1994 resulted in over 95 per cent of our suppliers producing a meaningful environmental policy and action plan. In 1991 this figure was less than 10 per cent.

In 1995 we replaced the SEA with QUEST. QUEST stands for **QU**ality, **E**thics and **S**afe**T**y and is the process through which we assess both the quality and environmental performance of our supply base via ten principles.

For each environmental QUEST principle, suppliers are awarded a grade from A to E. An A grade is reserved for leadership, commitment and innovation and an E grade for a major problem which contravenes our environmental policy. The grades in between reflect good, average and poor performance.

We award our suppliers these grades based on different aspects of their environmental programme which reflect our own priorities. These are

- Environmental Policy and Awareness (Quest 6)
- Environmental Action and Achievements (Quest 7)
- Working Conditions in Developing Countries (Quest 8)
- Packaging and Environmental Claims (Quest 9)
- Timber (Quest 10)

Results

Our Millennium targets required suppliers to achieve a grade B for QUEST principles 6, 7, 8 and 9 – **84 per cent achieved this standard**; and grade A for QUEST principle 10 – **99.1 per cent of all products achieved 3rd party independent certification confirming the source was from well-managed forestry**.

Timber

About 24 per cent of B&Q's turnover is accounted for by timber and timber products such as wallpaper, tool handles and toilet seats, which come from over 145 suppliers in 40 countries.

In 1990, B&Q embarked on research into timber to find out about forest management in the supply chain and drafted a policy. The most important part of the policy is that it applies to all timber, both tropical and temperate. During forest visits B&Q found well-managed tropical forests and poorly managed temperate ones. In 1991, B&Q announced two targets: that by the end of 1993 it would identify all its sources of timber and that by the end of 1995 all its timber products would come from well-managed forests.

B&Q achieved both targets, but for the second target the company had to depend on its own process of internal scrutiny. This threw up several problems and proved that a system of credible independent certification is necessary to prove to its customers that the timber sold really is from well-managed forests.

This is why we set a third target: by the end of 1999, B&Q will only purchase timber-based products from forests independently certified by a certifier accredited by the Forest Stewardship Council (FSC). The FSC is a global organisation which has set the principles of good forest management against which forest-specific standards can be measured and can check the quality of the forest certifier's work. **99.1 per cent of all products achieved 3rd party independent certification confirming the timber was from well-managed forestry**.

Although the problems of independent certification and the FSC have been intensely complex, with many issues still to be resolved, B&Q believes that independent certification is the way forward for retailers and customers alike.

Product and packaging disposal

Through QUEST for suppliers, packaging is being reduced or omitted, material recyclability improved and post-consumer recycled content increased. As part of the overall supplier assessment process, suppliers are required to design products so that, wherever possible, they can be easily taken apart and the components recycled. For example, in 1996 B&Q decided to remove the tray from our own-label wooden toilet seat. This was made from polystyrene, which is difficult for customers to recycle. A further advantage was that the number of seats which could go into a 40ft container for shipping increased from 3300 to 4500, making an overall financial saving of over £100,000 a year.

Paint

As the UK's largest retailer of decorative paints, varnishes, wood treatments and speciality coatings, we recognise that we have a particular responsibility to find solutions to the environmental problems associated with paints. In 1997, to address this and other issues associated with our paint products, we introduced the B&Q Paint Policy and Labelling Scheme. This programme was launched nationwide at the beginning of 1998.

Peat

Our policy on peat has formed a central part of our environmental policy since 1991 when we made a commitment to stop purchasing peat extracted from bogs classified as a Site of Special Scientific Interest (SSSI) and to encourage research and development of peat-free alternatives.

Working conditions in developing countries

Environmental responsibility is merging with social responsibility. Nowhere is this better demonstrated than the growing accountability retailers and major brands now have for factories they buy from in developing nations. B&Q is convinced that we must tackle the issues associated with our wider trading neighbours country by country, through partnerships with development agencies across the world. We started with the Philippines and India, and in 1998 our work expanded into China.

Example project: India

Production in India of brassware, hand-knotted rugs and coir doormats for B&Q has now been surveyed for social and environmental impact by a locally based independent social development charity, providing third-party verification and expertise. B&Q was the first retailer to stock rugs which come from looms certified by Rugmark as not using illegal or exploited child labour. Rugmark is an independent charity supported by Christian Aid and Oxfam. ■

Packaging and disposal

Is the furniture designed to be easily repaired or to be discarded? Is it possible to replace worn or soiled items such as textile coverings and foam padding in chairs? If not, what are the disposal options?

Blankets can be used to protect furniture during transportation. Your manufacturer should also take action to recover used packaging for recycling. Packaging is expensive to dispose of, so it is in your interests to make sure that the manufacturer has taken steps to reduce it.

Comparing office furniture manufacturers

As well as standard questions you should ask all suppliers on policies and management systems, examples of the kind of questions you should be asking your office furniture manufacturer are:

- What are your sources of wood?
- Is wood purchased from independently certified, sustainably managed sources?
- Do you have a waste management programme?
- Do you use plastic foams, wood preservatives, formaldehyde, or solvent-based lacquer?
- What packaging do you use?
- Do you have distribution initiatives to reduce environmental impact?
- Do your products have recyclable or repairable parts?

Summary guidelines

✔ Avoid tropical hardwoods and check raw material sources. Wood products should be from independently certified, sustainably managed sources
✔ Consider renovation of worn furniture
✔ Consider wood substitutes made from recycled materials
✔ Avoid products where ozone depleting chemicals are used as a blowing agent for foams
✔ Avoid solvent-based wood preservatives, lacquers and adhesives
✔ Avoid adhesives containing formaldehyde and solvents
✔ Consider design for re-use and end-of-life disposal
✔ Investigate packaging recyclable content, recyclability and retrieval

OFFICE FURNIITURE

Purchasing

PAPER

🍁 Environmental issues

The key environmental issues associated with paper production and use are:

- loss of natural habitats to intensive tree farming;
- pollution from manufacture;
- energy usage;
- waste disposal; landfill and incineration.

In 1998 the UK used over 12 million tonnes of paper and board of which 4.7 million tonnes were made from recycled pulp from the UK and abroad, giving a recycling rate of 40 per cent. This huge market for virgin pulp means that there is pressure on the paper industry to produce trees quickly, leading to intensive tree farming.

Forestry practice

The paper industry plants more trees than it chops down, but in doing so natural habitats are destroyed to make way for intensive forestry. This is happening in the UK, particularly in Scotland. The majority of tree planting in the UK has taken place in the Scottish uplands and covers a significant proportion of the Scottish countryside.

Ploughing of deep peat for forestry in areas such as the Flow Country of Caithness and Sutherland contributes to global warming and destroys these unique habitats, as they are planted with conifers. Peat acts as a sink for carbon dioxide, locking the gas up chemically within its structure. When bogs are ploughed and drained, peat dries and decomposes, releasing the trapped carbon dioxide into the atmosphere.

Single species plantations (monocultures), especially those using exotic species, are unable to support the range of plant, insect, bird and mammal life found in more diverse old growth forests. Monocultures provide one basic habitat and food source; if a species is not adapted to that particular niche, it will not survive.

The prime source of supply for European paper is Scandinavia but there has been an increase in the use of eucalyptus, predominantly from plantations in Brazil and Portugal. Eucalyptus grows eight times faster than pine, which contributes to its value for paper making, but it also has significant negative effects upon the environment. The speed of its growth is responsible for lowering the water table in many areas. As the water table falls, top soil dries out and becomes less compacted and is therefore more susceptible to loss through wind and flooding. Soil acidification also occurs as the trees leach nutrients from the soil, thereby decreasing its ability to support vegetation without the addition of fertilisers.

In Brazil and Portugal the spread of extensive eucalyptus plantations has led to the loss of adequate water supplies for farm land, leading to the loss of crops and failed harvests, conditions which can precede drought.

Manufacturing problems

Bleaching agents

Paper pulp can be bleached with chlorine gas (used to break down lignin, which is a natural glue in wood) and a variety of chemicals including hydrogen peroxide and hypochlorite to achieve whiteness. The resulting effluent, called bleach liquor, has been found to contain over 300 compounds, many of which are dangerous toxins. One of the groups of compounds which cause major concern are dioxins; these are highly toxic and accumulate in the fatty tissue of fish, from where they can pass into the food chain.

Effluent

Wastewater effluent from pulp and paper manufacture can contain up to 1000 organic and inorganic compounds. Waste organic materials, those which can biodegrade, are measured by biochemical oxygen demand (BOD), that is, the amount of oxygen required to break the compounds down to their constituent parts. Effluent discharges from paper mills have been found to cause eutrophication, which occurs when an excess of nutrients enter a water course or body and over-enrich the water. This enrichment causes an explosion in the growth of algae (blooming) which consume any available oxygen and threaten plant and animal life. Algal blooms can also lead to the production of foul-smelling substances such as hydrogen sulphide and ammonia; the resulting water cannot be used for human consumption and can represent a threat to human life.

The following are the major recognised indicators of paper mill effluent:

- Chemical oxygen demand (COD): a measurement of total emissions of organic matter; the prime parameter for emissions to water.
- Absorbable organic halogens (AOX): a measurement of chlorinated organics from the bleaching of chemical pulps; the secondary parameter for emissions to water.
- Sulphur: the parameter used for emission to air. Sulphur is a major contributory factor to acid rain. The major source of sulphur emissions is burning fossil fuels.

Different maximum acceptable levels for mill performance are set by the various labelling schemes, and a number of mills have been awarded ISO 14001.

Additives

Optical brightening agents (OBAs) increase the whiteness of materials by absorbing radiant energy; when added to off-white colours, the blue-white OBAs create a brighter white appearance. OBAs have been found to be carcinogenic.

Mineral loadings are added in the papermaking process to create an even surface and feel to the end product. Most loadings and coatings currently used are china clay (kaolin) and chalk (calcium carbonate). The quarrying of such raw materials creates unsightly areas, dust and heavy traffic movement. In some areas it can also cause damage to important wildlife habitats.

Improvements to the manufacturing process

Oxygen bleaching

Oxygen pre-bleaching is designed to reduce the amount of chlorine bleaching necessary in the pulping process, which means fewer organochlorines are formed. Pulp is then washed and oxygen bleached several times to improve the whiteness. The oxygen used in this process can be recycled and, as oxygen is cheaper than chlorine, many mills are changing their operation. Elemental chlorine-free (ECF) and totally chlorine-free (TCF) pulp is also produced using reduced amounts of chlorine.

Improving efficiency

Many mills have invested heavily in changing their bleaching processes. By improving the efficiency of the pulping process, more impurities can be removed prior to bleaching, reducing the degree of subsequent bleaching required and, therefore, the formation of organochlorines.

Recycled paper

Making paper from recycled pulp uses less energy and, if correctly sorted, no bleach as the pulp was whitened when originally manufactured. The whiteness of recycled paper is achieved either by using unprinted white waste or by de-inking printed white waste paper. The de-inking process is done with detergents, water and compressed air and is not significantly polluting. When bleaching is needed, hydrogen peroxide can be used which is less damaging than chlorine. Optical brightening agents are not used in the production of recycled papers.

Waste paper and pulp can be recycled a number of times, although 15–20 per cent of the fibres become too small to use and fall through the papermaking screens as a sludge residue. Some uses have been found for such material as a fertiliser and as a spillage control product; sludge is recycled into absorbent granules which can be used to soak up hazardous spillages.

Disposal

Paper accounts for over a third of our waste, and is mainly disposed of to landfill sites or incinerators. There is little need for paper to be landfilled or incinerated; it can be recycled easily, will certainly reduce your disposal costs as it can represent over 70 per cent of total waste, and may even generate revenue. *See Chapters 3 and 7, Office Waste and Communication* ➘ for further information on waste and recycling.

Labelling systems and industry standards

The environmental classification of paper is a vital consideration when assessing the environmental credentials of a particular type of paper. The terms recycled paper or environmentally friendly mean very little without such classification. The following labelling schemes for recycled paper are in operation, but more detailed information on the content of different paper grades can be obtained from The Paper Federation of Great Britain. *See Chapter 10, Contacts and Resources* ➘

National Association of Paper Merchants (NAPM)

In order to qualify for the Mark, a paper or board must be manufactured from a minimum of 75 per cent genuine paper and board waste, which can come from converters, printers or household and office waste.

Blue Angel

This is a German scheme, awarding a Blue Angel label to paper which is 100 per cent recycled, of which at least 51 per cent is post-consumer waste.

The Blue Angel Award also indicates superior environmental performance. This scheme is directed by advisory committees of academics in Germany (they also advise the German government on legislation) and has run for several years. The scheme considers the materials used in manufacture, emissions, energy consumption and disposal and safety issues in the assessment of environmental performance.

EU Eco-label

Eco-labelling criteria have been set for copier paper and converted paper products (including envelopes) to provide a recognised environmental standard (see Eco-label section at the start of this chapter). Any virgin wood fibres used must come from forests where sustainable forest management is practised.

Nordic White Swan

The objective of the White Swan label is to encourage production methods with minimum environmental impacts. Fine papers can be made from virgin pulp or recycled fibres: it is the effect the manufacturing process has on the environment, rather than the selection of raw materials, which is assessed.

Chlorine-free

The term environmentally friendly is often used for chlorine-free papers. However, chlorine is now recognised as a pollutant. There are labelling systems for chlorine-free papers and chlorine gas is becoming far less widely used. *See Oxygen Bleaching, page 111*

☞ Practical action

Reduce demand for virgin paper

Pressure on natural habitats will be reduced if demand for new timber is also reduced. Reduce your usage, re-use and recycle your paper and close the recycling loop by using recycled papers. This will also reduce the volume of waste going to landfill/incineration.

Encourage recognised forestry standards

Demand accurate information from your paper supplier about forestry practices. Check the source of the wood pulp used.

Issues outlined concerning forestry in the Office Furniture section of this chapter apply equally to paper. The objectives of the Forestry Stewardship Council scheme and the WWF 95 Plus Group should be adopted as good practice in paper purchasing.

Encourage improvements in mill performance

It is important to quantify the environmental standards of the mill which manufactures your paper. It is unrealistic to be able to test these standards yourself; however, reputable paper merchants will be able to provide you with information regarding the measures of effluent from the relevant mill; alternatively this information can be sought from the mill direct. Enquire whether your paper suppliers have mills which have been awarded ISO 14001 or have an EMS in place.

Introduce recycled papers

Recycled paper uses less energy, requires less bleaching and chemical use than papers produced with virgin pulp whilst also closing the recycling loop.

Good quality recycled papers are widely available for use as copier, letterhead, presentation and even art and design purposes.

Build in the use of recycled papers at the tender stage of all relevant tender documents and contracts – office equipment, printers and paper supply.

Reduce the weight of paper used: 90 g/m paper is an alternative to 100/110 g/m for letterhead.

Ensure compatibility with office equipment

It is important to consider the servicing contract on your photocopiers when considering a suitable brand of copier paper. Check with your copier manufacturer that the paper you have chosen will not contravene your service contract. Some machines may need adjusting. *See Chapter 10, Contacts and Resources* ↘

Recycled printing papers

Design for recycled papers

Maximise your use of the different textures and finishes available in recycled papers and design to that. Don't design for virgin paper and then print on recycled! Work with your printer/designer to develop the use of recycled papers. Printing machines may need adjusting. High-quality, cost effective products are available in recycled fibre. Your choice of paper also affects its ultimate recyclability. The majority of laminated finishes cannot be recycled without the use of chemicals; therefore, we do not recommend their use. Alternative finishes such as water-glaze are available.

⚠ Common problems

Cost

Recycled papers used to be perceived as expensive. However, they are now available at prices which are competitive with virgin papers. If your supplier appreciates that you are serious about using recycled paper and you are prepared to commit yourself to using it, you should be able to negotiate a competitive price. Be persistent!

Quality

New developments in papermaking technology have made possible the production of recycled papers which compare in terms of appearance, quality and performance with virgin grades. Laser printer and photocopier guaranteed recycled papers are now common. It should be possible to match most virgin papers currently in use.

Perception

Changing people's attitudes to the use of recycled paper can be a major challenge but it can often be based on prejudice or a failed attempt to use recycled papers some years previously. Modern recycled papers have come a long way; though it may not look it, this book is printed on recycled paper!

Case Study 4.8

SUBJECT: **Paper Mill Environmental Performance**

ORGANISATION: **Inveresk plc**

LOCATION: **Inverkeithing, Fife, and Alloa, Central Scotland**

STAFF: **400**

Background

Specialist papermaker Inveresk PLC is a market leader in recycled paper, producing the widely-used Repeat range of 100 per cent recycled papers. Although the company is proud of its market-leading recycled range, Inveresk can boast many less public environmental achievements.

Internally, Inveresk has a strategic and far-reaching environmental policy, which is rigorously implemented in all aspects of paper production. This policy states that it will meet and, where possible, improve on legal environmental requirements and develop knowledge of the environmental impact of its processes and products, seeking to move towards long-term sustainable principles.

Minimising the release of waste materials into the environment, reducing the use of fossil fuels by good practice and investment in both manufacturing and transportation to minimise the impact on the environment are an integral part of Inveresk's day-to-day operation.

Inveresk produces more than 25,000 tonnes of recycled grades annually at Caldwells Mill, Inverkeithing, Fife, and Kilbagie Mill, Alloa – the company's Graphic Papers mills.

At the £8 million de-inking plant at Kilbagie Mill – one of just two of its kind in the UK and the only one in Scotland – 30,000 tonnes of waste paper is diverted from landfill each year. Effluent crumble from the plant is used as soil conditioner in farms in Fife and Central Scotland.

Action

Inveresk's Environmental Policy is regularly reviewed so that it is up-to-date and meets the company's objective, which is ultimately to become a sustainable business.

All mills have installed modern two-stage biological effluent treatment plants to effectively treat waste water. Some mills are recycling their treated waste water, thereby reducing the environmental impact of water abstraction. Where possible, mills are recycling the paper crumble from the effluent treatment plants to improve the quality of agricultural land.

Four of Inveresk's five mills have implemented ISO 14001 Environmental Management Systems and two have Integrated Pollution Control (IPC) authorisation. The fifth mill in the group is working towards implementing ISO 14001 by this spring.

The company produces an annual health, safety and environmental report which objectively measures each year's progress.

Results

Inveresk Graphic Papers's market-leading Repeat range of printing, laser, coloured and stationery products, is 100 per cent recycled using the Kilbagie de-inking plant. The range is fully guaranteed for laser, ink-jet and offset printing as well as plain paper faxing and one and two-sided copying.

All mills have set-up task teams to actively improve energy efficiency, to reduce costs and reduce greenhouse gas emissions.

Kilbagie Mill, in Alloa, Central Scotland, was the first graphic paper mill worldwide to receive Forest Stewardship Council (FSC) certification in July, 1999. This means the mill can produce, on request, paper which is maximum 75 per cent recycled and minimum 25 per cent FSC-endorsed virgin pulp.

FSC certification guarantees to customers that the paper is derived from a sustainable and managed forest which preserves indigenous wildlife. The chain-of-custody means that every supplier also adheres to FSC standards.

Inveresk's 100 per cent recycled Repeat range has gained three major environmental awards – from Her Majesty's Stationery Office, the National Association of Paper Merchants and the German Blue Angel mark.

Issued by Beattie Media on behalf of Inveresk PLC.

Contact: Suzy Powell/Laurna O'Donnell. Tel 0131 220 8269/0468 911 540 ∎

Summary guidelines

✔ Reduce your paper consumption
✔ Make sure that the recycled copier paper you choose is compatible with your office equipment and will not affect equipment warranties
✔ Make sure that any virgin pulp content in the paper you choose is ECF or TCF and is from an independently certified, sustainably managed forest
✔ Request information regarding mill environmental performance and aim to use mills with ISO/EMAS accreditation
✔ Demand accurate information from your paper merchant, and don't be put off

PAPER

Compatibility with equipment

Test the paper you intend to use and work with your suppliers. Some manufacturers and service companies blame machine faults on recycled paper and say that this is not covered by the warranty. Test the paper first and check your warranty.

CATERING AND CLEANING

🍁 Environmental issues

There is a strong link between health, safety and environmental issues, all of which must be considered when assessing cleaning contracts. Cleaning substances can represent significant health and safety risks and if released into watercourses in sufficient quantities these substances can harm plant and animal life.

Encouraging your cleaning and catering contractors to select more environmentally benign substances reduces environmental effects and health and safety risks. The major concerns are the use of acids, alkalis, bleaches and solvents (particularly if mixed). All of these cause air and water pollution, so correct disposal is important. Disposal of these substances to drain may require a licence from your local water company (depending on the concentration).

Acids

Acids are widely used in cleaning products, most commonly hydrochloric and phosphoric. Dilution of acids with water produces heat as a by-product, which can lead to an explosive reaction. Acids should always be added to water, not vice versa. If any acid is mixed with an alkali (also used in cleaning products) a reaction occurs which may be explosive. If acid is added to bleach, the poisonous gas chlorine is released.

Alkalis

Alkalis are often found in cleaning products used for dishwashing machines, removing greasy deposits, paint stripping and as concrete cleaners. Common alkalis are: sodium hydroxide (caustic soda), sodium metasilicate and borax (sodium borate decahydrate) and bleach (see below). Alkali substances can be carefully diluted with water but should not be mixed with acids as this will cause an explosive reaction.

Bleach

Bleach is a strongly alkaline solution of sodium hypochlorite in water; it can cause harm to human and animal health (if ingested) and to ecosystems if released in a concentrated form. Bleach should not be mixed with any other cleaning compounds and should only be diluted with water.

Solvents

Solvents cause the emission of VOCs, which contribute to photochemical smog, are low level air pollutants and also act as ozone depleters. Solvents retain their hazardous properties when mixed with other substances; they are used in many cleaning preparations and pose special problems; their volatility and reaction on the skin can lead to rapid absorption into the body and skin effects. Some are highly flammable, and most can be decomposed by heat into highly toxic products. They are used in pure form for specialist tasks, for example, chewing gum removal.

Phosphates

Phosphates are an environmental concern, but do not have health and safety implications. They are used in dishwasher powders, multi-purpose cleaning agents and scouring cleaners. Phosphates can cause eutrophication, which occurs when an excess of nutrients (such as phosphates) enter a watercourse or body and over-enrich the water. This enrichment causes an explosion in the growth of algae (blooming) which consume any available oxygen and threaten plant and animal life. Algal blooms can also lead to the production of foul-smelling substances such as hydrogen sulphide and ammonia; the resulting water cannot be used for human consumption and can provide a threat to human life.

Packaging and disposal

In addition to the products used, packaging material relating to cleaning products also has an environmental impact.

 Practical action

Alternative cleaning products

Cleaning contractors often provide their own cleaning products, but it is important to establish the following:

Material type and selection

Find out which substances are used on-site and the environmental criteria used for product selection. The range of products should be kept to a minimum to reduce health and safety risks and administration under COSHH.

Hazard identification

Replace hazardous materials with less hazardous alternatives such as water-based products to reduce environmental impact and health and safety risks.

Reducing the impact of packaging

Use concentrates, refillable containers and packaging material made from recycled material.

Summary guidelines

✔ Minimise the range of products used on site
✔ Minimise the use of hazardous substances or replace completely
✔ Ensure separation of acids, alkalis, bleaches and solvents
✔ Ensure adequate training of cleaning staff in correct usage and awareness of hazards
✔ Ensure correct disposal of cleaning fluids and containers
✔ Maximise usage of concentrates and refillable containers to reduce packaging
✔ Use washroom consumables and cleaning supplies manufactured from recycled material
✔ Purchase bulk packaged catering products where possible
✔ Avoid the purchase of individually packaged catering supplies such as individual milk portions (jiggers)

CATERING AND CLEANING

Case Study 4.9

SUBJECT: **Cleaning Services**

ORGANISATION: **Monthind Clean**

LOCATION: **Colchester**

STAFF: **800**

Background

Many of Monthind's clients need a push! They all want to be green and they see the sense in minimising their waste but the idea of measuring this waste, of undertaking a scoping audit to see exactly what it costs them each year, is awesome. Often they are so immersed in their core business that they haven't the resources, the people or the time to sort out their rubbish.

Action

Monthind, as their cleaning contractor, point them in the right direction, and provide most of the answers – how many black sacks are used a night, how many 1100 litre bins go to landfill each week, sometimes even how many plastic vending cups they use each week. They can also give them a list of the contents of their bins – frightening:

Office paper, plastic files, 5-litre plastic bottles, old IT equipment, a typist's chair with split upholstery, food waste, and of course cardboard boxes, cardboard boxes, cardboard boxes.

Many customers do not realise the cost of sending this to landfill. Monthind start by making a list and then by making suggestions:

- What can be recycled?
- Can someone else utilise the IT equipment?
- What can be compacted?
- Can packaging be returned to the manufacturers?
- What can Monthind or the client re-use themselves?
- This has to be a partnership.

To be effective, all recycling systems must be supported by the cleaners. The cleaners must understand the benefits in it for them, such as less lifting and better housekeeping plus their special responsibility to the environment.

Monthind, as the client's cleaning company, belong as part of the team. It is their cleaners who 'police' the process and show customers, by example, how the process works. For systems to be sustainable long-term it is essential to have committed input from the cleaners.

So often recycling systems are introduced with great enthusiasm and goodwill but so often this lapses – paper creeps into the general waste bins and the ratio of rubbish going to landfill increases once again – it needs constant monitoring. Cleaners are closest to the problem, closest to the offenders. By highlighting these, Monthind are able to bring concerns to the attention of the customer and gently bring things back on line.

Results

Monthind Clean sets up the recycling scheme as part of their full waste management system. This helps the cleaners, reduces the risk of back strain from lifting heavy bins and gives more time for detailed cleaning. It improves housekeeping (no more screwed-up paper around the bin or under the desk, fewer open bins full of unsightly waste).

A complete waste management system with colour coded bins eradicates black sacks totally and can be set up to recycle cans, toner cartridges, paper, cardboard, files – indeed almost anything. Anything which can be returned, re-used or recycled cuts the ever-increasing cost of rubbish going to landfill and its associated damage to the environment. If the waste management system is set up properly it can also cut the cleaning costs. Remember, up to 25 per cent of cleaning time is spent dealing with the removal of waste.

One of the real benefits in introducing an environmental policy is in bringing together employees. It enables them to buy into the idea and they work together as a team to meet a common objective they voluntarily wish to achieve. The knock-on effect of this is better communication throughout the business and a good team spirit. ■

Washroom consumables

Use toilet paper and hand-towels made from recycled material. There is no consensus on the life-cycle assessment of hot air dryers versus using towels; on balance, the overall environmental impact is similar. Use refuse sacks manufactured from recycled plastic.

Disposables

There is a problem with the use of recycled materials for food hygiene products due to the risk of residual contamination. On average, disposable catering products contain 30 per cent recycled material, but this tends to be recycled at source, that is, at the production stage. Plates can be manufactured from recycled paper and card, but need to be given a thicker coating of plastic which rather defeats the object of recycling! A more practical option is to reduce the usage of disposables and extend the use of recycled products.

There are a number of products commonly used within catering which can be replaced with environmentally preferable options:

- Individual milk and cream cartons (jiggers), designed for single use, create unnecessary packaging. Phase them out and use jugs where possible. Coasters can also be dispensed with.
- An in-house water purification system is a cost-effective alternative to buying in mineral water and can produce still and sparkling water. This means bottles can

Case Study 4.10

SUBJECT: **Catering Contractors**

ORGANISATION: **Crofton Halls**

LOCATION: **Orpington, Kent**

STAFF: **10**

Background

The Crofton Halls are community halls providing meeting facilities for the local community, operated by Bromley Council. The facilities comprise a small meeting room (60 max), small hall (160 max) and the main hall with a capacity of 350/500 max.

The halls are used by a broad range of community groups including: playgroups, disability groups and social functions including weddings. The halls have about 155,000 visitors per year, many on a regular basis. Consequently there are excellent opportunities to promote environmental action to individuals which will encourage a change of behaviour at home.

The organisation also manages other civic halls in Bromley including Anerley Town Hall and Play Centre, The Great Hall, Bromley Civic, and The Public Hall in Beckenham. The aim is to use Crofton Halls as a pilot project which can be extended to the other sites.

Action

There is considerable potential to work with catering contractors to reduce the quantity of disposable products, particularly plastic vending cups. We recommend the development of an Environmental Policy for the halls which can be circulated to contractors to raise awareness of waste and environmental issues. Some of the waste from functions and parties includes materials which may be suitable for the playgroup (eg balloons and bunting).

Results

- Encourage caterers to use the durable products provided as an alternative to plastic cups.
- Consider an additional charge to caterers who use disposable products to give an added incentive.
- Avoid the use of individual sachets such as sugar, milk and cream jiggers. Replace with milk jug and sugar bowls.
- Promote your Environmental Policy to caterers in advance.
- Liaise with the playgroup/Waste Alert regarding the re-use of materials.
- Re-negotiate waste disposal charges once the quantity of waste has been reduced due to recycling and waste reduction measures. ■

be re-used instead of being recycled.
- Take-away bags can be manufactured from recycled Kraft paper. This is acceptable since they are secondary packaging and not in direct contact with the food. Encourage re-use: for example, you could credit staff for returned take-away bags.
- Serviettes are available manufactured from recycled material.

A company which annually bought almost 7000 bottles of mineral water for client use at an estimated cost of £3614 decided to extend the water purification system that was already in place for staff use. The change resulted in total savings of over £5500.

PRINTING

Legislation

Printworks come under local authority air pollution control under the Environmental Protection Act 1990 because of the potential for solvent emissions to air. The Act introduced a new system of pollution control which recognised that emissions to one medium (air/water etc) can have an effect upon another. The Act authorised a range of 'prescribed processes and substances'; highly polluting industries are covered by Part A and regulated by the Environment Agency via Integrated Pollution Control. Part B processes are regulated under local authority air pollution control. Printing is a prescribed process under Part B if 20 tonnes or more of printing ink, metal coatings or 25 tonnes or more of organic solvents are used in any 12-month period.

🍁 Environmental issues

Printing processes

The main environmental issue associated with printing processes is the use of organic solvents. Organic solvent use gives rise to the release of VOCs, a major ozone-depleting substance (see Solvents in Catering and Cleaning section). Printworks account for approximately 10 per cent of the tonnes of VOCs emitted by industry.

VOC emissions arise in printing from: inks and ink thinning, press cleaning and washing, pre-print press cleaning and reclamation processes and the use of alcohol-based solvents (see Table 4.1). Organic solvents are also used in other printing processes to clean ink off the presses after print runs.

Table 4.1 *Printing processes and sources of VOC emissions*

Process	Description	Typical use	VOC sources
Flexography (includes Letterpress)	Relief letterpress printing using rubber rollers or photopolymer plates on presses	For packaging, eg print on cartons and labels	VOC-forming solvent-based inks
Lithography (Offset)	Flat surface process where only image areas of printing plate attract the ink Uses alcohol or water-based fountain solution	Corporate print: brochures, annual reports Magazine and newspaper production	VOC-forming solvent-based cleaning products Isopropyl or other solvent in fountain solution – Magazine printing VOC-forming solvent-based inks
Gravure	Recesses on a printing cylinder are filled with ink which is then 'lifted' by contact with the paper	Long run printing eg magazines and catalogues (This process is only used by a few large magazine printers who are already capturing and recycling solvent emissions)	VOC-forming solvent-based inks
Screen	Ink is squeezed through a stencil and applied to the printing substrate	Posters, fabrics/textiles	VOC-forming solvent-based inks

Inks

Inks comprise pigments, solvents and oil. Solvent-based inks are a source of VOCs. Some inks have been especially formulated to resist dispersion in water which can cause problems when printed material is de-inked as part of the recycling process. Pigments may also contain heavy metals such as lead, which can be harmful to human health and the environment. Other metals are also used in printing inks; in sufficient quantities, these metals can be harmful to flora and fauna.

Lithographic inks are traditionally based on mineral oils, a non-renewable resource.

Any product which relies on evaporation for drying purposes is a potential source of VOCs. This includes heatset, flexographic, gravure and screen printing inks.

Case Study 4.11

SUBJECT: **Printers**

ORGANISATION: **Copyprint UK Ltd**

LOCATION: **Vauxhall**

STAFF: **40**

Background

Copyprint UK is a medium-sized print and design company based in Vauxhall, South London. The company provides an extensive range of services including design, plate making, printing from single colour to four colour, lithographic and print finishing. The company has a large number of blue chip clients, many of whom have environmental policies and report publicly on their environmental performance.

Action

The majority of waste is paper, cardboard, plastic wrapping and wooden pallets. A paper recycling scheme is in place for white and coloured paper, for which revenue is received. Some unused paper is donated to local schools or listed on our waste exchange.

An agreement has been made with suppliers to take back pallets – approximately 40 per month – for re-use (these were previously landfilled). All printer cartridges are returned to the supplier.

Chemical wastes, including containers, inks, rags and washing solutions, from the printing processes are collected by a specialist company. The developer is now recycled and the silver is recovered, thus saving £50 per week. Metal plates are now cleaned and re-used, potentially saving £400/month. Copyprint has also switched from conventional inks to using vegetable-based inks, thus lessening their overall impact on the environment.

The company has also made progress in energy saving. The computers and other items of electrical equipment are now set to 'power down' mode when not in use. 50 energy-saving fluorescent tubes have been installed saving 8 per cent on energy costs or approximately £200 per year.

Copyprint has also revised their purchasing system, now buying in bulk. This has reduced purchasing related costs by £200 per month.

Copyprint is also taking a leading role in encouraging other businesses within the estate to start waste minimisation projects so facilities can eventually be shared amongst a group of businesses, such as recycling fluorescent tubes.

Results

Copyprint UK has recognised that taking environmental issues seriously will help the company and attract or retain customers that require good environmental practice from suppliers. The company has formed an environmental committee and is seeking to develop an environmental policy with an action plan and quantified targets. They have also shown that through waste minimisation measures there can be substantial savings in related costs. Currently this is amounting to over £5000 per year and is probably higher when considering the paper and plates that are being recycled.

For more information contact Fintan Harrold, Print Manager, Copyprint(UK)Ltd. Tel: 020 7735 0956 ∎

☞ Practical action

Ask your printer for environmentally preferable alternatives

Printing involves a series of complex interactions between inks, processes and specific outputs. It is therefore difficult to draw together specific environmental best practice standards for inks and printing as these may not apply to the specific job you may require. Nevertheless, the following sets out the types of products that are currently available. It is important to discuss environmental issues with your printer; they should:

- be aware of the environmental effects of their business;
- be taking steps to minimise and manage their effects;
- be able to demonstrate an ongoing commitment to using non-solvent-based solutions and inks.

Many printers who comply with legislation will already be demonstrating good practice. As a consumer of a service you have buying power. Printers should be keen to respond to enquiries and customer requests. If you feel that they are not keeping you abreast of the latest developments you do not have to continue using them!

Printing

Press washes

In the past year interest has been shown in citrus fruit-based solvents. However, they have not been widely used because their smell becomes sickly with ongoing use and they have been implicated as possible carcinogens.

Chemically modified vegetable oil-based washes are available from most suppliers, which are effective but can be disliked by press operators. Such products are widely used in Germany, Scandinavia and the USA but it may take legislative pressure to force their use in the UK.

Low viscosity solvent washes provide an environmentally preferable alternative to traditional products as they emit few or no VOCs. A solvent free water-based cleaner is also available.

Summary guidelines

✔ Obtain details of the environmental policy of your printer or any printer you expect to use

✔ Ensure that your printer has a policy for reducing VOC-forming solvent use and can demonstrate achievements

✔ Integrate a requirement to use the most environmentally preferable processes, inks, solutions and washes in tender documentation

✔ Encourage your printer to maximise the use of non-solvent-based fountain solutions, press washes and inks

✔ Encourage your printer to maximise the use of inks that do not contain heavy metals where available

✔ Encourage your printer to communicate with their suppliers to ensure that they are kept up to date on, and supplied with, the latest environmentally preferable products and raw materials

✔ Ensure that your printer keeps you up to date with the latest developments in solvent reduction and replacement

✔ Remember that as a consumer of a service you have buying power

PRINTING

Fountain solutions

Used in lithographic printing, fountain solutions are the largest source of VOCs. Vegetable oil-based alternatives have not sold well to date because printers feel they do not perform as well as alcohol-based solutions. Solutions containing high boiling alcohols which do not evaporate as easily as traditional solutions and thus release less VOCs are widely used in Denmark and Italy.

Waterless litho technology, which uses high viscosity inks and results in a reduction in waste paper production and ink use is widespread in the USA.

Inks

Environmentally preferable inks exclude heavy metals and have low solvent content (most water-based products contain only 5–8 per cent of organic solvent). Water-based and UV curing inks emit no VOCs, either during manufacture or when used by the printer. Inks are also available based on rape seed or soya bean oil in place of mineral oil, thus maximizing use of renewable resources.

VOC control can be avoided with the use of flexographic inks formulated for drying using ultraviolet light. However, UV curing lamps give rise to low level ozone emissions which can cause or exacerbate respiratory illness.

GROUNDS MAINTENANCE

Developing good practice for the management of grounds, parks, and playing fields promotes a strong environmental message to the public, staff and pupils. Enhancing the wildlife value of grounds and plants, whether indoor or outdoor, can provide a useful way of making people think about their connections with the environment. Though many offices do not have large areas of grounds, many have indoor plants and may even have small outside areas that could be enhanced with a pond or wildlife area. Encouraging wildlife value is also increasingly important to schools and local authorities; as the guardians of areas of park, ground and countryside, they have a responsibility to develop and promote best practice.

Environmental issues

The main environmental issue associated with purchasing products for grounds maintenance is chemical use. Herbicides and pesticides, if inappropriately chosen and used, can provide a major threat to plant, animal and bird species. Pesticides and herbicides can wash into water courses through surface water drainage during rain and can damage both water quality and biodiversity.

The use of peat for horticulture and grounds maintenance has become an issue of major environmental concern, lowland raised peat bogs being those which are most threatened at present. Many bogs, including those being actively used for peat extraction, are sites of national and international wildlife importance. Extraction of peat for commercial purposes is the single biggest threat to peat bogs in the UK.

Groups such as Friends of the Earth and conservation bodies such as English Nature have made progress in protecting sensitive areas of peatland but the main opportunity to reduce the threat is to find alternatives and to encourage their use.

DIY stores such as B&Q have made progress in introducing growing media utilising peat-free alternatives and have had some success at encouraging customer take-up through education and competitive pricing. The quality of peat-free compost has grown dramatically since the early 1990s. Alternatives to peat compost include bark chips, cocoa shell mulch, coir (derived from coconuts), spent mushroom compost and composted green waste.

Legislation

Chemicals for use within grounds maintenance have become more tightly controlled in recent years; the Control of Pesticides Regulations 1996 cover the advertisement, sale, storage and use of pesticides and two statutory codes of practice under the regulations define procedures for pesticide suppliers for their safe use. They are also covered by Control of Substances Hazardous to Health Regulations (COSHH) 1988.

 **Practical action**

Chemical use

Use of non-residual chemicals is essential to avoid the build-up of harmful chemicals on the ground or within plants and animals.

A contact weed wiper, through which herbicide is directly applied to specific plants, is an accurate method of herbicide application and avoids the danger to other plants, animals and to humans that can occur through the drifting of chemicals from spraying. Spraying should not take place if the wind is above force 2.

Plant native species

Encourage planting of native species – they support more types of insects than non-native ones because insects have evolved with those trees and shrubs over time. Select species to match those in the local area. Many nurseries are now providing mixtures of native trees; if you can't find one, try the British Trust for Conservation Volunteers (BTCV). Some shrubs (eg buckthorn) can harbour cereal pests and ideally should not be planted in abundance close to arable land. Slow growing shrubs such as crab apple, field maple and hawthorn require less maintenance than fast growing trees.

Summary guidelines

✔ Avoid the use of chemicals
✔ Avoid the use of peat
✔ Encourage organic methods
✔ Where chemical use is necessary follow good practice guidelines
✔ Promote biodiversity by removing nutrients from site, encouraging native species and avoiding soil disturbance
✔ Use the advice of experts such as your local Wildlife Trust or County Ecologist for specific advice
✔ Integrate best practice standards into your grounds maintenance contracts
✔ Avoid trimming and cutting between March and July

GROUNDS MAINTENANCE

Relax mowing regimes

Try not to cut between March and July while birds are breeding and butterflies are on the wing. Some verges will be fertile and produce vast amounts of coarse growth; these may need to be cut more regularly. Verges on poor soils (eg sand, chalk or very wet areas) usually contain more plants and will need cutting less frequently, perhaps only once or twice a year. Green waste removed from mowing and maintenance can be composted and used in areas where nutrients are required.

As with mowing grass verges, the value of grass often lies with both its structural diversity and species composition. Areas of long grass are vital in the winter for over-wintering insects (including butterfly eggs and larva) and in the summer for ground nesting birds. Shorter areas in which flowers are promoted will provide valuable nectar sources for butterflies, bees and other insects. In order to promote this, a relaxation of mowing during the spring and summer is all that is required; even raising the cutter bar will allow some plants to

Case Study 4.12

SUBJECT: **Assessing Supply Chain Performance**

ORGANISATION: **NHS Supplies**

LOCATION: **Reading**

STAFF: **1900**

Background

NHS Supplies is a special health authority, formed in 1991 as the purchasing and supply arm of the NHS in England. It influences around half of the £7 billion the NHS spends on goods and services each year.

It is the NHS' own centre of expertise on supply issues, taking a strategic perspective on supply on behalf of the health service. It works with NHS trusts, health authorities and suppliers and 98 per cent of trusts choose to use NHS Supplies for some or all of their purchasing needs.

From 1 April 2000, NHS Supplies evolved into two separate organisations, the NHS Purchasing and Supply Agency, an executive Agency of the Department of Health, while the existing warehousing and logistics functions will become the NHS Logistics Authority.

NHS Supplies has adopted a systematic approach to addressing environmental issues by implementing an EMS across the organisation, for certification to the international standard ISO 14001 by June 2000.

This will enable NHS Supplies to demonstrate legislative compliance, continual improvement in environmental performance and to send the strongest possible signal to the NHS supply chain that good environmental management is essential for the delivery of efficient and effective healthcare.

Action

Efforts to date have been focused on identifying methods of reducing the environmental impact of NHS Supplies' operations. Standard techniques, such as energy efficiency and waste minimisation, are being introduced to achieve these aims, but NHS Supplies' activities also impinge upon the environmental impacts arising at Trust-level – for example through packaging, which arises as waste on trust sites. To help reduce this waste burden NHS Supplies deploys, wherever possible, reusable totes instead of cardboard boxes to deliver ward-level orders.

NHS Supplies also has significant scope to influence trusts' environmental performance indirectly via specification of environmentally sensitive products and services. It is currently exploring ways of incorporating environmental criteria in national purchasing contracts in compliance with public procurement regulatory demands. To this end, buying teams have been given a series of performance indicators against which future progress can be measured. These include:

- Proportion of contracts offering 'environmentally preferable products'.
- Proportion of contracts incorporating 'green' specifications.
- Proportion of tenders evaluated using life-cycle costings.
- Proportion of contracts supported by substantiated environmental information.
- 'Environmental ranking' of supplier base.

Results

NHS Supplies provides information and guidance on legislation and protocols to encourage NHS trusts to reduce the impact of their purchasing activity and enable them, through the provision of appropriate environmental information relating to products and suppliers, to make more environmentally-informed purchasing decisions.

In 1995, before NHS Supplies became a national organisation, the NHS Supplies Central Division commissioned an Environmental Waste Project with finance from the NHS Executive (West Midlands). The study identified the adverse environmental impacts of major products and recommended ways in which these could be reduced. It also pinpointed product categories with a low environmental impact and highlighted these products in the stock catalogue. While some of these environmental 'flags' still remain, NHS Supplies is now reviewing approaches to providing such information in the future in light of feedback from 88 per cent of English trusts suggesting that 70 per cent of them would use such information in their purchasing decisions, where it had been identified as legitimate to do so.

In summary, NHS Supplies has recognised the importance of responsible environmental management in the provision of efficient and effective healthcare and is committed to working with its stakeholders to achieve real environmental improvements throughout the NHS supply chain. ■

flower. This may also save a great deal of money; one city council spends an estimated £500,000 per year on grass cutting.

Management practice

Maximise the ecological value and biodiversity of ground features. Never trim hedgerows before the end of July; you may be prosecuted under the Wildlife and Countryside Act if nesting birds are disturbed. Preferably cut in January/February after berries have gone. Ideally, unless there is a specific pest problem, trim every second or third year; try to leave sections uncut, especially at hedge junctions.

If large trees become a safety hazard, is it possible to pollard or trim rather than remove them? If there are no standards (trees which are larger than the surrounding vegetation), can some hedge plants be marked and left to grow on?

Parks and recreation grounds

Try working with the County Ecologist, perhaps producing a brief management plan for the best sites (which need be no more than two pages and a map). These should detail the conservation work planned over the forthcoming 5 to 10 year period. Sites where this extra effort will bring greatest benefits include those adjacent to existing nature reserves or woodlands and historic sites, where relict flora often holds on in discreet corners or even on the walls of crumbling ruins. Promote organic methods: further information on organic gardening can be obtained from the Henry Doubleday Research Association. *See Chapter 10, Contacts and Resources* ↘

CHAPTER SUMMARY

❑ Follow and use the standard purchasing principles and tools in the introduction to this chapter

❑ Look at areas where you can reduce consumption

❑ Make sure that the manufacturers and suppliers of any product you purchase can provide you with information on the environmentally preferable products that they produce/provide

❑ Integrate environmental criteria into tender and contract documentation

❑ Use the information in this Manual to help you to identify environmentally preferable products

❑ Avoid any products that require COSHH sheets or contain hazardous materials

❑ Avoid disposable products

❑ Purchase products that can be easily re-used or recycled

CHAPTER 5
Building Management

INTRODUCTION

Buildings are responsible for about 50 per cent of the UK's annual emissions of carbon dioxide. Therefore, your office represents a significant proportion of the environmental impacts of your organisation, particularly if you are in the service sector, where the core business is office based. Sound office practice needs to be considered in the assessment of overall corporate environmental performance.

Low utility consumption is a sign of an efficient and well-managed office with a pleasant working environment. Conversely, energy wastage is an indicator of poor management.

Energy use in offices has risen sharply in recent years as a result of the growth in information technology and air conditioning. Energy is the largest controllable outgoing in running office buildings, averaging 10–25 per cent of total service costs. Using simple efficiency measures, fuel bills can often be reduced by 20 per cent.

This chapter will help you to improve the way you manage your office building and enable you to implement effective energy efficiency and water saving measures. It is designed to help you to develop your own plan of action, incorporating as few or as many measures as applicable. In the first section, building management, how your offices are maintained and managed is discussed with particular reference to hazardous wastes, office equipment and general maintenance. Energy and water use are discussed in terms of general actions you should take to kick-start an improvement programme and ensure it is successful. Practical action is given to allow you to tackle the main utility users in the office: heating and cooling; office equipment and lighting; and kitchen and washroom areas.

There are legislative requirements which apply to the management of your building. These include: the Duty of Care and Special Waste Regulations, the Montreal Protocol and the Control of Substances Hazardous to Health (COSHH) Regulations. Many areas of the building management function are frequently contracted out; you must make sure that your contractors are complying with these regulations on your behalf.

A refurbishment programme provides an excellent opportunity to invest in new technology for an energy-efficient building. Office equipment is an area of high energy use. It also has health and safety risks which need to be minimised. Energy efficiency measures have clear commercial and environmental benefits.

There is often room for improved management control, particularly in the areas of fabric maintenance and refurbishment programmes. You may have a purchasing

policy in which the use of unsustainably produced wood for your furniture requirements is banned, but has this been communicated to your fabric maintenance
contractors? Fabric maintenance can represent significant loopholes in your overall
environmental policy. Be aware of what is purchased on your behalf! *See Chapter 4,
Purchasing* ⤴

🍁 Environmental issues

Environmental issues around building maintenance and utilities management are
discussed in the relevant subsections.

Government and industry initiatives

Building Research Establishment Environmental Assessment Method (BREEAM)

The Building Research Establishment (BRE) recognises the environmental impact of
buildings and the potential for reducing environmental damage by improving their
design, in their Building Research Establishment Environmental Assessment
Method (BREEAM).

The environmental impact of buildings can be radically reduced by the application of cost-effective technology. A certificate is provided by the BRE, based on an
independent assessment; builders will be able to use assessments in their publicity
and buyers will have a record of the way in which their building has been designed
according to environmental criteria. BREEAM is a very useful mechanism for assessing the environmental impact of new and existing buildings.

Building Services Research and Information Association (BSRIA)

The BSRIA published a strategy for environmental care in building design, construction and ultimate demolition. The Environmental Code of Practice for Buildings and
their Services guidance document provides a common language for all concerned in
the building process: client, architect, quantity surveyor, designer, services and facilities manager. The Code spans the life cycle of any building – whether commercial,
industrial or residential – from concept to demolition. It asserts that, with skill and
foresight, environmental impact can be reduced at little or no increase in overall cost.

Construction Industry Environmental Forum

The Construction Industry Environmental Forum is a partnership project between
the Construction Industry Research and Information Association (CIRIA), the
Building Research Establishment (BRE) and the Building Services Research and
Information Association (BSRIA). The forum addresses the needs of the construction and building industry to respond to environmental issues and aims to identify
opportunities for innovation and promote solutions to environmental problems.

Building
Management

HAZARDOUS WASTE

Legislation

The legislation on general waste is detailed in Chapter 3, Office Waste ⤴

There are a number of everyday materials which many offices will have for maintenance or cleaning purposes which have hazardous properties. Hazardous materials are those which in their storage or use are considered to be potentially harmful to human health or the environment. Under the Duty of Care, all of these materials must be properly disposed of. In addition, a number of these materials are covered by the new Special Waste Regulations.

Special Waste Regulations 1996

The Special Waste Regulations set out the provisions for the keeping, treatment and disposal of controlled wastes that are dangerous or difficult to manage. Their main purpose is to provide an effective system of control that ensures that special waste is soundly managed from its production until final destination for disposal or recovery. They replace the Control of Pollution (Special Waste) Regulations 1980 and implement European legislation on hazardous waste.

Waste is defined as 'special' if it appears on the European Hazardous Waste List and it possesses certain hazardous properties or it is a prescription-only medicine. The exception to this is that household wastes are not special. Special wastes include widely used products such as oils, lead and nickel cadmium (NiCd) batteries, acids, flammable liquids, and solvents. Those commonly used in the office are covered in more detail below.

If you are dealing with special wastes you must pre-notify the local or area Environment Agency office in the area to which the waste is being taken by filling in a consignment note. You must keep a copy of all consignment notes. A fee is charged for each consignment.

Breaking the regulations is punishable by a fine and/or imprisonment.

Clinical waste

Most healthcare wastes come under the Special Waste Regulations. However, some may not meet the hazardous thresholds in the Regulations and in these cases the duty of care provisions of the Environmental Protection Act should be followed (see Chapter 3, Office Waste). Clinical waste is defined in the Controlled Waste Regulations 1992 under the Environmental Protection Act as:

'Any waste which consists wholly or partly of human or animal tissue, blood or other body fluids, excretions, drugs or other pharmaceutical products, swabs or dressings, or syringes, needles or other sharp instruments, being waste which unless rendered safe may prove hazardous to any person coming into contact with it; and

Any other waste arising from medical, nursing, dental, veterinary, pharma-ceutical or similar practice, investigation, treatment, care, teaching or research, or the collection of blood for transfusion, being waste which may cause infection to any persons coming into contact with it.' (NSCA, 1999)

Guidance on the treatment and management of clinical waste is given in Waste Management Paper No 25 available from the Environment Agency.

Government and industry initiatives

National Household Hazardous Waste Forum
This forum, managed by Save Waste and Prosper (SWAP), engages in dialogue with the government, industry associations and non-governmental bodies on the future impact of waste regulations and on the national waste strategy. The information they provide focuses on household waste but is also relevant to offices.

Practical action

Do not purchase hazardous materials
Materials that are hazardous to humans or the environment require much greater control during use and disposal. They are therefore expensive. Wherever possible you should seek to use an alternative material, such as water-based paints. *See Chapter 4, Purchasing*

Identify special wastes
To identify whether you have any materials that require disposal as special waste you will need to follow the steps outlined in the Special Waste Regulations 1996 and the Department of the Environment, Transport and the Regions Circular 6/96 (see Legislation section on page 134). The Environment Agency will also help you with any queries you have.

Follow special waste consignment note system
In addition to the provisions of the Duty of Care for special waste, you must follow these steps:

Step 1 Before any special waste leaves your site you must pre-notify the local area Environment Agency office in the area to which the waste is being taken. This is done by completing parts A and B of a five-copy consignment note.
Step 2 You must send one copy to the Regulator for the area where the waste is going. This must be done at least three working days, but not more than one month, before the waste is to be moved.
Step 3 When the waste is removed the carrier must complete part C to the form. You must then sign part D. You must keep a copy of the consignment note and give the other three to the carrier.

There is a fee charged by the Environment Agency for each consignment.

Waste oil

Never pour waste oil down the drain; this is illegal as well as environmentally damaging. Waste oils can be recycled. Oil can be re-refined into new lubricating oil, laundered and returned to the company that supplied it for re-use or cleaned to produce a fuel product. Used car engine oil can be taken to an oil bank for recycling. Large quantities of waste oil, generated at sites such as a garage, should be collected by a registered contractor who will buy it from you.

Follow the Environment Agency Oil Care at Work code:
- Site your storage tank within an oil tight bund wall on an impervious base. Make sure that valves and pipes are contained within the bund.
- Make sure that the bund has no drain which would allow oil to escape.
- Don't overfill your tank; check the amount of oil already in the tank before receiving a delivery.
- Supervise all deliveries; stop the delivery if there are any leaks or overflows.
- Clearly mark all pipework to show the type of oil and where it leads, and lock all valves and gauges securely after a delivery.

If an oil spill occurs:
Try to stop the oil from entering any drains or watercourses using earth or sandbags to absorb it. Never hose it down. Call the Environment Agency Emergency Hotline free on 0800 807060

The Environment Agency's Pollution Prevention Guidelines provide advice on statutory responsibilities and good practice. *See Chapter 10, Contacts and Resources*⤵

Paint

All paint waste containing halogenated solvents is special waste. This will include old paint tins that contain some waste paint. To minimise your special waste you should purchase water-based paints. Some decorative paints now have a label indicating their solvent content; for example, B & Q label all their paints with the solvent content. *See Chapter 4, Purchasing*⤴

Batteries

Lead, mercury dry cells and NiCd batteries are covered by the special waste requirements. For other batteries large quantities should not be concentrated in disposal but diluted with other wastes. The normal Duty of Care procedures should also be followed.

⚠ Common problems

No clear disposal route

If staff are not aware of an authorised disposal route for special wastes, they will end up in the general waste or hidden in a store room. Ensure all staff are aware of the correct procedures for dealing with special waste and who they should contact with any queries.

Contractors

Contractors have been known to leave difficult and special wastes on site to avoid the cost of disposal. Ensure that proof of correct disposal for all materials is written into contractual agreements.

Storerooms

Storage areas and workshops tend to be a haven for old chemicals, solvents and other maintenance materials. Ensure these areas are cleared out periodically and obsolete materials disposed of correctly. Disposing of special waste in bulk will save money, but do not wait until storage becomes a hazard.

Summary guidelines

✔ Assess all of your wastes to see if they require disposal as special waste
✔ Check that contractors are removing hazardous wastes and disposing of them correctly
✔ Follow the Special Waste Regulations Consignment Note System
✔ Follow the Environment Agency Oil Care at Work Code

HAZARDOUS WASTE

OFFICE EQUIPMENT

Environmental issues

Your choice of office equipment manufacturer and servicing contractor has important implications for your environmental, and health and safety policies. The main environmental concerns are emissions of ozone and dust during operation and the end of life disposal of the machine and component parts. Symptoms of indoor air pollution caused by laser printers and photocopiers include headaches, catarrh and an unpleasantly dry working environment. The dry working environment is exacerbated by high room temperatures.

Ozone

Copiers and printers rely on high voltages to make the toner powder stick temporarily to a print drum, before its transfer to paper. This process generates ozone. Most laser printers and copiers have a built-in filter to extract the ozone from the exhaust fumes. They contain activated carbon to break down ozone and, when new, reduce ozone to well below the Health and Safety Executive (HSE) levels. However, when inadequately maintained or used in small rooms, these machines can release dangerous amounts of ozone.

Dust

Dust is given off by paper and toner. The amount of dust from the toner varies from machine to machine and is also dependent on the type of paper used. Copiers can give off electrostatically charged toner dust; this can cause irritation in the respiratory tract when inhaled. Carbon particles in toner used in photocopiers are normally no smaller than 0.005 mm, making them too large to cause bronchial disorders. However, carbon particles used in toner for laser printers and colour photocopiers are smaller than 0.005 mm. If these particles are inhaled they can be hazardous to health. Manufacturers must produce (Control of Substances Hazardous to Health) COSHH Hazard sheets with details on the components, the health hazards associated with them and how toner should be handled. This includes special requirements for exposure control.

Computers

VDUs emit various types of radiation. A significant proportion of the radiation consists of pulsed EMFs (electromagnetic fields) of between 15 kHz and pulsed 50 kHz fields. The exposure to electrical fields and the expected damage to the operator depends on the strength of the field, the distance from the field source and the length of exposures over a long period of time. Headaches, irritability, tiredness and skin complaints can result from this static electricity.

☞ Practical action

Ventilation

High usage photocopiers should be located in a specific, well-ventilated room. If large quantities of printed material are produced, extractor fans should be fitted on the machinery, and the air conducted directly out of the building.

Ozone filters

Make sure copiers are fitted with filters and make sure that filter changing is included in the service agreement. In areas of poor ventilation or heavy usage, supplementary filters should be fitted. They are more powerful and remove ozone, toner and paper dust from the laser printer and clean the office air in the immediate vicinity.

COSHH

Ensure correct handling of toner under COSHH and obtain detailed assessments from the manufacturer. Use toner with minimal hazardous materials (details will be on the COSHH sheets) to minimise health and safety risks. Use disposable gloves when replacing toner; clean up any spilt toner and wash your hands thoroughly. Use protective clothing and possibly a mask when replacing loose toner (plan to change over to cartridges). Toner must not smudge or be released into the surroundings.

Plants

Research by NASA (National Aeronautics and Space Administration) found that up to 87 per cent of poisonous toxins found in office buildings can be absorbed with the right selection of plants. By breathing in carbon dioxide and contaminated air, they help to improve the air quality in an office by providing a natural filtering system. Mother-in-law's tongue is found to be particularly effective!

Workstation health and safety

The Health and Safety Display Screen Equipment Regulations 1992 require that workstation design and operation considers health and safety issues. It is important to consider the positioning of visual display units (VDUs), since EMFs are at their highest at the sides, rear and tops of VDU terminals, rather than the front. Therefore the number of hours at a terminal may not be a reliable indicator of exposure. Ideally, operators should not work within one metre of the sides or back of adjacent VDUs unless the machines have been tested and confirmed to emit only low levels of non-ionising radiation. Workstation assessments should be carried out for any employees spending over 25 per cent of their working day using a VDU.

Mainframe machine rooms

Space

Machine rooms are often run unmanned; therefore, false ceilings and windows may not be necessary. Fewer building materials are needed and valuable, naturally lit office space can be kept for employees!

Lighting

Lighting can be arranged in blocks so that it can be switched on where needed and left off elsewhere. Note that vertical illumination may be necessary for maintenance purposes.

Cabling

The cable management system should be flexible to accommodate changes in machines. Flexibility is also needed in power distribution and communication cable systems.

Heat recovery

Machine rooms generate a lot of heat. This can be recovered to help heat the remainder of the building. There needs to be sufficient filtered fresh air to pressurise the machine room to prevent the ingress of contaminants (dust, for example).

Building Management

Summary guidelines

✔ Ensure adequate ventilation in the office, particularly printing and photocopying areas
✔ Arrange office equipment to avoid prolonged exposure to photocopiers, printers, computers and VDUs
✔ Take breaks from your VDU screen in line with Health and Safety Guidelines
✔ Use plants to improve air quality in the office
✔ Carry out workstation assessments according to the Health and Safety Display Screen Equipment Regulations 1992
✔ Save office space and energy by maximising the efficiency of mainframe computer rooms

OFFICE EQUIPMENT

Energy efficiency

Power-saving devices should be fitted for maximum efficiency. They can be used to make sure that only those machines which are necessary to run the system remain on at all times. This will consequently reduce power demands and heat generation. Clearly label which machines have to stay on for 24 hours and turn the others off when possible.

Fire protection

Traditionally, halon flooding equipment has been installed as fire protection in computer rooms. Under the Montreal Protocol halon production has been phased out since it is a very powerful ozone depleter. An acceptable alternative is the use of a sprinkler system, with an automatic cut-off of electricity in an emergency, or passive detection, for example, smoke alarms. *See Fire Protection later in this chapter*➘

FABRIC MAINTENANCE

Most organisations contract out the fabric maintenance of their building(s). Implementing sound environmental controls can reduce costs and make sure your environmental position is not weakened by your subcontractors.

Environmental issues

Plasterboard

Plasterboard is manufactured from gypsum. The quarrying of raw materials destroys areas of the countryside, damages wildlife habitats and creates dust and heavy traffic movements.

Industrial gypsum can also be used in plasterboard. This is produced in power stations during the desulphurisation process; activity in this process may cause concentrations of heavy metals to build up. There is concern that the resulting materials may have health risks.

Paint and varnish

The major environmental issue with paint and varnishes is their use of solvents. Solvent-based paints can be replaced by low-solvent or water-based alternatives. *See Chapter 4, Purchasing, for information on the environmental issues of solvents and the eco-labelling scheme*➚

Solvent-based paints are also hazardous in disposal and come under the Special Waste Regulations.

Batteries

Around 600 million batteries are used in the UK every year. Chemical reactions continue in old batteries that can result in hazardous metals leaching into the environment causing adverse effects to humans and wildlife and vegetation damage. Wet batteries containing both lead and acid can be particularly damaging if disposed of in an uncontrolled way. Batteries used to contain low levels of toxic metals, particularly mercury. This has been almost eliminated from batteries since 1994.

NiCd and lead acid batteries can be recycled; there are currently no facilities for recycling other batteries. *See Chapter 4, Purchasing*

Oils

The biggest oil incidents have been spills by tankers such as the *Sea Empress* off the coast of Wales in 1996. However, small quantities of oil can also cause major damage to watercourses and groundwater if it is spilt or disposed of inappropriately. Oil forms a film on the surface of rivers and lakes that makes it difficult for fish to breathe by reducing the amount of oxygen in the water. Just 5 litres of oil can cover and poison a small lake. Oil will also coat animals and plants that come into contact with it.

Timber products

Timber from unknown or unsustainable sources should not be used. Use timber suppliers accredited by the Forest Stewardship Council (FSC) where possible. Softwood timbers and temperate hardwoods are considered to be from sustainable sources; in the case of tropical hardwoods you should be able to demonstrate that the timber comes from a well-managed, sustainable source. *See Chapter 4, Purchasing, for more information on sourcing wood products*

Composite timber products

Plywood should not contain tropical hardwoods or wood from unknown or unsustainable origins. Ensure your contractor can supply information on the species of wood used in the plywood and country of origin.

☞ Practical action

The practical action outlined below is equally applicable to new construction, everyday maintenance and refurbishment programmes where the quantity of materials both purchased and disposed of is substantial.

Materials

Make sure environmental and energy efficiency criteria are considered in the selection of materials on-site. Refurbishment programmes provide an excellent opportunity to develop environmental purchasing objectives. In the case of a large refurbishment programme, there will be a structured tender process: environmental criteria should be built in at the tender stage. For example, specify water-based rather than solvent-based paints. This reduces the environmental impacts of your activities and avoids potential disposal problems. Make sure your policies are extended to subcontractors. *See Chapter 4, Purchasing*

Usage

Obsolete materials often end up in the skip due to lack of storage space. There may also be scope to reduce the quantities of materials ordered to minimise wastage. Efficient project planning and choice of materials can facilitate re-use. For example, 20 cans of paint from staging builders Andy Knight Ltd were re-used by the charity training centre Foundation for Human Development during refurbishment.

Re-use or recycle obsolete materials

Find alternative disposal routes for materials currently going into the skip to significantly reduce your disposal costs and divert valuable raw materials from landfill. Typically these will be timber, metals, furniture and carpets. There are a number of organisations that will take obsolete materials; contact local charities and the Recycling Officer at your local authority for more details. Waste minimisation clubs such as Waste Alert (London) will often be able to help match materials to charities and other businesses.

For example: 50 exhibition quality carpets were collected from Waste Alert member Allframes and re-used by the Foundation for Human Development. The carpets weighed approximately 1.3 tonnes and saved Allframes over £600 in disposal costs.

Contractors

Waste Disposal

Make sure contractors are complying with the Duty of Care Regulations, Special Waste Regulations and COSHH on your behalf. This includes the disposal of hazardous and special waste. Check the training procedure of the supplier: the environmental controls need to be understood at all levels of the organisation. *See Hazardous Waste, Practical Action, page 135* ↵

Summary guidelines

✔ Incorporate environmental performance and energy efficiency considerations into maintenance material and product specifications

✔ Ensure that your policies on materials extend to contractors

✔ Use efficient planning and ordering of materials to minimise waste

✔ Find alternative routes for materials currently going to landfill, eg timber, fittings, furniture and carpets. Contact your local waste minimisation club for more information

✔ Ensure that contractors are complying with all the relevant waste and health and safety legislation on your behalf. Check their training procedures on all levels

FABRIC MAINTENANCE

REFRIGERANTS: CFCs AND HCFCs

Chlorofluorocarbons (CFCs) and hydrochlorofluorocarbons (HCFCs) are extensively used as refrigerants and are needed to operate many existing refrigeration and air conditioning systems. Although owners of refrigeration plant have a duty of care to ensure that CFCs and HCFCs are not released into the atmosphere, they can escape through leakage or during maintenance. Even if you have a properly installed, well-maintained system, you could still lose your refrigerant through accident or equipment failure.

It is vital that you formulate a strategy to achieve a smooth, cost-effective change-over to non-CFC and HCFC refrigerants and comply with existing and future legislation.

Legislation

The Montreal Protocol

In 1987 the Montreal Protocol was ratified by 60 countries, which committed themselves to reducing the production and use of ozone-depleting substances such as CFCs and halons. The production of CFCs was banned in 1994 and new legislation (June 2000) bans the use of CFCs (being principally R11, R12 and R502) from the end of 2000. In addition the manufacture of HCFCs (principally R22) will be banned by 2008.

For replacements for CFCs the product R134a is a reasonable consideration depending on application. The replacements for R22 are generally seen as R407c and/or R410a. Contact the Department of Trade and Industry or the Refrigerants Users Group for more information.

Environmental issues

CFCs

CFCs are ozone-depleting chemicals and potent greenhouse gases. Over the past years, scientists have realised that CFCs are destroying the stratospheric ozone layer that protects the earth's surface from ultraviolet radiation. Increased ultraviolet light near the earth's surface can increase the incidence of skin cancer and damage plants, animals and whole ecosystems.

The manufacture and import of new CFCs was banned in the European Union on 1 January 1996. Less developed countries need to phase out by 2010.

HCFCs

HCFCs are also ozone-depleting substances but have one-twentieth of the ozone depletion potential (ODP) of CFCs. They are being used as transitional substances to replace CFCs. The widely used refrigerant R22 is an HCFC and is still manufactured. HCFCs currently are due to be phased out in 2015. Usage in new systems should therefore be avoided.

143

HFCs

Hydrofluorocarbons (HFCs) have zero ODP. However, these chemicals are very powerful global warming gases; HFC 134a has a global warming potential (GWP) of 1300. HFCs are only a medium-term option and were banned in some refrigeration equipment after 1999.

Government and industry initiatives

Refrigerant Users Group (RUG)

RUG is a non-profit-making, limited company, funded by its members – any company that uses refrigerants and who will therefore have to operate within the CFC ban. RUG staff run a database and library of information and members are kept up-to-date on all refrigerant issues through regular newsletters.

 ## Practical action

Plan for alternatives

In the longer term you will need to have a strategy for retrofitting your equipment to run alternative refrigerants or replacing it with new equipment.

Minimise leakage

In the short term, improved standards of maintenance, minor equipment modifications and better work practices can substantially reduce losses of refrigerant gases. Poor maintenance is the common reason for coolant escaping into the atmosphere. Specify automatic refrigerant pumps and leak detection systems for new build or refurbishment.

Find an alternative substance

Your alternative should fulfil the following environmental criteria:

* Zero ODP.
* Zero or very low GWP.
* Energy efficient.

The hydrocarbons propane and butane meet all these criteria.

Summary guidelines

✔ Switch to a fluid with zero ODP and GWP
✔ If possible, find a retrofittable replacement
✔ Clarify any safety issues arising from the new fluid
✔ Minimise leakage in your current system and make sure it is regularly maintained

REFRIGERANTS: CFCs AND HCFCs

FIRE PROTECTION: HALON

Halons are extremely efficient fire-fighting agents, the most popular being known chemically as Halon 1211 and 1301, or known by their trade names as BCF and BTM respectively. They are used in portable systems in green and sometimes red hand-held extinguishers and wheeled units, or in fixed installations such as computer rooms.

🍁 Environmental issues

Halons deplete the ozone layer at a rate 16 times faster than CFCs.

Legislation

A revision of the Montreal Protocol in Copenhagen in November 1992 banned the production and import of new halon at the end of 1993. Under new legislation (June 2000) halons are banned for use after 31 December 2002. The legislation requires that installed systems using halon are fully decommissioned by 31 December 2003. You will not be able to use halon for topping up or maintenance after the end of December 2002. Some of the information in this section is based on the DTI guide *Halon Phase Out: Advice on Alternatives and Guidelines for Users*. Contact the DTI for further information.

Government and industry initiatives

Halon Users National Consortium Limited (HUNC)

The Halon Users National Consortium Limited (HUNC) is an independent, non-profit-making organisation which was set up by halon users and the fire industry with the support of government. HUNC's aim is to ensure that the existing stocks are safely managed down to zero. They will advise on:

- how to dispose of and recycle halons;
- where to find recycled halon to keep critical systems operating;
- alternatives to halon.

☞ Practical action

Plan for alternatives

Reassess your continued use of halon and switch to an alternative or replacement agent if possible.

Consider the following issues when selecting an alternative to halons:

- Fire fighting effectiveness.
- Damage to equipment from use.
- Ease of installation.
- Suitability of the area for a gaseous system.
- The hazards it presents for occupants.
- Environmental performance.

Recycle

Halon can be recycled very effectively and, since production ceased, recycling has become an important source of supply. Manage your own stock or bank by topping it up with your own decommissioned and reclaimed halon. However, this is an expensive and unreliable option.

Establish compatibility with existing equipment

When considering an alternative, establish whether it is compatible with your existing equipment. Some replacements tend to take up more space than halons, therefore you would need larger extinguishers.

Current alternatives

Carbon dioxide

Carbon dioxide (CO_2) has zero ODP, is colourless, odourless and clean. As its density is greater than oxygen, in a flooding system it will quickly take over the oxygen in the area, making breathing extremely difficult. Carbon dioxide takes up more room than halon (more equipment may be needed) and works by providing a blanket of heavy gas that reduces oxygen to a point where combustion is no longer possible. Systems can be automatic or manual; however, when an area is occupied it needs to be switched to manual. On a manual setting your company needs to have excellent detection systems allowing the system to be set so evacuation can take place before the CO_2 is turned on.

Water sprinkler systems

This is the most common type of fixed fire protection. Do not use this system on live electrical equipment fires and flammable liquids. Compared to halon, water is slow to react to fires, and machinery may be subject to some damage.

Fine water spray systems

These are relatively new to fire fighting. Since the application rate is less than that of a sprinkler system, some of the water damage possible is avoided, making it suitable for computer rooms. Fine sprays can be used on flammable liquids and live electrical equipment but not on substances such as reactive metals.

Foam systems

Low, medium and high expansion foams act by forming a barrier between fire and the supply of oxygen. They are not effective against running or spray fires. Foam can be destroyed by some liquid fuels (alcohol, for example) by chemical reaction, so make sure the right foam is chosen.

Dry powder systems

These are capable of rapid extinguishment, but provide very little cooling. Once the powder has settled it becomes ineffective. There are different powders suitable for different applications. All types of powder are unpleasant to breathe and are not recommended for occupied areas. They also settle after use and add to the post-fire clean-up.

Detection only

This is a method of fighting fires manually with extinguishers, hose reels or by the Fire Brigade with the introduction of a highly sensitive smoke detection system.

Alternative gaseous agents

These are direct alternatives to halons that are electrically non-conductive and leave no residue. They fall into two categories: inert gas systems and halocarbon gas agents. When considering these you should seek further information from the British Fire Protection Systems Association who produce a code of practice for gaseous fire fighting systems (BFPSA, 1995).

Inert gases

Inert gas systems are natural gases from natural sources. They have zero ODP and no global warming potential. Inert gas systems include: Argonite, Inergen and argon. See Table 5.1.

Halocarbon gas agents

Hydrofluorocarbons (HFCs) and perfluoro-carbons (PFCs) have an important role in fire fighting. They do not harm the ozone layer and are not therefore covered by the Montreal Protocol. These gases are, however, powerful greenhouse gases. They should therefore only be used where careful analysis shows them to be the best alternative.

Building Management

Summary guidelines

✔ Advise your insurance company that you intend to change your fire fighting equipment
✔ Clarify the health and safety issues
✔ Maximise use of existing equipment
✔ Minimise leakage in your current system and undertake regular maintenance
✔ Replace and recycle your halon
✔ Plan a complete replacement programme for all halon containing equipment

FIRE PROTECTION: HALON

Table 5.1 *Gaseous agents and their GWP (based on material from DTI, 1995b)*

Trade name	Chemical designation	Chemical name/ gas blend	GWP
CEA-410	FC-3-1-10	Perfluorobutane	7900
FM-200	HFC227ea	Heptafluorobutane	3300
FE 13	HFC23	Trifluoropropane	12100
Argonite	IG-55	Argon, nitrogen	0
Inergen	IG-541	Argon, nitrogen, carbon dioxide	0
Argon	IG-01	Argon	0

ENERGY

 ## Environmental issues

Environmental disasters such as oil spills and the threat of global warming and radioactive pollution are rarely considered to be an office issue; however, these and other less dramatic impacts of energy use are some of the key environmental issues we face. The extraction, generation and use of energy can all have a major impact on the environment. Energy efficiency in the office can provide an immediate and cost effective response to these impacts.

Extraction and transport

The UK relies on a significant amount of imported non-renewable fuels such as coal, oil and gas. The transportation of oil in particular can cause serious and long lasting pollution. Oil spills from tankers like the *Sea Empress* off the coast of Wales and the *Erika* off the coast of Brittany have caused enormous damage to sensitive habitats. Oil rigs and pipelines have their own associated environmental impacts and are potentially high risk polluters.

Burning of fossil fuels

When fossil fuels such as gas, oil and coal are burnt to produce electricity or heat, a number of gases including carbon dioxide, nitrogen oxides, sulphur dioxide and particulates are released into the atmosphere. These emissions are major contributors to acid rain and the greenhouse gases. Only one-third of the energy from the fuel burnt actually leaves the power station as useful energy.

Greenhouse effect (global warming)

Certain trace gases (for example water vapour, carbon dioxide, methane, nitrous oxides) form an insulating blanket around the earth. This blanket allows the sun's rays through, but prevents some of the heat radiated back from the earth escaping. This heat retention can be likened to the role of glass in a greenhouse. These gases are a natural phenomenon, and without their effect the Earth would be uninhabitable.

While the greenhouse effect is a natural and essential condition, emissions from human activities are increasing the concentrations of several key gases, in particular carbon dioxide and methane. Scientists cannot yet understand exactly what effect this increase in gases will have on our weather and climate. The 1995 report by the International Panel on Climate Change (IPCC) concludes: 'The balance of evidence suggest that there is a discernible human influence on global climate.' The Panel warns that if current trends persist we may see a warming of the globe by 2 degrees Celsius by 2100. Climate change on this scale will have wide-ranging impact. For example, the rise in sea level could flood low lying areas such as London.

Direct energy use and emissions from business, including the electricity generation that powers business and business transport, account for over 40 per cent of UK greenhouse gas emissions. On average 100 m^2 of office space produces 14 tonnes of CO_2 each year. Reducing these emissions is key to our response to the challenge of climate change.

Acidification

Acidification, sometimes referred to as acid rain, is caused by emissions of sulphur dioxide (SO_2), nitrogen oxides (NO_x) and ammonia. The major sources of SO_2 and NO_x emissions are the burning of fossil fuels and transport respectively; ammonia causes local acidification, mostly as a result of farming techniques. Acidification of soils results in loss of plant nutrients, threatening the long-term productivity of forests. Tree damage and poisoned lakes are widespread in northern Europe. Water becomes more corrosive to a variety of materials including metals and concrete, which can cause damage to piping systems and may be a health hazard. In the UK, acid rain's main effect is building corrosion.

A number of measures are being used to reduce the emissions of acidifying gases from the UK. The UK is committed to reduce sulphur dioxide emissions (on 1980 levels) by 80 per cent by 2010. Cars fitted with three-way catalytic converters emit 70–90 per cent less NO_x than those without. Similarly, emissions from combustion plants can be reduced by 90 per cent using current technology.

Nuclear power

Over 20 per cent of our electricity is generated through the use of nuclear power. Although nuclear power does not contribute to the greenhouse effect, it creates a legacy of radioactive waste that will be potentially lethal for thousands of years. The costs associated with managing this risk have contributed to making nuclear power uneconomic and no new power stations are planned in the UK.

Government and industry initiatives

Energy Efficiency Best Practice Programme (EEBPP)

This DETR and DTI-funded programme provides impartial, authoritative informa-

Building Management

tion on energy efficiency techniques and technologies in industry and buildings. This information is disseminated through publications, videos and software, together with seminars, workshops and other events.

Make a Corporate Commitment (MACC2)

The Government has recently relaunched its 'Corporate Commitment' campaign. The aim is to stimulate organisations in both the private and public sectors to do their bit in the national drive to greater sustainability.

Top management will be encouraged to publicly commit to specific self-declared targets for improving performance in those aspects of their operations that have significant impacts. Improved performance might be in one or more areas; for example, waste, water consumption, emissions, energy, or transport. Those wanting help in meeting their commitments will be encouraged to take full advantage of the free and impartial advice from the government's best practice programmes as well as help from other sources.

The Climate Change Levy

The Climate Change Levy will apply to the energy bills of all UK businesses and public sector organisations from April 2001. The levy aims to encourage reductions in the use of non-renewable forms of energy as well as providing support for energy efficiency and renewable energy generation (including wind, solar and tidal power).

The levy in 2001 will be charged as follows:

Electricity	0.43p/kWh
Gas and coal	0.15p/kWh
LPG	0.07p/kWh

Exemptions will include certain forms of 'renewable' energy (including wind, solar, tidal and electricity from waste) some combined heat and power plants, natural gas in Northern Ireland and other energy used in certain industrial processes. However, most organisations can make savings by improving energy efficiency and therefore reducing their energy use. There will be an Enhanced Capital Allowances scheme which will allow companies to claim back tax against 100 per cent of the costs of plant and machinery that meet energy efficiency criteria, for one year. This scheme will initially include boilers, pipe insulation, lighting and refrigeration systems, with all 'eligible' products placed on the UK Energy Technology List (available after November 2000 at www.eca.gov.uk).

HM Customs & Excise Climate Change Levy Helpdesk: Tel: 0161 827 0332

ALTERNATIVE ENERGY

Environmental and cost concerns have driven the development of, and increasing number of, alternative energy sources. This chapter discusses the main types of commercially viable energy sources but is not exhaustive. *Contact the Centre for Alternative Technology for more information – see Chapter 10, Contacts and Resources* ⮡

 Environmental issues

Consumers can make dramatic improvements in their environmental performance through considerate energy purchasing. Technologies such as wind, solar and wave power do not use non-renewable resources and have no emissions of carbon dioxide or other air pollutants. Combined heat and power plants make use of the by-product of conventional electricity generation (heat) to feed heating systems for buildings or directly for industrial processes, resulting in high levels of efficiency and reduced carbon dioxide emissions.

Government and industry initiatives

Future Energy

Future Energy accredits electricity tariffs which support or invest in electricity from the full range of renewable energy sources. Exacting criteria are applied and the checking process is carried out by the independent government-backed organisation, the Energy Saving Trust.

Non Fossil Fuel Obligation (NFFO)

The government is encouraging the development of alternative energy sources such as wind and solar power through the Non Fossil Fuel Obligation (NFFO). Under the NFFO–5 order, electricity suppliers in England and Wales are required to enter into contracts with renewable energy developers.

☞ Practical action

Consider renewable energy

Generating your own power from renewable sources will require capital investment, but the payback can be impressive. Keep abreast of ever improving technology and always consider renewables when specifying energy supply for new buildings or major extensions. For example: The viewing gallery of the former *Glasgow Herald* building in Glasgow has been transformed into a 'zero-energy' building experiment with a host of renewable energy generation technologies including photovoltaic solar panels and wind turbines. Rather than relying on large wind or solar farms, the concept is that buildings should carry enough generating capacity to supply the bulk of their own needs.

Building Management

Case Study 5.1

SUBJECT: **Renewable Energy and CO$_2$ Reductions**

ORGANISATION: **The Co-operative Bank**

LOCATION: **National**

STAFF: **3911**

Background

The Co-operative Bank celebrated its 125th anniversary in 1997 and at the same time announced the introduction of a Partnership approach, which included measuring performance in line with the bank's ethical and environmental commitments. The bank has approximately 1.75 million customers and published its second Partnership Report in 1998.

Action

In 1998, the Co-operative Bank committed to reduce its emissions of CO$_2$ per customer account by 20 per cent of 1997 levels. This target was based on the UK government's original negotiating position at the Kyoto Climate Change conference in December 1997. The bank achieved this target after just one year.

Green energy is now being used at the bank's London, Manchester and Stockport offices. London is supplied with electricity generated from an east London sewage sludge incinerator; Manchester is supplied with hydro-electric power generated on the Manchester Ship Canal and Stockport is supplied by a landfill gas scheme in St Helens. Previously, the vast bulk of electricity for these offices was supplied by fossil fuels.

The bank is now the biggest purchaser in the UK of electricity from alternative energy sources, with just under 50 per cent of its electricity supply coming from renewable energy. Assuming everything else is equal, this will lead to an estimated cut in the bank's annual net CO$_2$ emissions per customer account by more than 40 per cent.

Last year it set a new target of a 60 per cent reduction, 60 per cent being the amount that scientists agree is needed globally to prevent irreversible environmental damage.

The bank also supports a Community Woodlands initiative which results in an additional carbon offset of 2.5 per cent per year.

Results

- A reduction in emissions of CO$_2$ of 9.8 per cent or 1,295 tonnes.
- A reduction in emissions per customer account of 40 per cent.
- Gas consumption reduced by 860,453 kWh or 8.7 per cent.

For more details refer to http://www.co-operativebank.co.uk/ 97_suppliers_ecological.html ∎

Solar

There are three main ways in which solar energy is used.

1 Passive solar design uses the form and fabric of a building to capture energy from the sun and so reduce the building's needs for artificial light and heat.
2 Active solar heating employs solar collectors (often on a south-facing roof) to capture and store the sun's heat via water storage systems and use the heat primarily for water heating.
3 Photovoltaic cells involve the direct conversion of light energy from the sun into electricity by means of specially prepared semiconductors. Solar photovoltaic cells are arranged in panels on the roof or external walls of buildings.

Wind

Wind power is now cheaper than coal or nuclear power in the UK. There are already over 400 wind turbines generating power for the grids, while many small machines produce electricity for local use. The British Wind Energy Association's target is for 10 per cent of the country's electricity to be wind-generated by 2025. The UK's windy climate is ideal for wind power but resistance from local people over visual pollution is common. There is potential to develop wind farms at sea using similar technology.

Hydro Electric Power (HEP)

Electrical power can be derived from water in three ways:

1 Hydro-power devices rely on falling water to generate electricity by allowing it to pass through specially designed water turbines; the modern version of the traditional water wheel.
2 Tidal power stations generate electricity by capturing the water of tidal rise and passing it through turbines.
3 Wave power devices are designed to absorb the energy of the waves.

Tidal and wave power are not commercially available at present but demonstration projects are continually assessing the viability of these methods.

Combined Heat and Power (CHP)

Combined heat and power (CHP), or cogeneration, is set to play a major role in carbon dioxide reduction strategies. With over 1300 CHP installations in the UK, CHP is a growing sector, one which the EC hopes to double by 2010. CHP makes use of the heat that is produced in electricity generation (from most fuels) to feed heating systems for buildings or directly for industrial processes. The heat produced in the process is recovered to heat water which is then used to supply heat to the site. High levels of efficiency and reduced carbon dioxide emissions are achieved. CHP is not cost effective in all buildings and needs to be evaluated on a case by case basis. CHP plants are particularly suited to sites requiring year-round heat demand such as nursing homes, hotels, leisure centres and 24-hour production sites.

Building Management

Summary guidelines

✔ Consider renewable technologies when specifying new buildings or major extensions

✔ Assess the feasibility of using combined heat and power in your building or new site

✔ Consider sourcing all or a proportion of your energy supply from renewable resources

✔ Contact Future Energy for a list of electricity companies offering accredited Green Tariffs

ALTERNATIVE ENERGY

For example, the BBC has installed a CHP scheme at Television Centre in London which is predicted to reduce annual CO_2 emissions by 12,553 tonnes.

Green tariffs

Green energy purchasing is gaining an increasingly high profile within business. When combined with an effective energy efficiency policy, purchasing 'green energy' maximises the contribution a business can make to achieve the UK's CO_2 reduction targets. *See Chapter 4, Purchasing*

Most energy suppliers are now offering options to buy electricity from renewable or 'green' sources. There are two main payment options:

• The amount of energy you purchase each year is matched by your energy supplier's purchases from renewable sources.

• You pay into a fund to support future investments in renewable energy.

ASSESSING ENERGY USE

Energy is the largest controllable outgoing in running office buildings. Consumption, and therefore cost, can be reduced by at least 10 per cent at no cost. With investment, further reductions are achievable. Energy can be saved in many ways.

Practical action

Companies often see energy efficiency as purely a technical problem; however, the key to efficient energy use is good management. The aim of energy management is to minimise cost while maintaining high standards of service. It is important to give responsibility for energy management to a named person who can coordinate your approach.

Gain senior management support

To encourage senior management commitment you need to present the business case by establishing the energy costs. Find out what you paid for all your energy sources over the previous year. This may come as a shock. A good way of highlighting the costs is to relate the savings of a small reduction in energy costs to the equivalent increase in sales that would have the same impact on the bottom line.

Calculating your energy costs

The information you need to make these calculations can be obtained from your fuel bills. These should cover at least a full year and be the actual cost, not an estimate by the utility company. If your bills are quarterly or based on estimates, arrange for monthly meter readings. A lot can be learnt just from looking at the monthly pattern of fuel use.

It is essential to establish your baselines from which to work.

As a rule, use total annual cost; annual costs per m^2 (treated floor area) and annual cost per member of staff. You may also wish to record the proportion of your energy supply sourced through a 'green tariff'.

Treated floor area (TFA) is the gross floor area (total area inside external walls) excluding plant rooms and other areas not heated (eg stores, covered car parks and roof spaces). Ideally it should be measured, but an estimate of treated floor area can be made by multiplying the gross floor area by 0.9.

Complete Table 5.2 to calculate your energy costs per square metre of treated floor area. In most offices electricity bills are higher than gas or oil and usage often varies more widely than fossil fuel use. It is therefore essential that you consider electricity and fossil fuel use separately.

Calculate your energy costs per member of staff. *See Chapter 9, Environmental Reporting* ↘

Table 5.2 *Energy costs per square metre of treated floor area*

	Total annual cost (£)		Treated floor area (m^2)		Annual cost (£/m^2)
Gas		÷		=	
Oil		÷		=	
Coal		÷		=	
Electricity		÷		=	
Total annual cost £					
Total annual cost £/m^2					

Table 5.3 *Energy costs per member of staff*

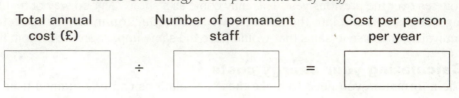

Total annual cost (£)		Number of permanent staff		Cost per person per year
	÷		=	

Tariffs

There is a potential 10–15 per cent saving to be made by changing to the right energy tariff. Your energy supplier and tariff should be reviewed to ensure you are using the most appropriate for your building's needs. For example, a growth in use of computers or other equipment which need to remain switched on overnight will make tariffs with low night use rates more economical.

A key part of energy management is regular continued metering of your consumption on a monthly (or even weekly) basis. This information will help you to assess the success of measures implemented. It will also allow you to monitor and report progress to senior management and staff so as to build commitment to energy efficiency.

More detailed analysis of energy consumption can be carried out by, for instance, relating heating use to weather or degree-days. For further information contact the Energy Efficiency Best Practice Programme (EEBPP).

Table 5.4 *Carbon dioxide emissions per square metre of office space*

	Annual kWh		Treated floor area (m^2)		Annual kWh/m^2		CO_2 conversion factors		CO_2 emissions $kg/m^2/year$
Gas		÷		=		X	0.19	=	
Oil		÷		=		X	0.25	=	
Coal		÷		=		X	0.30	=	
Total fossil fuel kWh/m^2									
Total electricity kWh/m^2		÷		=		X	0.44	=	
Total CO_2 emissions $kg/m^2/year$									

Calculating your emissions

Complete Table 5.4, using actual meter readings, to calculate your carbon dioxide emissions.

Compare your baseline figures with industry benchmarks. *See Chapter 9, Environmental Reporting* ⤵

Motivate your staff

When examining energy use most people start by gathering information, such as meter readings, and move on to consider investment in new equipment. These are both important. However, unless you encourage a culture change amongst your staff in the way they use energy, any amount of technology will have little impact.

Few people are excited by energy management. This provides the energy manager trying to involve staff with a challenge. A guide from the EEBPP, *Managing and Motivating Staff to Save Energy,* (1995a) gives ideas including the following ways of encouraging people.

- Ask people what they know, think and suggest about your use of energy and how they could contribute to reducing it.
- Agree objectives, targets and monitoring duties with your staff.
- Give incentives, rewards, feedback on results and thanks. *See Chapter 7, Communication* ⤵

Building Management

REDUCING ENERGY USE

☞ Practical action

Heating and cooling

In an air-conditioned office it can take up to half the energy again to remove the heat generated by office equipment as it takes to run the equipment. Air-conditioning is often over-specified and in some cases can be avoided altogether.

Check the room temperature

Reducing the temperature of a room by one degree can cut the heating bill by as much as 10 per cent. Check that thermostats are positioned and set correctly (16–19 degrees). Fit tamper-proof thermostats if necessary! Turn off heating in unused rooms. Avoid the use of electric heaters.

Check when heating is on

Make sure that heating is off or reduced outside working hours. Fit seven-day timer switches to vending machines and other appropriate equipment and sensor controls in places not in constant use. Consider using thermostatic radiator valves in areas where occupancy varies and ensure all radiators are not obstructed.

Check windows and outside doors
All windows and outside doors should be closed when heating is on. Install automatic door-closure devices on external doors to cut down heat loss.

Install insulation and draught proofing
The insulation of the loft, boilers and pipes will help prevent heat loss. The most important pipes to wrap are the hottest ones and the ones in the coldest places. Draught-proofing can prevent heat loss from roofs, doors and walls. Carry out the penny test: is there more than a penny's width gap beneath your door? If so, draught-proof it.

Reduce temperature of stored hot water
Hot water is often too hot and needs to be mixed with cold water before use. The thermostat should be turned down to a minimum of 60 degrees. Any lower than this can increase the risk of Legionnaires' disease.

Condensing boilers
Condensing boilers use a large heat exchanger to recover heat from flue gases, offering a 10 per cent gain in efficiency. New boiler(s) you install should be of the condensing type.

Use natural ventilation
Minimise areas of air-conditioning by using mechanical or natural ventilation. You do not need to provide air-conditioning for all areas of your office. Most people like to be able to open their window. Air-conditioned buildings use about twice as much energy as naturally ventilated buildings.

Ensure air-conditioning is not over-specified
The amount of heat that computers generate is frequently calculated using maximum power demand figures. This gives a distorted figure since it is based on the peaks of energy use rather than an average figure. This leads to many buildings being over-specified in terms of air-conditioning needs. *See Office Equipment section below for more information* ↘

Make sure cooling and heating are not on together
They often are!

Check air-conditioning times
Any need for air-conditioning outside office hours will only be for small areas of your office.

Set temperature controls to at least 24 degrees
Do not set the air-conditioning to come on before the temperature gets to at least 24 degrees. Even a slight increase in temperature setting can give a substantial reduction in your energy bills.

Case Study 5.2

SUBJECT: **Energy Efficiency**

ORGANISATION: **Reed Business Information**

LOCATION: **Quadrant House, Sutton, Surrey**

STAFF: **1500**

Background

Quadrant House is the head office for Reed Business Information, a major magazine publisher with approximately 150 titles. The building is a large air-conditioned office built in 1980, housing 1500 staff.

Action

Several large-scale projects have been undertaken over a number of years to reduce energy consumption. A building energy management system is used to monitor plant operation, air-conditioning, and chiller use and then adjust time programmes and control operation to ensure pumps, fans and cooling towers operate only when needed and use of the main chillers is restricted.

Originally, lights were controlled from a large switch panel in the corridors and many lights were left switched on unnecessarily. An automatic lighting control system now schedules lights to go off at periods throughout the day. The system was programmed to turn perimeter lights off at 10am and 1pm when daylight was sufficient and to switch internal lights off hourly after 6pm. Any adverse reaction from the lights going off was dealt with by altering the local lighting controls in each zone. Lighting in overlit areas has been reduced by arranging for two out of three fittings to be lit in the daytime and one in three at night. Decorative tungsten lights in the restaurant and reception areas were replaced with lower wattage bulbs and 2000 office light fittings in Quadrant House were modified from 2 x 85 watt fluorescent tubes to a single 70 watt triphosphor tube with a high frequency fixed-output ballast and specular reflector fitted to each. The result of this measure alone was a reduction in lighting energy consumption in excess of 50 per cent and increased light levels.

The funding required for these improvements was generated through a centralised energy management contract.

Results

As a result of these changes in energy management, electricity consumption has been reduced by 15 per cent and gas consumption by 67 per cent. These measures reduced carbon dioxide emissions (CO_2 per square metre) from the building by 27 per cent. ∎

Don't use the windows to regulate the temperature!
If the office is too hot or even too cold, people often open the windows to remedy the situation; in reality, your heating and cooling controls need attention.

Building Energy Management Systems (BEMS)
These offer the most sophisticated energy control by using micro-electronics to automatically monitor and control all the building's services.

Office equipment
Office equipment is now second only to heating as a major user of energy in most offices. The use of office equipment is doubling every few years and consumes around £300 million worth of energy each year. Computers, fax machines, copiers and vending machines can account for up to 70 per cent of energy use in some offices.

Investigate energy consumption
Calculate the true energy consumption of equipment. The nameplate rating is often based on maximum power demand. In practice, energy usage can be substantially lower. A typical PC uses £240 of electricity during its lifespan (4 years). However, equipment consumption varies dramatically with age, maintenance, model and manufacturer. Ask your suppliers or manufacturers to supply data on the average power consumed under typical operating conditions and the standby and low energy consumption for new equipment. Consider whole life energy cost savings; it may save you money in the long run to pay more initially. This information will also help you to calculate your air-conditioning requirements. *See Heating and Cooling section above* ➔

Launch a switch-off campaign
One-third of all PCs are left on overnight or over the weekend. Prevent this waste of energy by implementing an energy-saving policy to switch off machines when they are not in use. Insist that staff switch off at least their computer monitors (these use the most energy) when not in use, including when they are away from their desks for meetings or lunch. Turning off machines for any lengthy breaks during the day can achieve up to 60 per cent energy savings. To avoid residual background power consumption, switch equipment off at the plug when it is not needed.

A switch-off campaign will also reduce the costs of air-conditioning by reducing the heat generated by office equipment.

The DETR provide free posters and stickers to encourage switching off office equipment and other energy saving tips.

Enable energy-saving features
Most equipment can be set to go into stand-by or power-down (automatic switch off) mode after a predetermined time. Ensure all equipment has this facility activated, as machines are often set up with it disabled. Contrary to popular under-standing, screen savers do not save energy.

Share printers wherever possible
This will reduce the energy demands of printers standing idle.

⚠ Common problems

Lack of knowledge of the cost of energy
Establishing your energy costs is an essential starting point to address scepticism about the point of change. Small reductions in controllable costs such as energy can result in the same improvement to your profitability as a large increase in sales.

Lack of management responsibility
Energy can fall between different people's responsibilities and never be managed effectively. Give responsibility to a specific member of staff.

No board level support
If the board is not initially interested in energy efficiency you need to make an effective presentation of the business case. This can be more powerful if you have had success with some small-scale initiatives before looking to the board for support.

No money
Many of the actions outlined in this section require little or no investment. If you have no capital at the start, use the returns on the low cost measures to finance investment. This will enable a comprehensive energy efficiency programme to be managed with no initial funding.

Boredom
Few people are excited by energy management. Overcome this by involving staff, encouraging their ideas and rewarding commitment.

Summary guidelines

✔ Set up a management structure for energy

✔ Investigate your current energy costs and carbon dioxide emissions

✔ Motivate staff by involving them in the project and providing feedback on progress

✔ Check that your heating and air-conditioning are only on in the right areas at times when they are needed and at the most efficient temperatures

✔ Investigate energy saving technologies such as condensing boilers

✔ Set targets for improvement and review your progress regularly

REDUCING ENERGY USE

Building Management

LIGHTING

🍁 Environmental issues

Inefficient lighting systems use more energy. This contributes to acid rain and global warming. You can save significant amounts of energy and money simply by introducing more efficient lighting. Your choice of lighting can also affect staff productivity levels. Approximately 80,000,000 fluorescent tubes are disposed of annually in the UK. Fluorescent tubes contain mercury, cadmium and lead. *See Chapter 3, Office Waste* ↗

If every household in the UK replaced one conventional 100 watt lightbulb with one 20 watt compact fluorescent bulb, the nation would save all the electricity generated by one large power station (NatWest Group, 1997)

Choice of lighting

Tungsten bulbs

The standard tungsten bulb is very cheap to purchase but has a short life span and is very inefficient in its use of energy. Tungsten bulbs produce light by passing an electrical current through a fine wire filament, which becomes 'white hot'. Ninety-five per cent of this light is turned into heat, which can add to the workload of an air-conditioning system. Long usage results in brittle filaments which break due to vibration or heat expansion when the light is turned on.

Tungsten halogen lamps

These can be used to replace tungsten spotlights for desk and display lighting with energy savings of about 50 per cent.

Compact fluorescent lamps (CFLs)

CFLs are a relatively new form of lighting which use about 20–25 per cent of the electricity for a similar conventional lighting level. Their initial cost is higher but they last up to eight times as long as tungsten bulbs and are now common for domestic and office use. These lamps are not suitable for use in passive infra-red (PIR) fittings or in circuits using dimmer switches.

Fluorescent tubes

Fluorescent tubes are widely used in offices. They use about 18 per cent of the electricity of a tungsten bulb and less energy than a CFL. Fluorescent lamps produce light by applying electrical energy to either end of a tube containing inert gas plus a little mercury, creating an electrical arc. This method of lighting is more cost- and energy-efficient than tungsten lighting and fluorescent tubes produce very little heat compared to lamps. The useful life span of fluorescent lamps is approximately 7500 hours. Control gear is necessary for fluorescent tubes to start up and maintain light output and modern electronic controls are becoming increasingly efficient.

Slimline fluorescent tubes

Slimline fluorescent tubes are thinner in diameter (26 mm) and shorter than standard fluorescent tubes. With the reduction in size they produce an instant saving in the amount of energy required to give off light. Replacing standard fluorescent tubes with slimline fluorescent tubes will produce approximately 8 per cent energy savings.

Triphosphor fluorescent lighting

These tubes last longer and are more energy efficient that a standard fluorescent tube particularly when used with modern electronic control gear. They typically use 16.5 per cent of the energy of a tungsten bulb.

Daylight fluorescent

Daylight fluorescent tubes simulate the full colour and beneficial ultraviolet spectrum of natural daylight. These daylight tubes help to create a more healthy working environment by reducing fatigue. They may help seasonal affective disorder (SAD) sufferers, who suffer a cyclic form of depression linked to the reduced light levels of autumn and winter months. These lamps use the same amount of energy as a standard fluorescent. They are particularly useful in areas with no natural light such as basements, which can be depressing to work in.

Metal halide and sodium discharge lamps

These are suitable for lighting large areas such as car parks and warehouses. They are usually more efficient than fluorescent lights although this varies by type. Low pressure sodium lamps are the most efficient but are not suited to rapid switching.

☞ Practical action

Action on lighting will be a key part of your overall energy efficiency programme. There are a number of controls that can be used to make your lighting more efficient.

Time controls

These allow you to set lights to switch off automatically at set times to match the working day. Time switching may be used to switch off lighting at regular intervals, forcing occupants to reassess their lighting and to turn lights on only if required.

Presence detection controls

Acoustic, ultrasonic or infra-red sensors may be used to switch lights on or off automatically when somebody enters or leaves an area. It is important to set the timing correctly on these, particularly in toilets! Fit presence detector switches in places not in constant use, for instance, lavatories and meeting rooms.

Daylight detectors

These can switch off or dim lights according to the levels of natural light in the office and so maximise the use of natural light.

Building Management

Use natural light

Maximise your use of natural light. Keep all windows clean and make sure lights can be switched off manually, particularly near windows, or install daylight sensors. Remove fluorescent tubes in overlit areas.

Install low-energy lighting

Modern fluorescent tubes are vastly more efficient than tungsten lamps and are continuing to improve in efficiency. The low energy consumption and longer life of modern lamps will mean they show a good return on their initial investment. Whenever lighting is upgraded, use the opportunity to install the most efficient option available.

Improve lighting efficiency

All types of lamp lose efficiency with time (less light is given off and more energy used). Introduce a relamping programme where all lights are replaced at the same time, so that all fittings are running to full capacity. This programme will save on maintenance and disposal costs and will ensure consistent lighting levels.

Run a 'switch off' campaign

Increase staff awareness of energy efficiency; encourage staff to be diligent and turn lights off whenever possible. It is a common misconception that a burst of energy is required each time lights are switched on; this is not the case.

⚠ Common problems

Summary guidelines

- ✔ Maximise use of natural light
- ✔ Introduce a relamping programme – invest in energy-efficient lighting
- ✔ Install timer and sensor controls in areas not in constant use
- ✔ Implement a 'switch off' campaign – dispel the myths!
- ✔ Make staff aware of lighting controls and responsibility for switching off at the end of the day

LIGHTING

Misconceptions

'Switching fluorescent lights on and off uses more energy than leaving them on.'

Not true! A 1.8 m tube left on unnecessarily for 15 minutes uses 72,000 joules of energy. The energy used to start the tube is less than 150 joules. Over a 15-minute break the energy used is 500 times greater if the lights are left on.

'Switching lights on and off shortens their life.'

Not true! Leaving lights on for extended periods also shortens their life and if lights are switched off for more than 20 minutes there is a net gain in lamp life.

Lack of awareness

Staff are often not aware of how lighting is controlled – banks of switches need labels – or who should switch off lights at the end of the day.

WATER

Water is an increasingly scarce and therefore expensive commodity. The true cost of water is higher than the supply and sewerage charges alone. The true cost should include the energy taken to heat and deliver the water in your building. Therefore, energy costs should be used as an important additional driver for reducing water use. *See Energy earlier in this chapter*

🍁 Environmental issues

In England and Wales, as in many parts of the world, the balance between water supply and demand is an increasingly vital issue. Over the last decade, the demand for water in the UK has reached unprecedented levels and there is a trend towards a reduction in average rainfall, often leading to water shortages. In the future, organisations are liable to see tighter restrictions on their use of water and further increases in charges for metered water, yet most businesses are still not aware of how much they are using. Over two-thirds of water use in the average office takes place in the washroom, where substantial savings can often be made.

Legislation

Water Industry Act 1991

It is an offence for occupiers of trade premises to discharge trade effluents into a public sewer unless authorised by the sewerage undertaker.

To obtain a consent to discharge, occupiers of trade premises must make an application to the sewerage undertaker. The consent may impose conditions such as the rate, quantity and composition of effluent.

Water Resources Act 1991

It is an offence to cause or to knowingly permit any poisonous, noxious or polluting matter or any solid waste matter to enter any controlled waters. Application for consent to discharge to controlled waters must be made to the Environment Agency. If consent is granted, the Agency will set conditions to ensure compliance with statutory water quality objectives.

Government and industry initiatives

National Water Demand Management Centre (NWDMC)

The NWDMC was established in 1993 in recognition of the important role that demand management has to play in ensuring the sustainable use of water resources; the need for appreciation of the political, technical and economic considerations surrounding demand management and a need to raise awareness and influence key players.

Buildings that Save Water

A project run by the Construction Industry Research and Information Association (CIRIA), 'Buildings that Save Water', is investigating greywater and rainwater recycling demonstration systems with the aim of providing sound design and operation guidance. A technical report and best practice manual is due to be published in June 2000. Contact CIRIA Customer Services.

 Practical action

Assess usage

Consider where water is used in your organisation. Use this information to make targeted savings. Any saving in water consumption is not only a direct reduction in purchasing costs but also leads to an associated saving in wastewater disposal costs and improves your environmental performance.

Cost

The cost of water supply as a utility is often mistakenly considered to be too low to be of concern to offices. Water bills are split into two components; the purchase price, usually charged per m^3, and the disposal price – your water discharged to sewer – also charged per m^3. Both of these charges are set to rise at a rate greater than inflation. This may be all your accounts department actually pays for water; however, to identify the true cost of water to your organisation you should add pumping costs: pumping and distributing water around the site and building incurs energy costs; and maintenance costs: pumps, meters and pipework all incur maintenance costs, not to mention possible treatment and capital costs associated with meeting increasing demand for water.

Metering

Almost half of the water companies in the UK now offer free installation of water meters on request and all but three companies now have more cost-reflective tariffs for customers who use large amounts of water. Meters of different sizes have associated standing charges, for example £41 for a 15 mm meter to £1128 for a 150 mm meter.

Calculating your water use

Use your water bills to calculate the amount of water that you use and how much you spend on water supply and sewerage annually.

Use Table 5.5 to calculate a baseline of water use per member of staff. NB. 1 m^3 is equivalent to 1000 litres.

Refer to Chapter 9, Environmental Reporting, to compare your performance with industry benchmarks ↘

Table 5.5 *Water use per person per year*

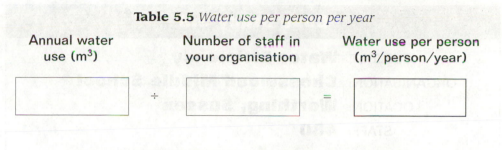

Annual water use (m³)		Number of staff in your organisation		Water use per person (m³/person/year)
	÷		=	

Table 5.6 *Water costs per person per year*

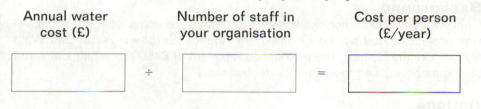

Annual water cost (£)		Number of staff in your organisation		Cost per person (£/year)
	÷		=	

Washrooms

Over two-thirds of water use in the average office takes place in toilets and washrooms. Up to 20 per cent of water is used for urinal flushing and 30 per cent through taps.

New legislation came into force in July 1999 which set a maximum cistern volume for new toilets. This is 6 litres for single flush toilets, and 4 litres short flush and 6 litres long flush for dual flush toilets.

WC cistern dams

Water displacement devices, sometimes known as cistern dams, are generally low cost and easy to fit. Most water companies will provide cistern dams free of charge; if not, improvise using a solid object such as a housebrick or a plastic bottle filled with water. You may need to experiment with different sized objects to ensure adequate flushing is maintained. They can save between 1.5 and 4 litres per flush.

Washroom controls

Complete washroom control systems that limit hot and cold water supply as well as lighting and ventilation are now available. Infra-red sensors react to anyone entering the washroom and activate all the services. The services are then only available for the time period set in the control unit. This makes it impossible to leave a tap running, avoids overflowing and flooding, and separate urinal flushing systems are not needed.

Taps

Fit push-button taps to save up to half the water used through taps. Push-button taps cannot be left on accidentally, help prevent floods in the event of a sink getting blocked and are more reliable than hydraulic models, especially in areas of bad limescale.

Case Study 5.3

SUBJECT: **Water Efficiency**

ORGANISATION: **Chesswood Middle School**

LOCATION: **Worthing, Sussex**

STAFF: **480**

Background

Chesswood Middle School was chosen to participate in a pilot water minimisation project funded by the Environment Agency, Southern Water and West Sussex County Council. The project had a budget of £4500 to implement water saving measures and record their effectiveness.

Actions

- Infra-red urinal controls installed in male toilet blocks.
- Retrofit push taps with built-in flow restrictors fitted to all washroom taps.
- Flow restrictors fitted to taps in the classrooms and replacement plugs provided.
- Save-a-flush bags (plastic bags filled with a moisture-retaining compound) installed in all toilet cisterns. These devices save approximately 1 litre per flush and work effectively in most cisterns.
- Water butts on down pipes to collect rainwater for garden watering.
- Three outside meters (to account for external water use) and one logger for the main meter installed.

The project is currently part way to completion. Following the installation of each efficiency measure, the water meters will be monitored for three weeks.

Results

Infra-red urinal controls reduced water consumption by 60 per cent, a saving of £2000 per year. These units cost £900 to install, making the payback period less than six months. This high saving was partially because the previous system was faulty, but was welcomed all the same! The push taps saved a further 9 per cent and were welcomed by the caretaker, who was previously subjected to regularly flooded toilet blocks; the toilet paper down the sink trick no longer works! It is expected that this combination of measures will dramatically reduce the school's water bills and has led to a much better understanding of where the water was being used and how best to reduce consumption. The project was completed by the end of April 2000.

For more information contact Southern Water. Tel 01903 835 342 ∎

Urinals

Retrofit existing urinals with deodorising pads to remove the need for water flushing, or consider installation of waterless urinals if refurbishment is due. Potential savings are between £70 and £170 per urinal per year.

Automatic flush controllers on urinal systems ensure that the cistern only flushes during office hours or after use rather than continuously. These devices can reduce water use and costs by 50 per cent.

Maintenance

Check your pipes for leaks: leaks can cost you large amounts of money and can cause damage to the building. Check your meter readings regularly and carefully – if you are paying for water that you cannot account for, you may have a leak.

Ensure that taps and pipework are regularly maintained; a tap dripping once per second wastes 4750 litres of water annually.

Talk to your supplier

You may be able to save money by negotiating with your supplier. If you have reduced your water consumption or no longer use sprinkler or hoses to water gardens you may be eligible for reduced charges.

Your water supplier should also be able to supply you with a range of water saving tips and may be able to conduct visits and provide advice on minimising water.

Landscaping

Using a sprinkler to water gardens and landscaped areas can use up to 1020 litres of water an hour.

- Water early in the evening to reduce evaporation losses.
- Use low volume watering devices such as seep hoses
- Use mulches or ground covering plants to lower soil temperature and reduce evaporation.
- Plant drought resistant plants or ensure appropriate plants are in the right locations for their requirements, ie thirsty plants in shady areas.
- Use hosepipe trigger controls to avoid their being left on.

Greywater and rainwater recycling

Systems for recycling greywater (water from showers and wash basins) and rainwater can reduce mains consumption by up to 90 per cent. Despite this, greywater and rainwater recovery systems have not been widely adopted in the UK. Some of the barriers to uptake are the relatively unproven technology of total recovery systems, associated unproven cost benefit, a lack of standard for rainwater or greywater systems and a lack of design guidance. Use water butts to collect rainwater from guttering, and use this water for small gardens.

Case Study 5.4

SUBJECT: **Water Efficiency**

ORGANISATION: **Three Valleys Water – Environmental Studies Centre**

LOCATION: **Bushey, Herts**

STAFF: **4 [Environmental Studies Centre]**

Background

Three Valleys Water provides drinking water to some 2.4 million customers in the Northern Home Counties and parts of North London. In 1997 the company built an Environmental Studies Centre at the Clay Lane Treatment Works in Bushey to meet the increasing number of educational and environmental requests. Over 5000 people visited the centre in its first year. The Centre has received two awards for links between education and business and has registered for the Eco-Centres Award Scheme.

Action

Through education, Three Valleys Water is making children aware of water usage and the environment. Literature to back up practical activities is being created for school use and free trees are supplied to local schools. Centre staff give talks in schools and have developed a range of activities cross-referenced to the National Curriculum.

At the Centre water-conscious gardens, a tree nursery, a butterfly garden and sensory garden have been established. A joint venture is planned with *Gardening Which* to trial watering devices.

The water-conscious gardens demonstrate simple water-saving techniques to the public and the gardens are used to teach local NVQ students. The Centre is writing a series of information leaflets to encourage good gardening techniques and booklets aimed to support the government's home study agreement.

Experiments are taking place with a local further education college to develop patio boxes that require no watering. This project is interesting several groups, from OAPs or those with bad backs to designers.

Results

The Environmental Studies Centre's activities promote a very positive message about Three Valleys Water. The Centre has been in existence for a little over one year but has already had an impact on local schools and on staff attitudes to water and energy use and composting kitchen waste. The whole garden development and ongoing trials have the potential to meet the needs of many diverse interested groups but, most of all, to help the environment. ■

⚠ Common problems

Blockages

Using cistern dams in modern toilets is not always viable due to restricted water flow which can result in blockages. Newer designs of cistern dam such as Save-a-flush (a plastic bag filled with a moisture-retaining compound, retains one litre per flush) are more suitable. Monitor toilets closely after fitting dams and experiment with various sizes if necessary.

Summary guidelines

✔ Assess your water usage; determine where the most water is used

✔ Check your bills; review standing charges and tariffs

✔ Upgrade your washrooms to minimise water wastage

✔ Adapt your landscaping practices and collect rainwater in water butts for watering

WATER

Building Management

CHAPTER SUMMARY

❑ Follow Special Waste Regulations for disposal of hazardous materials

❑ Consider the health and safety issues of office equipment

❑ Maximise the opportunities of refurbishment programmes to invest in energy efficiency measures

❑ Replace refrigerant with chemicals that do not damage the ozone layer and do not contribute to global warming

❑ Implement a lighting replacement programme and switch-off campaign

❑ Implement a water-saving programme focusing on major areas of usage, typically washrooms and landscaping

CHAPTER 6
Transport

INTRODUCTION

Travel, and cars in particular, has revolutionized the way we live. But the way we choose to travel has a price: for health, for the economy and for the environment. Motor travel continues to rise by approximately 2 per cent every year and the DETR's most recent National Road Traffic Forecasts (1997) predict that traffic will increase by up to 51 per cent between 1996 and 2016. It is now generally accepted that traffic jams cost time and money, create pollution and take the pleasure out of driving, and there is a growing public consensus for change and a new approach to transport management.

Transport is an area that people tend not think about when considering the environmental effects of their office. Offices can be heavy users of transport, both in commuting and business travel. Company car sales account for half of all new cars purchased and have a higher mileage than privately registered cars. The environmental effects of your transport needs may therefore be a significant part of the overall environmental impact of your offices. Efficient use of transport will also improve business effectiveness and profitability.

The guide *The Company, The Fleet And The Environment* (Energy Efficiency Best Practice Programme, 1995) concludes that:

> *'Experience shows that effective fleet management releases typical savings of 10 per cent. With fleet cars costing £5,000 or more each year, an average fleet of 100 cars could save £50,000. For many companies, turnover would have to increase by £0.5 million or more to make a comparable contribution to profits!'*

These benefits are certain to increase. Congestion is set to increase and the government is expected to increase fuel duty to reduce the growing greenhouse gas emissions.

This chapter is divided into commuting and business travel. It explains how your organisation can provide facilities and encouragement to allow staff to reduce their car dependency when travelling to work. The chapter also looks at ways of reducing the impact, and cost, of the company car. To enable you to prioritise the key areas to target when reducing, the chapter begins with a hierarchy of transport solutions.

Transport hierarchy

The environmental issues surrounding transport are complex and can make approaching the issue confusing. In Chapter 3, Office Waste, we looked at the government's waste hierarchy, which provides a guide to dealing with your waste. We have developed a transport hierarchy that provides a simple rule of thumb to reducing the environmental effects of your transport:

1   Reduce the need to travel at all through better planning and use of communication technology.
2   Switch from energy intensive and polluting vehicles to more efficient transport modes such as public transport, cycling and walking.
3   Make sure vehicles are efficient and well maintained.

The guidance given in this chapter follows this hierarchy. Within the two main sections of commuting and business travel, subjects are covered in order of their level in the hierarchy.

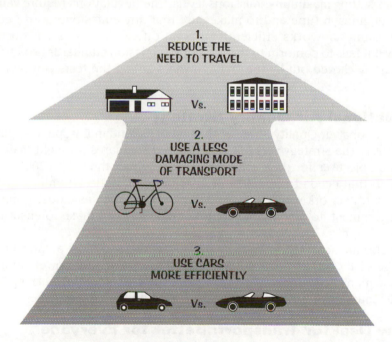

Figure 6.1 *The transport hierarchy*

Board-level commitment

Company cars are heavily linked to remuneration. Vehicle allocation, free fuel and parking are policy areas that will require board level agreement. Senior managers are often very reluctant to lose their luxury car! Equally, significant expenditure on video or teleconferencing to reduce the need to travel will require board agreement. It is therefore important when tackling transport to make sure top level commitment is there to back initiatives.

Senior management need to understand the business case. The main benefits are: the potential for significant savings and that tackling a sensitive issue such as transport will show that the organisation has a genuine commitment to environmental improvement. You are also likely to receive more support if transport initiatives are linked with the organisation's overall environmental programme. An environmental programme that ignores transport will lack credibility.

Legislation

Emissions and maintenance

The emission of pollutants from road vehicles is governed by the Road Vehicles (Construction and Use) Regulations made under the Road Traffic Act 1988. These have been amended a number of times, partly to comply with European Union Directives setting maximum emissions levels. The Regulations require vehicle users to keep engines in tune and to make sure that any emission control equipment, such as catalysts, works efficiently. It is an offence to use a car on the public highway if it fails to conform to the prescribed emission standards. Roadside checks are regularly carried out by the DVLA; owners failing the tests can be fined up to £5000.

The National Air Quality Strategy

The UK National Air Quality Strategy, the first of its kind in Europe, was published in March 1997. The Strategy sets out health-based standards for eight main air pollutants and objectives for their achievement throughout the UK by 2005. It identifies the action that needs to be taken at international, national and local level, and provides a framework which allows relevant parties, such as industry, business and local government, to identify the contributions they can make to ensuring that its objectives are met.

Vehicles are accepted to be the main air polluters in most areas and are therefore targeted for action. Local authorities will receive greater powers to manage air quality, which could include powers to tax non-residential parking, carry out roadside emissions tests and introduce a congestion pricing scheme.

A New Deal for Transport: Better for Everyone

The Transport White Paper, *A New Deal for Transport: Better for Everyone* published in summer 1998 (DETR, 1998), sets out how the government intends to create a better, more integrated transport system to tackle the problems of congestion and pollution, promote transport choice and reduce car dependency. The new approach incorporates:

- Local Transport Plans, to promote integration and traffic management, improve public transport and make it easier to walk and cycle.

- Better bus services, with local partnerships, exclusive contracts in some areas, extra help for rural buses, and concessionary fares for all elderly people.
- Better rail services, with a *Strategic Rail Authority*, a better deal for passengers and encouragement for rail freight.
- A one-stop national public transport information system to help plan seamless journeys.
- Revised planning guidance to reduce the need to travel.
- Better information, road maintenance and consumer protection for motorists.
- A *Commission for Integrated Transport* to keep up the momentum for continuing improvement.

Taxation

The Royal Commission on Environmental Pollution noted that the costs paid by transport users do not reflect the environmental damage and disbenefits caused by the use of land for transport infrastructure and by movements of vehicles. The use of economic instruments, such as pricing measures and taxation, is an important way of influencing travel choice and can help to ensure that all costs, including environmental costs, are reflected in the price of transport.

The costs of road travel could rise dramatically in the future. In the March 1998 Budget, petrol duty was raised by 7.3 per cent despite the abolition of the former fuel duty escalator. The Chancellor also announced that he would be considering the case for replacing the existing business mileage discounts with discounts for driving fewer private miles in company cars,

The government aims to introduce legislation to enable local authorities to levy a new parking charge on workplace parking. This charge would not apply to residential parking. Local councils will also be allowed to charge on congested roads, provided they plough back the money into transport improvements.

These charges will send a direct economic signal that traffic jams generate hidden economic, social and environmental costs. Workplace car parking charges can counter the effective subsidy of free parking space given to rush hour commuter car traffic. Road user charges can be pinpointed to tackle specific congestion hotspots in different areas at different times of day.

Environmental issues

Transport has a range of effects that have made it a key environmental issue. The environmental effects of transport are primarily caused by road vehicles due to their large numbers and the way they are used; for example, for short journeys with single passengers. Short haul air travel is increasing, but generates three times the CO_2 emissions of train travel. Walking and cycling have the least impact on the environment, create little pollution or noise, use little space and cause few accidents. They are also a good form of exercise!

Air pollution

When petrol or diesel is burnt for energy in an engine the main by-products are

Transport

water vapour and carbon dioxide (CO_2). Other pollutants are also produced because the burning process is not perfect.

Greenhouse effect

Surface based transport accounts for at least 22 per cent of UK carbon dioxide emissions, the most important greenhouse gas contributing to climate change. This level is rising as traffic growth continues to climb and is even higher if air travel is included. Other exhaust emissions such as nitrous oxide also contribute to the greenhouse effect. Following the Kyoto Conference on Climate Change in December 1997, the European Automobile Manufacturers Association agreed to reduce the CO_2 emissions from new passenger cars by over 25 per cent over the next ten years.

Increasing transport demand is a major obstacle to meeting the UK's international commitments to reduce emissions of carbon dioxide. In the 2000 Budget, the Chancellor extended the lower rate of vehicle excise duty (VED) for cars which have an engine capacity of up to 1200 cc. In addition, he announced that future company car tax would be based on the CO_2 emissions of the vehicle used by an individual.

Polluting emissions

All types of transport emit air pollutants; however, road vehicles are most significant, contributing over 50 per cent of the emissions of nitrogen oxides and over 75 per cent of carbon monoxide emissions in the UK.

At a local level the pollution from vehicle exhausts is linked to a range of health effects, in particular respiratory ailments.

Among the health issues raised are lead poisoning, particularly in children, and the carcinogenic effects of chemicals such as benzene. In addition, there has been an increase in the incidence of respiratory illness over recent years, particularly amongst children. It has been suggested that environmental factors such as air pollution could initiate asthma in previously healthy individuals or provoke or aggravate asthma symptoms in those who are already asthmatic.

Particles of matter such as carbon and unburned fuel and oils that are found in exhaust gases (known as particulates) are especially implicated in the causes of respiratory problems. Emissions from diesel engines contain higher levels of particulates. Smaller particles, known as PM10s, cause the greatest concern for health as they can penetrate the body's defences. An American study has suggested that particulates may be responsible for as many as 10,000 extra deaths a year in England and Wales (Royal Commission on Environmental Pollution, 1994). All London buses are expected to be fitted with particulate traps by 2005.

Petrol, diesel or alternative fuels

Until recently diesel cars were promoted as being greener due to their greater efficiency which leads to lower carbon dioxide emissions. However, the Committee on Medical Effects of Air Pollutants (1997) stated that on health grounds, with the current state of knowledge, diesel engine cars should not be recommended over petrol engine cars with catalytic converters. In urban areas, where most people live, diesel vehicles remain an important source of oxides of nitrogen (NO_x) and particulate emissions. Petrol cars fitted with 3-way catalytic converters also remain an important source of NO_x emissions and, in addition, of emissions of carbon monoxide (CO) and volatile organic compounds (VOCs). For petrol cars, this is primarily due to the predominance of short journeys in urban areas, often from cold starts, conditions under which the catalyst is much less effective at controlling pollutants. Both vehicle types produce carcinogenic substances in differing proportions, such as polycyclic aromatic hydrocarbon compounds (PAHs), benzene and 1,3-butadiene. Overall, therefore, comparison of the likely health impacts of the two vehicle types is difficult and definitive advice, on health grounds, of diesel versus petrol-powered light vehicles is not possible. However, concerns about the effects of particles on health in urban areas currently tip the balance in favour of petrol.

In the near future the comparison between petrol and diesel may alter and will also be complicated by a range of alternative fuels, the use of which is growing rapidly. Liquid petroleum gas (LPG) and compressed natural gas (CNG) both have significant net benefits over petrol in the reduction of air pollution and carbon dioxide emissions.

The Energy Savings Trust launched its Powershift programme in 1996 to boost the market for LPG, CNG and electricity powered vehicles. The scheme meets some of the cost between conventional and alternative vehicles or the cost of conversion. LPG costs half the price of unleaded petrol, the premium for alternative-fuelled vehicles continues to fall and the number of refuelling stations has increased dramatically.

Other impacts

Road accidents

Whilst the health impacts of air pollution are much disputed, there is no arguing with road accident figures. While these are amongst the lowest in Europe, they represent nearly two-fifths of all accidental deaths in the UK.

Noise

For the majority of people in the UK, road traffic is the main source of noise (Royal Commission on Environmental Pollution, 1994). At a local level, airports and aircraft flight paths can create serious problems. Although it has received less attention than air pollution, there is a growing body of evidence on the effect of noise on health. In particular it is linked to stress-related conditions such as raised blood pressure.

Noise is also a major reason why people avoid walking or cycling on busy roads and therefore acts as a deterrent to using more environmentally preferable modes of transport.

Congestion

Congestion imposes considerable direct costs on road users through longer journey times, journey time unreliability, increased fuel consumption, and frustration and discomfort for vehicle drivers and passengers. Estimates vary, but congestion certainly costs business billions of pounds every year.

Transport

177

It is estimated that UK drivers and passengers lost 1.6 billion business hours as a result of traffic congestion in 1996, and that 80 per cent of this total occurred in urban areas. The problem is particularly acute in the inner conurbations and during peak commuting periods. A significant contribution to this must be that, nationally, 70 per cent of the workforce drives to work, and of these, 75 per cent have parking provided by their employer. However, congestion can also be a problem in rural areas during holiday periods, at popular tourist locations, at special events and at bottlenecks on the trunk road network.

Congestion is a major contributor to air pollution, noise and nuisance, as discussed above; in addition, traffic congestion can also damage the viability and vitality of urban centres by discouraging visitors and encouraging relocation to out-of-town areas. Congestion makes it more difficult for bus operators to provide an efficient and reliable service, and makes use of the roads unpleasant for cyclists and pedestrians.

Maintenance and disposal

Disposal of worn-out car parts and final disposal of cars as scrap presents a major waste problem. Cars contain many hazardous or contaminated materials such as batteries, exhaust systems, tyres and oil that need to be carefully dealt with. Discarded vehicles result in 8 to 9 million tonnes of waste each year in the European Union. The proposed End of Life Vehicles Directive sets a target to re-use and/or recycle 80 per cent of the vehicle's weight. Under this proposal, the automotive industry is responsible for collection and recycling of vehicles to reduce the burden on public authorities in line with the Producer Responsibility Principle.

Government and industry initiatives

Travel Wise

Travel Wise was launched by Hertfordshire County Council in 1993 and is now a national campaign involving over 100 highway authorities. The aim of the Travel Wise campaign is to promote travel awareness and alternatives to car travel. The Travel Wise newsletter, *Changing Tracks,* reports quarterly on a wide range of local initiatives including Walk to School Week, staff car sharing schemes and park and ride sites.

Green Transport Plans (GTPs)

Commuting has been highlighted as a key factor in developing an integrated transport system in the UK and the government is encouraging business to implement Green Transport plans – bringing together transport and other business issues in a coordinated strategy – to relieve pressure on roads and car parking facilities, to save money and to improve businesses' environmental performance.

COMMUTING

Commuting to work creates a huge demand for transport. Between 1985 and 1999 the proportion of individuals travelling to work by car increased from 57 per cent to 70 per cent. More cars on the road mean more stress, more time wasted in traffic and more pollution. While no organisation can control the way staff get to work in the way they control business travel, it is possible to provide facilities and encouragement to reduce this burden.

Nottingham City Council has been at the forefront of promoting 'green commuter plans' for the city's employers. These plans help companies to set up a comprehensive approach to reducing the environmental impact, and often cost, of commuting. Green Commuter Plans are intended to be developed and implemented over a three-year period with a target to cut car commuting journeys by 30 per cent.

Green travel plans

 ## Practical action

Key features required to set up a plan include:

- Senior management commitment, including leading by example and appointment of a senior member of staff as the Staff Travel Coordinator.
- Staff travel survey to provide a baseline.
- A target to monitor and encourage progress.
- Extensive consultation with staff to overcome resistance to change and gain commitment.
- Use of work area travel plans in larger organisations.

Establishing a baseline
An important first step is to have an accurate idea of how your staff currently travel to work. This will provide you with a baseline figure from which to monitor improvements and allow you to target initiatives on areas with the most potential for improvement.

Survey staff travel
A survey of all staff, or of a representative sample, will allow you to gather information on current commuting patterns. Key information required is preferred mode of transport (and why, if possible) and distance travelled.

Get staff involved
A survey presents an opportunity to find out what measures would encourage staff to cycle or take public transport to work. This will yield useful information and will develop staff interest in the project.

Encourage participation

Organise a prize draw for those who have been involved in the survey to encourage participation. For example, Boots in Nottingham carried out a staff travel survey with a response rate of 85 per cent. Respondents were entered into a prize draw of a 'family of bicycles'.

Minimising commuting

For commuter travel, meeting the top level of the transport hierarchy, reducing the need to travel, demands radical thinking. Can you bring the office closer to staff or even let staff work from home so that they rarely need to come to the office? A variety of working practices are now commonplace. Location-independent working provides staff with the means to work from any building using a mobile phone and portable PC with a modem link. Teleworking refers to staff that work from a fixed base outside the organisation, for example, the home. Teleworking is not unique to large businesses; micro businesses can now operate through Telecentres – local resource centres. A number of small companies share the premises and reduce overheads by sharing resources and travel.

Studies have found that teleworkers produce more work and have lower support and property costs. This has been calculated as a 45 per cent gain in efficiency. The overall environmental effects of the teleworking trend are complex; however, working from home for just one day a fortnight will reduce an employee's commuting trips by 10 per cent. Management by results will ensure that employees do not abuse teleworking.

Nottingham City Council requires new staff to move within 20 miles of their workplace to qualify for its relocation package. In future, this may be changed to within five miles, with a more generous package for those who live closest.

☞ Practical action

Plan relocations

When moving to a new office, make sure it is near to residential areas and has good public transport access to minimise the distance staff have to commute.

Book accessible conference venues

Hold conferences at venues with good public transport links rather than those located at motorway junctions. Include instructions on how to travel by public transport as well as by road. This might be the first impression of your company and it can promote your environmental awareness.

Encourage home working

To develop home working, focus on one major benefit and use that to sell the idea. For instance, if the sales force of a company is hardly ever at their desks, could they work from home and save office space and costs?

Case Study 6.1

SUBJECT: **Green Transport Plans**

ORGANISATION: **Stockley Park Transport Plan**

LOCATION: **Stockley Park, Uxbridge, Middlesex**

STAFF: **6600**

Background

Stockley Park is Europe's leading business park, located near Heathrow. It launched the Stockley Park Transport Plan to improve the choice of travel available to the 6600 staff on the site for both environmental and commercial reasons. A travel survey showed that 30 per cent of employees were interested in car sharing and 60 per cent would use public transport some or all of the time – if it were improved! The results of this survey were key in the development of the transport plan, which included public transport improvements, car sharing, cycling, raising awareness and reducing dependency.

Action

Stockley Park subsidises two bus services, investing £120,000 a year. The additional funding has enabled the introduction of new, more spacious, branded buses on the main route.

To enable people to find suitable car share partners, Stockley Park Consortium have designed an innovative Internet system called 'Spark'. Users can register with the car share scheme and carry out a search for car share partners. Once a suitable match has been found, a map is viewed and the two people can email each other to set up an arrangement. Spark also provides an ideal forum for raising awareness of transport alternatives, providing information about cycling to work, public transport timetables and maps.

Online shopping at Tesco is also offered through 'Spark', enabling people to shop over the Internet at lunchtime, reducing car dependency. Promotion of the free, twice weekly shopper bus also forms part of the transport plan.

Employees are encouraged to cycle to work and the Stockley Park Bicycle User Group meets regularly. Many employees were involved in National Bike to Work Day and received a free breakfast and bike repair service.

Spending on the Transport Plan has now reached approximately £150,000 and the Stockley Park Consortium has pledged £2.3 million towards sustainable transport improvements, including the Heathrow North station at Hayes, the development of new bus routes and cycle routes.

Results

Stockley Park has been awarded 'Business Park of the Year' by the Institute of Transport Management in recognition of the lead taken by the consortium in implementing an innovative transport plan to reduce traffic congestion. ∎

Cash for car parking

Use incentives such as a cash payment to encourage those staff that do not need to drive to work to consider the alternatives.

Provide public transport information

A simple but essential part of reducing commuter travel is provision of information. Ensure current maps, timetables and other information are available to all staff by displaying in major staff meeting places and on your company's intranet if you have one. A national public transport information system is planned for 2000.

Discounted travel

Larger organisations are increasingly able to negotiate discounts with local public transport operators.

Staff at BAA Heathrow can purchase Travelcards that offer discounts on bus and rail services of up to 80 per cent.

Cycling

Cycling has great potential for implementing the second level of the hierarchy: using a less damaging mode of transport. The National Cycling Strategy published in 1996 aims to double cycle use by the year 2002 and quadruple it by 2012. It highlights the potential for the UK to dramatically increase its use of bicycles. 'In Switzerland there are more hills, Sweden has colder winters and Germany higher car owner-ship; yet each has five times the share of bicycle trips than the UK': Department of Transport (1996b).

The Strategy urges all companies to provide facilities for cyclists to increase the proportion of staff cycling to work. It also suggests providing financial incentives for employees to encourage cycle use and that 'Consideration be given to reallocat-ing car parking space to cycle parking as a potentially cost efficient use of land by commercial concerns'.

There can be a direct benefit to organisations from encouraging staff to cycle. The British Medical Association stated that cycling has considerable health advan-tages, particularly for preventing heart disease. Healthier staff means fewer days off sick. People who cycle to work also benefit from reduced travel costs and often a quicker, more convenient and more reliable mode of transport. The National Cycle Network, designed and built by Sustrans and supported by the Millennium Commission, will cover 8000 miles by 2005. This vastly improved network of specif-ically designed cycle lanes will go through the centre of most major towns and cities, enabling a far greater number of people to cycle safely to work.

☞ Practical action

Secure and sheltered cycle parking

Providing a secure, sheltered place to store bicycles is crucial to encouraging staff to cycle to work. Risking your bicycle being stolen is a major deterrent. A Sheffield stand, an inverted U-shaped bar which takes two bikes, costs from just £25. At the other end of the scale, a cycle cage holding 12 bikes with key or swipe card access costs from £1500. Alternatively, talk to your local authority about setting up cycle parking nearby and offer to cover part of the cost.

Changing facilities

The other facility needed is showers and changing areas. Neither the cyclist nor their colleagues will be keen on cycling miles to work if they have to wear the same clothes all day!

Lease and loan schemes

Consider offering an interest-free loan for bicycles and other necessary equipment such as helmets and waterproof clothing. Staff at HMV Music Stores can buy bicycles at a 10 per cent discount and spread the payments using an interest-free loan of up to £500.

Bicycle users groups

Form a Bicycle Users Group or BUG to encourage new cyclists to meet more experienced ones to discuss routes, safety and equipment. Some BUGs have a 'buddy' system for new or inexperienced cyclists.

Information and promotion

Use the health and environmental benefits of cycling to promote cycling to work to your staff. Sponsored 'Cycle to Work' days can persuade those who don't cycle to give it a go, but ensure there is a next step such as cycle training schemes, security marking for bikes, or follow-up events to maintain momentum.

Guarantee a taxi for emergencies

Giving staff the reassurance of a guaranteed taxi ride in the case of an emergency will overcome many of their concerns about doing without their car.

Public transport

Public transport may already be a widely used alternative to driving if your office is in a town centre. In this case simple measures such as providing timetables can be very successful at ensuring staff are making the most of available services. If you are out of town, most staff are less likely to be aware of local public transport services and higher profile initiatives will be needed to encourage a culture change away from the car.

 **Practical action**

Provide season ticket loans

Staff may be put off public transport by the initial cost of a season ticket, particularly if they are commuting into London. Some organisations give employees free Travelcards as part of their salary package, others such as British Telecom and Friends of the Earth offer their staff an interest-free loan for the ticket which enables the cost to be spread out.

Provide maps and timetables

Good information is a key to encouraging use of public transport. There should be points in the office where local public transport information, such as timetables and route maps, is held. Some of this information may be available on computer; London Transport have a guide to their services available on the Internet. Large companies may be able to obtain tailored information from bus companies.

Provide dedicated services

Another option for large companies is to build on existing public transport by providing company transport for local employees or a shuttle service to the local train or bus station.

Work with the Council and transport operators

Large organisations can accomplish a great deal by working with their local authority, which will be trying to encourage more use of public transport and cycling, and transport operators who have an interest in attracting more passengers.

An example of this partnership approach would be an employer working with a local bus operator to provide: discounted tickets for staff, services that fit in with the times staff want to travel and travel information targeted at staff. For instance, Nottingham City Council provides a staff discount travelcard scheme. Travelcards for the city's buses are sold to staff at a discount and sent directly to the workplace. The cost is then automatically deducted from the payroll. Park and ride season tickets for staff can be negotiated along the same lines.

'Leave your car at home' day

One of the barriers to switching from car to public transport is habit. An initiative to overcome this is to hold a 'leave your car at home' day. Many local authorities have run these successfully and linked them to Green Transport Week, which is held in June. The day will need to be publicised well in advance. Publicity such as a picture of the Chief Executive on a bicycle will help! The reward is that some of those staff that switch to a bus or bicycle for the day may decide to do so regularly.

Parking

Free parking spaces are an expensive perk that encourage staff to commute by car. Southampton University Hospitals have calculated that an average of £300 a year is spent on maintaining each of its parking spaces (including maintenance and opportunity costs). This figure is higher in expensive town centre areas. To encourage staff to use less polluting modes of transport you need to tackle this subsidy, as well as implementing the positive measures outlined above.

The cost of providing parking is likely to rise further as the government is considering giving local councils powers to tax non-residential parking to help curb air pollution. Reducing the need for car parking spaces will minimise direct costs and allow the opportunity cost of that land to be realised by using it for another purpose. Some of the profits can then be put back into encouraging other forms of transport to work.

☞ Practical action

Assess the cost of your car park

The first step to efficient car park management is to assess how many spaces you have available, who is using them, when they are used and how much they cost. The real cost of the parking should be allocated to specific work areas so it can be managed rather than hidden in overheads. The real cost includes the land, laying out, maintenance and management and loss of alternative uses.

Prevent unauthorised access

To prevent unauthorised access there is a range of equipment such as automatic card systems that allow quick entry and exit.

Assess who needs a parking space

Only staff that genuinely need to bring their cars to work should be given a parking permit.

Charge for parking space

Charge for parking spaces at a market rate and use the money to provide support for other modes of transport such as facilities for cyclists and loans towards public transport season tickets. Encourage staff to car-share with lower parking charges.

Car sharing

Car sharing is a relatively simple way to achieve more efficient use of the car, the final level of the transport hierarchy. Some of your staff may already be car sharing and this, along with the savings, means resistance is likely to be lower than to some of the measures described above.

Transport

 **Practical action**

Provide a notice-board
The simplest way to promote sharing is a dedicated notice-board or computer bulletin board where staff can exchange information to enable them to link up (you could publicise it as a dating agency for car sharing!). This also provides a focal point for publicising environmental initiatives and reporting progress back to staff.

Organise a database
To provide more active support for car sharing, an organisation can develop a database of those wishing to car-share and the locations from which they commute. The database should have a designated member of staff responsible for updating or it will swiftly become out of date.

Guarantee a taxi in emergencies
A guaranteed ride home by taxi in the event of an emergency should be made available to all staff who are car sharing.

Summary guidelines

✔ Plan new developments that minimise the need to travel and are accessible by public transport
✔ Promote home working where it is appropriate
✔ Provide secure facilities for bicycles
✔ Provide changing facilities for cyclists
✔ Offer loans for season tickets or other incentives to encourage staff to use public transport
✔ Charge for car parking spaces and use the proceeds to support cycling facilities, season ticket loans and car sharing
✔ Support car sharing by maintaining a database of those wanting to participate and their journey

COMMUTING

⚠ Common problems

Resistance to teleworking
Some organisations still see teleworking as an easy option. However, many companies have found that, in the right situation, it can save money and increase the efficiency of staff time.

Attachment to the car
Many people have never dreamt of using anything but their car for commuting. Measures to encourage less damaging modes of transport are therefore potentially controversial.

If staff see the initiatives as a management cost cutting exercise, imposed from above, they will fail; you cannot force staff to use the bus or cycle. Make sure you involve staff from the beginning and that your programme is seen positively, offering benefits to staff and the environment. In this context measures such as charging for car parking will be easier to introduce.

Case Study 6.2

SUBJECT: **Green Transport Plans**

ORGANISATION: **BAA**

LOCATION: **Heathrow**

STAFF: **57,000**

Background

BAA is the world's largest commercial operator of airports, owning and operating seven UK airports. Heathrow Airport is now the world's busiest international airport, handling over 60 million passengers and over 1.2 million tonnes of cargo a year. Heathrow is served by over 90 airlines flying to over 200 destinations. The airport provides direct employment for over 57,000 people and up to 82,000 jobs in the local area are dependent on the airport.

BAA Heathrow's environmental policy commits it to minimising the impact of its growing business on the environment and local communities through continuous improvement of its performance. This performance has been the subject of annual reports since 1993 and community reports have been published since 1996. In 1998/99 we merged these into one document reporting against the sustainable development 'triple bottom line' of environment, economic and social accounting. Surface transport, with its air quality, health and social equity implications, is one of the key issues addressed in the report.

Action

Heathrow is already the aviation hub of the world, but BAA's aim is to make it the world's leading public transport hub as well. In addition to setting targets for increasing the proportion of air passengers using public transport, the airport has initiated a staff green transport plan process. BAA Heathrow was one of the first to make progress in this area with publication in 1997 of the Heathrow Area Employee Travel Initiative. This was followed in 1998 by a consultation document outlining the purpose and potential benefits of a transport plan for BAA staff based at the airport. The emphasis was on encouraging and persuading staff to think about changing their travel patterns.

The consultation plan was distributed with the staff newspaper. Trade unions, key management staff and transport forum groups were also consulted. An independent agency was used to facilitate focus groups to gather the views of selected staff in more detail.

Results

The consultation process demonstrated that staff have a high general awareness of the travel initiatives that had been introduced at Heathrow including a staff travelcard (which permits discounted travel on a network of buses and trains covering all three of BAA's south-east airports) and free travel for staff

Transport

187

on local buses (over 650,000 trips in 1999). Some of the main messages were the need for flexible transport arrangements to meet shift working requirements, and the importance of high quality bus services.

The consultation also highlighted the importance of keeping staff informed of the travel options for getting to and from work. BAA Heathrow has designed Freeflow Heathrow, an award-winning campaign to raise awareness of travel issues at the airport. We also organise events such as Bike to Work Day and Car Free Day.

Further work is now underway to continue involving staff in transport planning and to bring about changes to travel behaviour. We are also seeking the commitment of other companies at the airport to produce their own staff travel plans in 2000. ■

Poor image of public transport

Many people see public transport as inefficient and expensive. Where reasonable services do exist, encouraging staff to try public transport or cycling may overcome this barrier. One way of doing this is by running a 'leave your car at home' day. *See Public Transport*

Lack of public transport

Where services are poor, large organisations can work with a transport operator and local authority to provide a better service.

Poor cycling facilities

On your own site you can provide changing and storage facilities for cyclists. You can also work with your local authority to develop better cycle paths in the local area.

Sainsbury's supermarket in Islington uses three pedi-cabs, each powered by a cyclist, to provide a pollution-free means to transport customers and their shopping home.

BUSINESS TRAVEL AND COMPANY CARS

Business travel and the company car fleet can be a major expense for an organisation. Maximising the efficiency of the car fleet and business travel is sound business practice. It can also produce substantial environmental improvements. Company cars account for almost 20 per cent of all car mileage in the UK despite representing only 8 per cent of all cars. Company policy on the purchase and use of company car fleets is therefore important for the environment. Company cars are generally much newer and better maintained than the average private car and therefore less polluting per unit of fuel consumed. However, they tend to have larger engine sizes and, as they account for a high proportion of the new vehicle fleet, they contribute to higher overall average fuel consumption both directly and through their influence on the stock of cars in the secondhand market. These drivers also tend to drive significantly further to and from work and those who receive free fuel drive further still.

☞ Practical action

Transport emissions ready-reckoners

Emissions from transport and their environmental effects are complex. At present carbon dioxide emissions are being prioritised by government and industry in light of international commitments to reduce our contribution to global warming.

Use Tables 6.1–6.3 to estimate the carbon dioxide emissions arising from your business travel and use this baseline figure to measure progress. Make a practical decision as to the amount of data you can collect at reasonable cost, proportionate to the environmental impact. For example, local travel by car may be difficult or expensive to calculate but if this is a significant proportion of your businesses travel, you may want to investigate means of measuring trips or distances.

The best data to collect is fuel use. This will reflect distance travelled as well as engine sizes and fuel efficiencies and will highlight direct rewards for using more efficient vehicles. Fuel consumption for the whole company fleet may be the easiest figure to obtain and can be used as a first step to working out overall emissions. Once this system is established, you can concentrate on collecting more accurate fuel use data, per car or department. This will enable you to make targeted and effective efficiency measures. The fuel consumption figures given in Table 6.1 are examples based on a fleet of ten diesel and ten petrol cars, travelling 30,000 miles each for a year. Assuming fuel efficiencies of 30 mpg and 38 mpg for a petrol and diesel car respectively, this would require 1000 gallons (30,000/30); 4600 litres of petrol or 3632 litres of diesel.

Conversion figures for LPG and CNG are 1.65 kg CO_2/l and 2.67 kg CO_2/kg, respectively should you have any vehicles running on these fuels.

Just this simple exercise allows a rough estimate of 204 tonnes of CO_2 emissions for the 20-car fleet. If you do not have access to fuel use data, record the distance travelled by each mode of travel and multiply by the relevant conversion factor as shown in Table 6.2.

Table 6.1 *CO_2 conversion figures for fuel use*

Fuel type (litre)	Amount per year		CO_2 per litre (kg)		Total CO_2 (kg)
Petrol	46,000	x	2.31	=	106,260
Diesel	36,320	x	2.68	=	97,338
Total					203,598

Table 6.2 *CO_2 emissions by transport mode*

Transport mode	CO_2 per km (kg)	Unit
Bus	1.28	vehicle km
Petrol car	0.20	vehicle km
Diesel car	0.12	vehicle km
Short haul flight	0.18	passenger km
Tube	0.11	passenger km
Long haul flight	0.11	passenger km
Train	0.06	passenger km
Source: DETR, 1999a		

In Table 6.3 we have included an example of this process. Schroders use petrol and diesel car and tube travel for corporate travel although this is not quantified at present and does not form a major part of the overall travel undertaken. However, they have been able to quantify rail and air travel, which is shown in Table 6.3.

Minimising business travel

UK industry could save £450 million per year by employing simple fleet management techniques. A typical company with a 400-strong company car fleet could save £50,000 per year and cut carbon dioxide emissions by 50 tonnes through simple techniques such as fuel consumption monitoring, journey planning and driver training.

Table 6.3 *Example ready-reckoner of CO_2 emissions from Schroders plc corporate annual travel*

Transport mode	Distance (million km)		CO_2 emission factor (kg per passenger kilometre)		Total CO_2 (tonnes)
Short haul flight	50.06	x	0.18	=	9011
Long haul flight	34.40	x	0.11	=	3784
Train – UK	2.68	x	0.06	=	161
– Eurostar	1.56	x	0.06	=	94
Total	88.70				13,050

Green Transport Plans (GTPs)

The Green Transport Plan is a management approach that analyses the key transport challenges and opportunities facing an employer and provides the structure for an integrated, strategic response. GTPs are becoming accepted part of business practice throughout the USA and Europe and all UK government departments are developing their own GTPs. The DETR has produced guidance on implementing a GTP in your organisation. *See Chapter 10, Contacts and Resources* ➘

Reducing the need to travel

British business managers spend nearly 11 hours behind the wheel each week – two of them in traffic jams – travelling to an average of six meetings (ETA, 1999).

While face-to-face meetings remain important to all organisations, the growth of communication technologies provides an alternative to the traditional business meeting. The savings achievable multiply as the distance increases. Consider the relative price of a phone call against an international flight!

However, technological solutions require considerable capital investment and logistical management of their own. Simple, low tech solutions such as better planning and logistics have been shown to have a major impact on the efficiency of freight and business transport. Tesco saved £720,000 a year, reduced their fleet mileage by 3 million miles and reduced their carbon dioxide emissions by 4600 tonnes a year by organising journeys to ensure that every vehicle has a return load; a common sense solution that many companies whatever the size of their fleet could learn from.

Short journeys are often disregarded as not worth monitoring, yet 58 per cent of all car journeys are less than 5 miles. A petrol car is not fully efficient until driven for 6 miles in an urban area, therefore these multiple journeys which produce more emissions and use more fuel may be a significant factor.

☞ Practical action

Use video and audio conferencing

Following the initial capital cost there is potential for considerable savings on travel costs and staff time, particularly where conferencing replaces international travel. Modern video communication products offer a wide range of facilities. For instance two screens can be used to maintain face-to-face contact while working with graphics and slides. Conference call technologies can be used to link small groups into virtual meetings or as a means of broadcasting information to large audiences with up to 1000 sites linked to a single call.

Coordinate meetings

Make sure that meetings and travel are coordinated by efficient journey planning. For instance, schedule meetings near to each other on the same day so only one trip is required or share a car with other staff going to the same location.

Plan staff commitments

Planning of staff commitments can also cut travel demand, particularly where work is split between two or more sites. When staff are seconded to other sites, providing hotel accommodation will avoid them having to make long round-trip journeys.

Using other transport modes

Use public transport for business travel

Make sure that, wherever practical, all business travel is by public transport. This can result in a more efficient use of staff time since it is possible to work on the train.

Encourage visitors to use public transport

Ensure that standard directions you provide to visitors cover access by public transport as well as by car. Maps should show bus routes and cycle lanes. Your marketing material is one of the first things a visitor sees about your organisation and is therefore important in communicating your environmental commitment.

Alternatives to the company car

How many of your staff really need a company car? Many companies now offer alternative packages that can save the company money, reduce environmental impact and satisfy their staff.

☞ Practical action

Provide an alternative package to the company car

An attractive and realistic alternative package might include cash and a season ticket to use on local public transport. This can save money on the cost of the car and on the cost of providing parking, which, as already mentioned, can be substantial.

Provide office pool bikes

Some organisations, such as Cambridgeshire County Council, provide office pool bicycles as an alternative to the car for short journeys.

Car choice

All cars use energy and cause pollution, so there is no such thing as a green car. The green choice is to reduce the company car fleet. However, you can make your car fleet more efficient and achieve significant savings by making sure that you purchase the right cars. More efficient models cause significantly less pollution than gas guzzlers. When choosing a car it is important to look at the whole life cost rather than simply the capital cost. A cheaper model may work out to be more expensive once issues such as fuel consumption and resale value are taken into account.

The Vehicle Certification Agency (1999) provides a comprehensive guide listing the fuel consumption, exhaust pollution levels and noise levels of most new petrol and diesel cars on sale in the UK. Small-engined cars such as the MCC Smart and Seat Arosa come out best in terms of emissions, fuel consumption and cost. *See Chapter 10, Contacts and Resources*

Practical action

Choose an efficient car

The key points to remember are:

- Miles per gallon, urban and non urban.
- Avoid 'sporty' models.
- Avoid cars with high acceleration.
- Avoid cars with high top speeds.

Monitor alternative fuels

The current position of petrol, diesel and alternative fuels was outlined in the section on the Environmental Effects of Transport. This position will change in the future and fleet managers need to monitor the relative merits of all available fuels.

Driving technique

Beyond car choice and maintenance, good driving technique can reduce fuel consumption by up to 25 per cent. This practice will also reduce the environmental impact of staff driving to work and their safety out of work hours.

Practical action

Train all drivers

There are a number of simple steps that drivers should take to lessen their impact on the environment.

- Drive off as soon as possible after starting the engine.
- Avoid harsh braking and acceleration; these are heavy fuel users.
- Slow down; driving at high speeds significantly increases fuel consumption. 40–55 mph is the most efficient speed.
- Turn the engine off if stuck in traffic for more than one minute.

These simple measures can mean a large reduction in harmful emissions as well as cost savings. If fuel use is being measured and managed, it is possible to monitor improvements and provide incentives to efficient drivers.

J Sainsbury plc has achieved an 8 per cent improvement in miles per gallon over two years as a result of changing car fleet manufacturer and issuing fuel efficiency driving guidelines.

Driver safety

Company car drivers have on average 30–50 per cent more accidents a year than comparable private car drivers. The average cost of a claim for accidental damage to a company car is about £1000, to which needs to be added the cost in lost time. Driver training can reduce these costs and the pain and trauma associated with them. Drivers who have attended driver training courses show reduced accident rates and greater fuel efficiency through a smoother driving style. These improvements are being recognised by many insurance companies through reduced premiums.

Plan ahead

Using route-planning software and real-time traffic information systems and combining trips can help ensure the fastest, least congested route.

Avoid excessive air-conditioning

Running air-conditioning continuously increases fuel consumption significantly.

Fuel

Fuel costs are an important part of the total costs involved in running a vehicle fleet and are likely to increase faster than most other elements of fleet budget. However, despite being the easiest variable cost to control, they are often disregarded by fleet operators as unavoidable. The use of petrol in cars is the fastest growing cause of greenhouse gases and it is expected that the government will continue to increase duty on these fuels to help reduce emissions.

Most companies award senior staff with larger cars and higher mileage allowances. These measures encourage the use of less fuel-efficient cars and more driving. The perk of free fuel leaves private motoring effectively free and therefore encourages greater distances to be travelled.

☞ Practical action

End free fuel for personal use

Organisations should end the perk of free fuel for personal use. Mileage allowances should be the same for all cars. These measures will encourage the selection of smaller cars and reduce the amount of driving.

Monitor fleet fuel use

Monitoring vehicle fuel performance is necessary to control the company car fleet. Monitoring techniques do not need to be highly technical; in fact the systems need to be simple to run to produce a clear picture without entailing excessive administrative cost. The main factors to consider are: the volume of fuel used, the associated cost and the distance travelled. These will provide a complete record of fuel performance by vehicle. Driver and vehicle performance can then be accurately monitored.

Maintenance

A well-maintained vehicle can be 10 per cent more efficient than one that is not regularly serviced. One in five roadside breakdowns are the result of bad vehicle maintenance. To minimise the costs and environmental impacts of your car fleet it is essential to keep it well maintained.

Practical action

Service your car fleet regularly

Regular servicing helps to ensure that your fleet is running at optimum efficiency. Use manufacturers' recommendations as the minimum level for service intervals. These services should check emissions to make sure they are at a minimum level. Your garage should be able to provide a record of the emission level. Other important areas are to make sure that tyre pressures are correct and that spark plug leads and connections are in good condition. Drivers need to be made aware of their responsibility for helping to ensure regular servicing.

Use a responsible garage

Make sure that the garage that carries out the maintenance of your company cars is environmentally responsible. Ask the garage for details of the environmental precautions it takes. Car maintenance involves washing down oily and greasy surfaces and changing oil at regular intervals. Car washing areas and any area where there may be oil spills should be designed to collect dirty water and prevent its discharge to drains. Waste oil and oily rags should be disposed of in accordance with the 1996 Special Waste Regulations and oil should never be emptied down the drain.

Use retreads for your tyres

Tyres are a major item of expenditure for a company car fleet; on average the third largest item in their operating budget after labour and fuel. Tyres are also a major waste stream that is difficult to dispose of. Retreaded tyres provide both environmental and cost benefits. Fleet managers have found tyre costs can be reduced by 50 per cent by retreading their tyre casings at least twice. This has led to retreads being widely used by transport based organisations such as professional hauliers and taxi companies.

Despite their mixed reputation, retreads are already widely in use. All aircraft use retreads; a typical jet aircraft will carry out somewhere in the region of 200 take-offs and landings on a set of tyres that will be remoulded 4 to 5 times before being disposed of. In the UK retreads are manufactured to strict legal standards. The retreader you use should work to the British Standard AU 144e, be a member of the Retread Manufacturers Association (RMA) and be certified to the ISO 9002 quality assurance standard. Such a manufacturer will be subject to regular audits to make sure they maintain high quality levels.

The environmental benefits of retreads are also considerable. To manufacture a new passenger car tyre takes on average 32 litres of oil and 7 kg of rubber compound. To retread the same tyre takes 11 litres of oil and 3 kg of rubber compound. The current savings for the UK from the use of retreads are 150 million litres of oil and 60,000 tonnes of rubber compound. Retreading also reduces the problems of dealing with scrap tyres. These advantages have led to government support for retreads.

Summary guidelines

✔ Implement a Green Transport Plan and promote initiatives throughout the company

✔ Reduce travel through use of communication technologies such as video-conferencing and planning of staff commitments

✔ Make sure that all business travel is by public transport where practicable

✔ Purchase/lease efficient cars and take into account their whole life costs

✔ Train drivers in advanced driving practice

✔ Monitor the fuel performance of all vehicles

✔ Make sure vehicles are well serviced and maintained by a responsible garage

✔ If fleet management is outsourced make sure the company has high environmental standards and minimum requirements are included in the contract

BUSINESS TRAVEL AND COMPANY CARS

⚠ Common problems

Contracting out

Many organisations choose to contract out the management of the company car fleet. Make sure that the standards detailed above are passed on to the management company and are written into the contractual agreement.

Cars and status

Cars are closely related to remuneration and status within many organisations. Measures that seek to encourage senior managers to use smaller cars are potentially highly controversial.

To overcome these problems the key is senior management commitment. The second important principle is to involve staff from the start. Tell your staff what is happening and make them feel part of a positive programme, otherwise they may be suspicious of any changes you introduce.

Sporty drivers

Good driving technique can reduce fuel consumption by up to 25 per cent, cut accidents and reduce maintenance costs. Driver training and fuel monitoring will curb any budding Damon Hills in your organisation!

Lack of knowledge of fuel cost

Many organisations have only an overall idea of the cost of company cars and business travel. This makes improvement difficult to monitor and report on.

To overcome this, use fuel cards to monitor the fuel consumption of individual drivers. There are major savings available from measures such as driver training which will be clearer if you can demonstrate them.

CHAPTER SUMMARY

- ❏ Use the transport hierarchy: reducing the need to travel, encouraging the use of less polluting modes of transport and improving the use of the car
- ❏ Gain top level commitment to reducing the cost and environmental impact of your transport
- ❏ Survey staff to assess commuting patterns and measure business mileage and related carbon dioxide emissions
- ❏ Plan office locations, meetings and business practices to reduce the need for staff to travel
- ❏ Encourage the use of cycling, public transport and car sharing for commuting and business travel
- ❏ Offer staff a realistic alternative package to the company car, such as a season ticket for public transport and a guaranteed taxi for emergencies
- ❏ Use an efficient and well-maintained company fleet

Transport

CHAPTER 7
Communication

INTRODUCTION

With the help of this Manual you will have highlighted a number of areas for environmental improvement in your office practices. The key to the successful implementation of these initiatives is a communication programme to encourage individual participation. This is a major challenge and needs to be relevant, focused and interesting.

Head Office staff can often feel removed from activities at site level and therefore not see the environment as relevant to them. This is very common with manufacturing companies where the focus on the programme is at site level. For example, Eastern Group has a high profile on environmental reporting and won the ACCA Award 1998. They were keen to develop an environmental awareness programme to involve office staff. The programme highlighted the link between office activities and energy use and generation supported by a series of fact sheets covering environmental issues and the action that staff can take in their daily activities. The focus was to relate the core business of electricity generation and green energy to office activities to make the environmental programme meaningful.

Make the link between daily office activities and broader environmental issues. Most people do care about the environment but do not link this to everyday working activities. Make the most of individual enthusiasm by involving keen staff in your programme. They are a valuable resource to motivate others and exert peer pressure.

This chapter identifies the issues to consider when planning initiatives, including launching a paper recycling scheme. We give practical guidance on communication tools to encourage participation, from simple posters to Internet sites, and running an environmental awareness training workshop. We highlight the key points to running a successful workshop, from good marketing to choosing good speakers. External communication is covered in more detail in Chapter 9, Environmental Reporting.

PROMOTING INDIVIDUAL ACTION

Securing individual commitment is the key to the success of your programme. Many environmental initiatives are actively dependent upon staff involvement, for example paper recycling schemes and energy efficiency campaigns. Staff need clear guidance on what they need to do to make it work and the environmental and business benefits of the schemes.

☞ Practical action

Obtain senior management commitment

Endorsement from a senior level is essential to communicating the importance of the environment programme. Establishing an environmental policy signed by senior management gives a mandate to the programme (see Chapter 2, Getting Started). Ensure management have a good understanding of the business issues.

Promote individual action

Individuals need to understand the connection between office practice and wider environmental issues. Give staff clear guidelines on what action they can take in their daily work activities and how they can make a difference. Promotion of the environment needs to be fun, creative and relevant to daily activities. Environmental issues, particularly waste, can be seen as very dull. Humour can be very effective in conveying your message.

Produce clear, relevant environmental information

Show the link between your organisation and the environment. Demonstrate the environmental impacts of your organisation and the environmental issues associated with those impacts. Use this to support environmental initiatives and highlight the contribution that each employee can make. Use simple facts such as 'Every tonne of paper we use contains wood from seventeen trees'.

Encourage participation

Identify keen staff and harness this enthusiasm by encouraging involvement. Keen individuals can exert considerable peer pressure. *See the section on Environment Teams in this chapter* ↘

Promote the business case

Explain the business reasons for your introduction of an environmental programme. Illustrate potential cost savings, forthcoming legislation and current best practice to remain competitive.

> ## Summary guidelines
>
> ✔ Explain the connection between work activities and environmental issues
> ✔ Make sure you have senior management commitment
> ✔ Produce clear and relevant information on the environmental programme
> ✔ Highlight any cost savings from environmental measures
> ✔ Promote the business case
>
> **PROMOTING INDIVIDUAL ACTION**

Communication

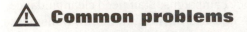

⚠ Common problems

Lack of senior management commitment

Environmental initiatives can quickly lose momentum without the support of management. However, it is important they are seen to walk the talk. Corporate travel policies and the thorny issue of company cars are often extremely contentious. *See Chapter 6, Transport* ⤴ Senior management can often be persuaded by cost savings!

Lack of knowledge and understanding

Many barriers are based upon a lack of knowledge. Provide clear, factual information to help overcome a lack of understanding. Becoming environmentally sound does not have to be a cost; going green saves you money.

COMMUNICATION TOOLS

Environmental initiatives need to be creatively promoted: don't send memos to launch your paper recycling scheme. The aim of your promotional activities is to motivate staff sufficiently to result in a change of behaviour. This is not an easy task.

☞ Practical action

Be creative

Electronic communication is a useful tool for communicating and supporting initiatives. Use daily bulletins on networks or log-in screens to promote initiatives and give feedback. For example, publicising your paper consumption and tonnage of waste to landfill will help to promote a forthcoming paper recycling launch. Do not send out a single-sided, two-page memo about waste reduction!

Work to your company culture

Schroders (investment bankers) have a strong culture of electronic communication to improve business efficiency. Details of the Environmental Policy and programme are communicated via intranet and Internet which includes specific environmental information on utility consumption and purchasing. Video and audio-conferencing is increasingly used for internal meetings, which has improved communication between offices. For example, the London Group Facilities Management team increasingly advises other European offices.

Create an identity for your environmental programme

This can be done graphically through a visual image or a cartoon character to brand the environmental programme. Running a competition for staff to design a character or image can be a useful way of promoting involvement and enthusiasm. For example, Her Majesty's Customs & Excise created a cartoon character, the 'Guzzler', for their energy efficiency programme, which is used on all material promoting the programme.

Enclosures in payslips

If you want something to be read, enclose it with your payslips. This can be an effective way of promoting an environmental programme but you should consider its use very carefully. Extra enclosures can be seen as creating waste.

Case Study 7.1

SUBJECT: **Communication Mechanisms**

ORGANISATION: **HM Customs and Excise**

LOCATION: **UK-wide**

STAFF: **23,000**

Background

HM Customs & Excise have a well-established environmental programme, driven and coordinated by the Energy Efficiency and Environmental Compliance Unit at New King's Beam House in Central London. Customs have over 300 sites throughout the UK from small VAT offices to Head Office buildings.

The communications network consists of an Energy and Environment Manager in each region supported by Environmental Care Officers at a local level. The Environmental Policy Manager was keen to support and encourage the ECOs and other staff by giving them clear factual information regarding environmental issues and guidance on the practical action that can be taken.

Action

Environmental information resources were developed for posting on the intranet to support the Customs & Excise Environmental Policy and link to performance indicators. Environmental Information Sheets were developed for the significant environmental impacts of the business: air pollution, climate change, water, waste, forestry and paper, sustainability, biodiversity, ozone depletion and acid rain. These explained the environmental issues in everyday terms and related them to daily activities. These were supported by Environmental Action Sheets for each issue and are linked to performance indicators (see Figure C.1).

Results

High-quality, relevant information is available to all staff in a very accessible form, linking daily activities to the Environmental Policy and performance measurements. ∎

Communication

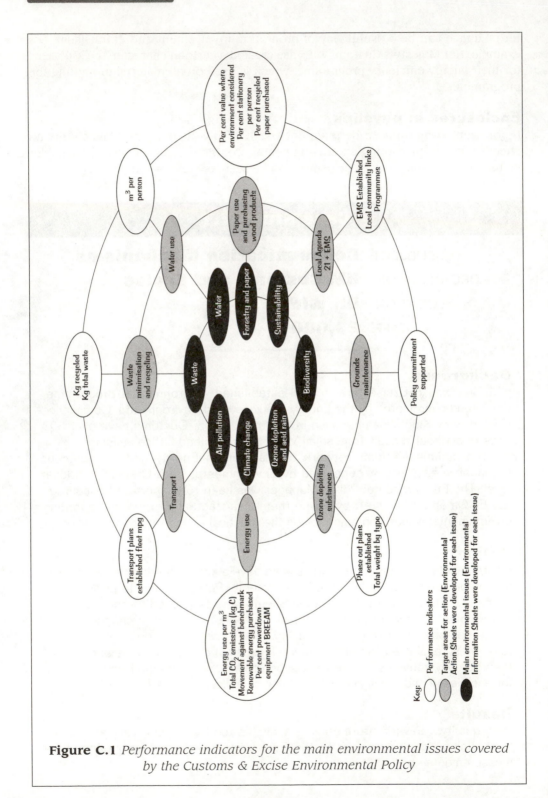

Figure C.1 *Performance indicators for the main environmental issues covered by the Customs & Excise Environmental Policy*

Produce guidelines for staff

Many organisations use their head office as a pilot project prior to extending initiatives to other areas. Producing guidelines that highlight lessons learned during the pilot can be a useful promotional tool. Guidelines that provide help and support are invaluable for promoting confidence and continuity. Include them in the Environment Management Manual. *See Chapter 8, Environmental Management* ➘

Summary guidelines

✔ Avoid paper based communication

✔ Utilise electronic communication where available

✔ Create an identity for the programme

✔ Reinforce the links between initiatives and environmental benefits

✔ Provide regular feedback

✔ Produce guidelines for staff

COMMUNICATION TOOLS

LAUNCHING AN INITIATIVE

Many environmental programmes start with recycling and are often driven by keen staff. **Promote waste minimisation prior to recycling**. Recycling is something which most staff can relate to and can involve everyone.

The following section looks at how to plan and implement a recycling scheme. Techniques and ideas are equally applicable to other initiatives or a wider environmental programme.

☞ Practical action

Planning

Plan your programme. A few poorly labelled, tatty boxes for recycling will not inspire cynics! The environment needs to be perceived as an essential, integral part of the way your organisation is run; not an optional extra.

Logistical problems are often overlooked before a recycling scheme is launched. Typical frustrations include not enough recycling bins, bins not emptied frequently enough or cleaners throwing out paper due to lack of communication. Good planning will avoid such problems. For example, identify areas for short-term storage of recyclables prior to launching the scheme, and let your cleaners know!

Recognise the implications of the initiative before starting. Failed initiatives are very damaging and it is then very difficult to re-launch. If your staff see a recycling scheme as chaotic, messy and more effort than throwing paper into general waste then they will feel negative about any further initiatives.

Communication

Case Study 7.2

SUBJECT: **Communication: International Environmental Survey (IES)**

ORGANISATION: **Ravens Wood School**

LOCATION: **Bromley, Kent**

STAFF: **1200**

Background

In 1997 the Ravens Wood School initiated an International Environmental Survey (IES) following Swedish comments that England was dirtier than Sweden and that Sweden received English pollution. The survey to test this hypothesis became the IES, a team of 15 pupils set up with representatives from years 7 to 10. The IES team has recently joined the Waste Alert programme in order to identify potential environmental improvement within the school activities to complement the work being conducted by the team.

Action

Currently, the IES team are designing a website which contains results gathered from the survey. The site outlines the project, stresses the importance of the environment and measures the attitudes of people towards environmental issues across the world, so as to inform politicians and decision-makers. Recently, a survey has been completed in Spanish and will be sent to Bolivia later this year.

The IES communications team use regular video-conferences to maintain relations with their Swedish counterparts. As the survey expands to different parts of the world, the team plans to use video-conferencing to facilitate the exchange of information and strengthen new contacts.

The team are also preparing a CD-ROM containing information on projects, current data and a copy of the team's project PowerPoint presentation. When completed, a sixth form GNVQ class will handle marketing and sales for the CD. As surveys with other countries develop, the CD will be updated and released in separate versions. The team has also produced a booklet containing survey results to be sent to companies and schools wishing for a range of information on public attitudes towards the environment.

Results

The IES has received widespread recognition, attracting the attention of a range of interested visitors. The use of communications technology has been invaluable in studying international attitudes on the environment. The team now aims to expand the project to France, Germany, Colombia, Australia, Norway, South Africa and Canada. ■

Involving cleaners and recycling contractors

Recycling schemes represent an additional system within the office. Communicate with your cleaning staff to make sure that they know how the new arrangements will work. Recycling schemes do not generally mean more work for cleaners, but they will have to change how they collect waste. Ensure the recycling scheme is built into your cleaning contract.

One company whose staff had thought they had been recycling paper for a number of years found out after a Wastebusters audit that their cleaners had not understood the system and were putting all the paper collected into general waste bins!

Make sure that arrangements with recycling companies suit your requirements. Liaise with your contractor over practical details: how you intend the scheme to work, where the waste can be collected from and frequency of collection. Coordinate collection times with the cleaning schedule and to establish communication channels between the recycling contractor and your organisation.

Marketing and publicity

Give the recycling programme a high profile; don't be discreet. Use strong, clear publicity material highlighting environmental benefits. Use posters at recycling points and notice-boards to remind staff. Display boards used in your reception or in the canteen will promote initiatives to staff and visitors and provide a central information point.

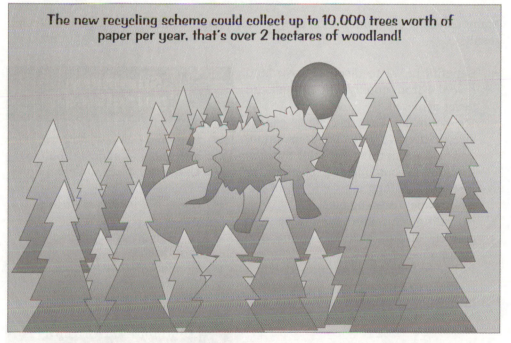

Figure 7.1 *Use posters to communicate your results*

Provide regular feedback

To maintain motivation, staff need to know how they are doing. Give regular feedback on progress and environmental benefits. Use electronic communication to produce updated results or highlight areas of weakness. Publish regular updates on the environmental programme that can form a regular feature in your in-house magazine. These are often seen by clients and can help to promote your environmental position externally.

Sponsorship and incentive schemes

Find ways to maintain interest. Incentive schemes are a successful, self-financing way of maintaining motivation. Some organisations achieve this by donating a percentage of cost savings and revenue to an environmental charity or staff social fund. A number of companies link their sponsorship programmes to the volume of paper collected. There are a number of forestry projects and imaginative sponsorship opportunities available. *See Chapter 10, Contacts and Resources* ↘

The environmental groups Friends of the Earth and WWF (World Wide Fund for Nature) have a number of major initiatives operating in conjunction with industry. There are a number of opportunities to sponsor local community projects. For example, sponsoring the production of an environmental video could assist schools with an environmental education programme.

⚠ Common problems

Many recycling programmes fail due to lack of communication, with the following results:

- Benefits in waste disposal costs and revenue from quality white paper are never achieved.
- The company sees recycling as expensive, ineffective and time consuming, and it does nothing for staff morale, resulting in contaminated schemes (for instance, vending cups end up in the white paper recycling bins).
- Recycling contractors are not keen to collect, due to lack of volume and contamination levels.
- Problems can be encountered when trying to re-launch the scheme at a later date.

> ### Summary guidelines
>
> ✔ Plan and communicate to overcome logistical problems
> ✔ Use internal communication channels
> ✔ Make it easy for staff to recycle
> ✔ Run a high-profile launch programme
> ✔ Provide regular feedback
> ✔ Create an incentive scheme
> ✔ Make it fun!
>
> **LAUNCHING AN INITIATIVE**

Case Study 7.3

SUBJECT: **Environmental Awareness Campaign**

ORGANISATION: **Shell International Limited**

LOCATION: **Shell Centre, London**

STAFF: **2800**

Background

Conservers in Shell was originally launched in Shell-Mex House in 1996. The thinking behind the initiative was for a greater 'Environmental Awareness' amongst Shell staff, thereby minimising the damage to 'our' planet and maximising reduction in Shell costs by being frugal, thrifty and responsible.

Action

This was achieved by way of an environmental campaign and exhibition. Staff were encouraged to change existing habits through determined perseverance, gentle persistence and influence. The main message was to promote the use of the 3Rs – Reduce, Re-use, Recycle – to change the culture towards waste management and use of resources within the office. One of the most successful initiatives was the 'office-bin-free' scheme: Conservers replaced all waste paper bins with desktop trays and desktop tidies (the former for paper recycling and the latter for non-recyclable waste, food stuffs, hankies, etc). This encouraged staff to segregate paper from waste, and more than ten tonnes of paper were being recycled every month from Shell-Mex House.

Results

Shell-Mex House closed at the end of 1999. However, the introduction of the Shell Conservers scheme had been very successful in raising awareness and the coordinators received a number of requests to see the scheme replicated at Shell Centre.

There was a network of 40+ Conservers within Shell-Mex House and they met quarterly to discuss ideas and new initiatives.

The scheme received a high profile and board level support as a runner-up in the first ever Chairman's HS&E awards chosen from 87 entries company-wide.

Conservers and Building Facilities Services are now in the process of implementing this scheme at Shell Centre, after successfully piloting it on the 21st floor. ∎

Communication

ENVIRONMENT TEAM

You cannot green the office on your own! The role of the person driving the programme is to act as a facilitator by encouraging and motivating others within your organisation. If a programme is based on the enthusiasm of one individual, which can often be the case with smaller organisations, there is a danger that the programme will come to a grinding halt if that person leaves.

Establishing an environment team is an effective way of disseminating information throughout your organisation and of spreading the responsibility for environmental issues.

☞ Practical action

Establish an environment team

Make sure that you have representation from across departments and different levels of your organisation; this will provide contact points within each department. Senior level representation will enhance the credibility of the group. Encourage involvement from keen staff. Environmental champions, people who become identified with the issue and who provide a useful focus, will effectively communicate the programme.

Northumberland Heath School, a primary school in Erith, London, is very active in communicating environmental initiatives and ensuring participation, including a team of litter pickers! There is an Eco-Committee of children with two representatives from years 3–6 (8–11 years) and an Adult Eco-Committee with a mix of staff, parents and governors. The children's Eco-Committee meet once a week at lunchtime and have developed an Eco-code in rhyming couplets. They are working towards becoming an Eco-School.

Select your chairperson

The chairperson should be senior and report back at board level. Ensure regular meetings and circulate agendas and minutes electronically to maintain a high level of awareness.

Internal communication forum

The team can help internal communication by bringing together people who do not generally work with each other. Excellent ideas, particularly regarding waste reduction measures, can come out of these meetings. There may already be informal initiatives in departments that can be extended throughout your organisation. Discuss any obstacles and how they can be overcome.

Identify and promote good practice, develop new initiatives and give feedback on existing schemes. Encourage suggestions for improvement and ensure that good ideas are recognised.

Introduce environmental awareness training

The team is a useful channel for environmental training to improve understanding and awareness of environmental issues amongst all staff. Suppliers such as recycling companies, paper merchants and toner cartridge companies will readily give presentations to staff to explain the processes involved. Visits can also be very useful; a trip to a landfill site can be a memorable experience!

Clarify the role of the team

Make sure team members feel that they have a role in promoting your programme. Where individuals and departments have made significant contributions they should be recognised.

Summary guidelines

✔ Choose keen staff who are potential environmental champions
✔ Choose a mix of staff from different departments and levels
✔ Make sure the environment team can report to senior management
✔ Give the team a defined role within your environmental programme
✔ Use the team to promote environmental awareness amongst all staff

ENVIRONMENT TEAM

⚠ Common problems

Lack of support

Environment teams become tired and bored if they become a talking shop but are not able to achieve anything because they cannot make funding decisions. Ensure that your committee has representatives from a senior level, endorsement from the board and a formal channel for ideas to be communicated.

Loss of motivation

Staff will lose interest if they feel the effort that they have contributed is not recognised or effectively implemented. This can be avoided by encouraging suggestions and providing regular feedback on the success of initiatives.

ENVIRONMENTAL AWARENESS TRAINING

Running an Environmental Awareness Training session will help to improve understanding and increase participation in your environmental programme. The aim of the training is to motivate people to take positive action to contribute to their immediate environment, both home and office. Raising awareness of the link between home, office and the local environment is important.

Communication

☞ Practical action

Representation from all departments

Ensure all departments are represented. Make sure you have a cross-section of departments and management levels to encourage communication and draw out specific issues. Specialist departments can often make important contributions to your programme.

For example, including the Production Department in the training session for London Weekend Television (LWT) resulted in obsolete production sets being passed on to local scrap schemes rather than being sent to landfill. News travels fast! This was followed-up by a call to Waste Alert South Thames (see page 41) from the Music Library at Granada (LWT is a Granada company) and 1000 sound effect CDs were passed on to Aylesbury Recycling – a community recycling programme creating jobs and training for disabled people.

Include suppliers

Consider including suppliers for catering, cleaning and maintenance. If your facilities management is contracted out, include your contractor. There is often considerable room for improvement in communication between contractor and client. Including suppliers in your training will improve understanding and chance of success. This can be developed into a separate event for suppliers. *See Chapter 4, Purchasing* ↗

Highlight existing good practice

Make sure you highlight successes. Your environment team may be extremely enthusiastic and have already achieved improvements, but need more support. Encourage them to do more by recognising good results.

Publicity and promotion

Use strong, relevant and concise wording to promote the event. To ensure success the programme needs to be promoted in a creative and interesting way so that it is meaningful. Avoid core business hours. Lunchtime can be popular, especially if food is provided.

Make sure training is appropriate

Training needs to take into account different levels of commitment and understanding within the organisation and be pitched at the right level. If the environmental programme is new to your organisation, the priority will be to present the business case for the environment rather than providing detailed assessments of environmental effects.

Workshop programme

Link the environmental policy and core business

Highlight the most significant environmental effects of the organisation, and explain the aims of the environmental policy and programme. Include quantified figures in terms of costs and environmental impact (eg tonnes of carbon dioxide). For example, for a bank the most significant environmental effect will be investment and lending decisions and consideration of environmental liability.

The environmental effects of the office in context

Give examples of the environmental effects of the office and how they relate to the broader effects of the company. Use examples of daily office activities to help put them into context, for example travel to work and how this relates to the carbon dioxide emissions of the company.

Existing good practice

Highlight examples of successful initiatives and give quantified results. Give feedback on tonnage of paper collected for recycling, the reduction in volume to landfill and the number of trees this equates to. Use benchmarks to give an assessment of current performance. *See Benchmarking, page 264*↘

Promote the importance of individual action

Give examples of actions that can be taken by all individuals in their daily work activities, for example double-sided copying or not printing out emails! Explain the environmental benefits of these actions.

Be creative

Use innovative training techniques to promote enthusiasm and generate ideas, and facilitate understanding of the issues. For example: role play can be a useful part of environmental awareness training. It is fun and can be a very effective way of getting a message across.

Allocate time for active participation

Avoid dry presentations on environmental issues. Assure participation through workshop sessions. Encourage suggestions for improvement; individuals who are actually doing the job and making decisions are in the best position to identify potential improvements to working practices. Include their ideas in the development of policy and action plans.

Wastebusters have developed a lively training resource aimed to get people thinking, called 'The Sloth Game'. This encourages discussion and involvement and the game focuses on how to achieve most by doing least! Participants are given a choice of actions for waste, recycling, energy and water and actions are rated by effort against potential cost savings. Participants are split up into groups to discuss the options; these generally get quite heated! The winning team achieves the greatest environmental improvements and cost savings with the least effort. A prize for the winning team adds additional incentive! More information from Wastebusters.

Participate in external seminars

Specific areas with significant environmental impacts need more specialist training. In a typical office these will be waste disposal, building management and purchasing.

Communication

Case Study 7.4

SUBJECT: **Environmental Theme Week**
ORGANISATION: **Unilever**
LOCATION: **Unilever House, City of London**
STAFF: **1000**

Background
The aim of the week was an awareness-raising exercise to identify current environmental performance within Unilever House, establish information resources and an intranet site for environmental issues, and give staff support and guidance as to what action they could take in the office and at home.

Action
The project was visually orientated and was based around the catchphrase *Message in a Bottle*. The caption and a logo were first used as a 'teaser', posted around the building and on all further information to develop a strong branding. The week itself consisted of a launch of the intranet site providing information on the environmental impacts of activities within the building together with suggestions for staff action. The final day of the week was based around a 'Green Lunch' using the staff restaurant as a base for the launch with a special green menu using organic food and an environmental theme. Staff were asked to enter a quiz for a mystery prize, the answers to which were contained in four tailored fact sheets looking at energy, water, waste and recycling. A display area with posters, videos and free gifts was also set up.

Results
The day was very successful, generating a great deal of interest and subsequent visits to the intranet site. The quiz generated over 200 responses, nearly 20 per cent of staff within the building. The week established a number of channels for environmental communication, and theme weeks on a variety of subjects will become a regular feature at Unilever House. ∎

Send staff on external seminars. Sharing experiences with other organisations can be very helpful. A recognition that other organisations are working with the same issues can be reassuring, build confidence and increase knowledge and understanding. The seminars run by the Environment Council's Business and Environment Programme are a good example. Organisations that are members are already committed to good practice. *See Chapter 10, Contacts and Resources* ↘

⚠ Common problems

- Getting people to turn up.
- Lack of senior management attendance.
- Not taken seriously.
- Environment seen as an optional extra for the greenies!
- Preaching to the converted.

Summary guidelines

✔ Make sure training is pitched at an appropriate level
✔ Be creative
✔ Use information that is relevant to your organisation
✔ Send staff to external seminars to share experience

ENVIRONMENTAL AWARENESS TRAINING

RUNNING A SUCCESSFUL EVENT

Local authorities, industry associations, government and regulators regularly organise external events to promote specific environmental issues to a wide range of audiences. Organising events is extremely time consuming, so make sure they are effective. It is extremely disheartening for everyone involved to put in a lot of work only to find that the event clashes with half-term and attendance is very poor. It is not unusual for delegates to be out-numbered by organisers!

☞ Practical action

Creative marketing

Develop creative marketing material to attract interest. Wastebusters launched a waste minimisation guide using the rationing theme from the Second World War, at the Imperial War Museum. Invitations were copies of ration books and individually addressed. Even if delegates were unable to attend, they remembered it!

Promotional material

Keep it concise and relevant. Sell the benefits of attending and show that you understand the issues for them. If your event is targeted at the hotel sector, give some hotel examples with cost savings achieved. Good practice examples from the industry can be very effective in generating interest, particularly if they are a competitor! Small businesses are short of time, resources and often don't see environmental issues as relevant. Show you are aware of the obstacles.

Use recycled paper and envelopes for promotional material. Email details and publicise on the web if facilities are available.

Communication

Choose an appropriate venue

Interesting local venues encourage attendance. The Environment Agency ran an event at London Zoo! It was very well attended and delegates had the chance to look round at lunchtime. Make sure the venue is accessible by public transport and give good directions.

Don't shoot yourself in the foot. It can be counterproductive to run a workshop on waste minimisation if your caterers use plastic cups, paper plates and there is excess food. Think about the messages you are putting across. Avoid the use of disposable products, particularly plastic vending cups and individual milk and cream jiggers. Be accurate on delegate numbers to avoid food wastage.

Appropriate time

Don't run a hospitality workshop at lunchtime! Avoid half-term holidays. Find out best times for your potential audience. Breakfast meetings are often popular. Don't let events drag on; keep to time.

Targeted mailing list

Avoid direct mail by developing targeted mailings. Use the contacts of other organisations involved in the event (eg local authorities). Make it easy for people to respond. Fax-backs work well.

Choose good speakers

They may be an industry expert, but can they present? Choose lively speakers who can engage the audience. Good practice case studies from organisations within the same industry or sector help people to relate to the issues and strengthen the message.

Visual aids and delegate packs

Make sure the venue provides PowerPoint facilities. Avoid use of lists of bullet points which can be very dull and switch people off. Visual aids should supplement rather than dominate the presentation. Keep printed information to a minimum. Avoid lengthy transcripts from each speaker; provide an email option. Ensure all paper and card used is from recycled paper.

Encourage active participation

Delegates generally like to be involved. Ensure that you allow sufficient time for discussion and active participation. People will get far more out of the event if they have had an opportunity to discuss the issues that are relevant to them. Encourage delegates to identify specific actions to take forward and to feedback progress achieved.

Common problems

Poor attendance

Dull marketing material ensures that your publicity material goes in the bin! Large untargeted direct mail campaigns will not be seen as relevant.

Case Study 7.5

SUBJECT: **Running a Successful Workshop – Hospitality Sector**

ORGANISATION: **Waste Alert, Camden**

LOCATION: **Hotel Ibis London Euston**

STAFF: **15**

Background

The hospitality industry is a major business sector throughout the Borough of Camden, with more than 120 businesses providing visitor accommodation. These range from international chains such as the Ibis London Euston, to small independently owned establishments. The hospitality sector, therefore, is a key focus area for Waste Alert Camden.

Action

A key factor in raising the awareness of hoteliers to the business benefits of environmental management was to bring them together at a workshop. The aim was to give them the opportunity to learn from existing best practice and to discuss with other like-minded professionals the perceived barriers to environmental improvements.

Results

The key elements of success can be divided as follows:

Venue

The Hotel Ibis London Euston was chosen as the venue for the workshop. The hotel had recently had a full environmental audit carried out for them by Wastebusters and was being promoted by Waste Alert Camden as a best practice case study. The hotel recognises the hospitality industry's responsibility to integrate environmental concerns in its operations and agreed to host the Waste Alert Camden hospitality workshop as a way of sharing their experiences. Holding the workshop at the Hotel helped to reduce the running costs of the workshop and was an attractive venue to the target audience, who were keen to see and hear what a local competitor with a recently refurbished hotel was up to!

Programme development

As background research for the workshop, the Club Manager liaised with key trade organisations including *Green Globe*, the *International Hotels Environmental Initiative* (IHEI) and the local region of the British Hospitality Association. This helped to identify existing best practice, resources and the most relevant issues to be covered in the workshop programme.

Communication

To achieve maximum interest and attendance, the Club Manager worked in close partnership with the Council's Tourism Development Officer. The Development Officer provided specialist advice about the local hospitality industry, sources of information, the most appropriate timing for the workshop and the key messages to be included and the presentation of the promotional material. The Development Officer also spoke at the workshop, highlighting wider issues such as international initiatives, future legislation, customer expectations, PR, industry environmental awards and the marketing advantages of hotels having good environmental performance within the highly competitive tourism industry.

The tools used during the workshop were specifically tailored to the hotel industry and industry-specific terms and examples were used as much as possible. There is nothing worse than using out-of-date, over-used information and inaccurate information as the basis of your workshop programme.

To add further expertise to the workshop, representatives from Thames Water and London Electricity Boards were invited to bring displays and information illustrating the services they could offer to businesses, to help them to reduce their utility bills. They were on hand throughout the workshop to provide advice and answer questions. In addition, they played an active role in the interactive sessions, adding valuable experience and information. To keep delegates fresh throughout the workshop, brief refreshment breaks were scheduled, with an opportunity for questions at the end of the day.

Recruitment of delegates

The Council's Tourism Development Officer provided an up to date and targeted mailing list. This enabled invitations to be sent to contacts at the right level at hotels throughout the Borough.

The invitations to the workshop were designed as fax-back forms, making it quick and easy for potential delegates to register. These were followed up with a comprehensive 'ring round' to increase the numbers attending. The Council provided additional support for this and for contacting the delegates the day before the workshop, to keep the workshop prominent in their minds. This also helped to build the delegates' confidence that the event was being run efficiently and to check they had all the details they needed. In the event of a delegate being unable to attend at short notice due to work pressures, they were much more likely to send another representative if the workshop organisers had recently contacted them. Try to develop a positive relationship with your delegates – even before they arrive – but don't go too far; nobody wants to be bothered by endless calls and wasteful mail shots. Invitations were backed up with coverage of the workshop in local and trade media and the Waste Alert newsletter.

Active participation

At the beginning of the workshop all delegates were asked to state what they hoped to get out of the workshop and were introduced straight away to the key points on the business case for environmental improvements. This helped to engage delegates immediately and enabled the workshop presenters to use examples given by the delegates to illustrate key points throughout workshop. The programme was designed to be as varied and as participatory as possible.

One of the key aims of the workshop was to enable the delegates to deal with the individual issues of their organisation. This was achieved by using a specially designed hotel process flow chart, 'A Guest's Eye View'. The aim was to map the typical route of a guest through a hotel and to help the hotel managers identify areas where their establishment could clean up both in terms of cost and environmental performance. It also provided hotel managers with an accessible and practical tool that they could take back into their workplace, to raise staff awareness of environmental issues. The chart could be used to facilitate staff brainstorming sessions, to identify priority areas and whom staff should be communicating with to minimise the impacts of a guest's stay in their hotel.

Feedback

All delegates were asked to complete a feedback form *before* they left the workshop. This enabled the Club Manager to carry out targeted follow-up after the workshop and to produce a full evaluation report of the event. The feedback from the workshop was very good. Delegates appreciated the chance to network and learn from each other. Nearly all indicated that they would be taking action as a result of the workshop. Hoteliers appreciated the timing and length of the event and having information on waste, energy and water in one hit – they are very busy people! Many have had instructions from head office to take action, and said they now felt better placed to do something positive. Many delegates said that the interactive approach was innovative and worthwhile and much better than listening to speakers! The representatives from Thames Water and London Electricity Boards were well used on the day and received a constant stream of enquiries.

Follow-up

Immediately after the workshop all delegates were sent follow-up information. They were also contacted several times by telephone to remind them of the ongoing support available to them through Waste Alert Camden and to monitor their progress – strike while the iron is hot! One third of the Club's members are from the hospitality sector and a follow-up workshop is planned to target those who did not attend the first event. ■

Lack of active participation

A frequent mistake is to have too many speakers and not to allow enough time for delegates to raise issues important to them. This tends to switch people off and they get bored.

Delegates at the wrong level

To get decision-makers to turn up, you need a very strong case. Where attendance is delegated, it can be seen as a bit of a 'jolly' and delegates may be more interested in getting away early for a train.

Disappearance at lunchtime!

It is very frustrating if there is a mass exodus and flurry of mobile phone activity at lunchtime. It is quite a challenge keeping people there all day. Make sure you have a strong afternoon programme.

Summary guidelines

✔ Chose good, relevant speakers
✔ Include case study organisations
✔ Targeted marketing campaign
✔ Accessible venue at appropriate time
✔ Ensure participation

RUNNING A SUCCESSFUL EVENT

GOOD PRACTICE GUIDELINES

The production of good practice guidelines can be a very useful way to extend successful initiatives throughout your organisation. Guidelines that provide help and support are invaluable for promoting confidence and continuity. A consistent approach to greening your office will also help to maximise the buying power of your organisation. For example, the inclusion of all sites in a national contract for paper recycling will help to ensure that smaller offices are able to have their paper collected. Equally, if you have guidelines which recommend specific brands of recycled paper this will help your purchasing department in their negotiations with suppliers.

Many organisations start their programme with pilot projects prior to extending initiatives to other areas. It is not necessary to audit every location to develop a corporate approach. The issues at sites with similar functions will essentially be the same.

The use of pilot projects allows you to test ideas and produce guidelines specific to your organisation that highlight lessons learnt during the pilot. It also enables you to control the development of the programme by a phased introduction.

☞ Practical action

Identify pilot locations

Choose a cross-section of sites and functions. Take into account regional differences, urban and rural locations and the number of staff. Small outlying offices will have different restraints and logistical problems from large city centre locations. Being seen to take these differences into account will add credibility to the programme. Smaller offices often feel rather overlooked. A realistic number of sites is between three and five.

Communicate your project objectives

Make sure that the aims of the project are communicated to the sites and individuals involved. Identify keen staff to help you take it forward and appoint a coordinator at each site. The attitude of the key staff at each site will help or hinder progress.

Conduct site audits

Use this Manual to conduct site audits and identify areas of improvement and potential cost saving. Highlight areas of existing good practice to give people encouragement. Identify logistical problems to ensure they are overcome. Find out what help people need.

Implement improvements

Following the audit findings, develop an improvement plan and monitor the results. Provide support and back-up and make sure teething problems are dealt with quickly. Use the results to develop best practice guidelines.

Publicise results

Make sure the pilot sites benefit from being guinea pigs! Involve them in the development of the guidelines and get their feedback. If the programme is launched formally, ask them to give a first hand account of the project. This will personalise the process and help people identify and relate to the project. Use as good practice examples in your annual report/environment report.

Launch best practice guidelines

Keep the guidelines concise and communicate electronically where possible. Provide practical guidance on the steps that need to be taken to introduce a range of initiatives, highlighting what can be done, how it can be done, who will do it and the potential cost savings.

Include contact points within your organisation and details of other useful organisations who can provide help and support. Illustrate the implementation of the guidelines with examples from the pilots, highlighting existing good practice and project achievements.

Summary guidelines

✔ Conduct audits of pilot locations
✔ Develop an improvement plan
✔ Implement initiatives at pilots and monitor results
✔ Develop and launch best practice guidelines
✔ Personalise the guidelines to your organisation with case study material
✔ Publicise results and make sure good practice is recognised

GOOD PRACTICE GUIDELINES

Communication

Set up an environmental forum

Encourage communication between sites and sharing of good practice through an environmental forum. Develop a regular environmental bulletin to keep people up to date with environmental trends and maintain interest and communicate electronically. This approach can help multinational organisations who are aiming for a consistent approach to environmental management. It can also help to bring regional and outlying offices on board. An environmental forum can also provide a good opportunity for organisations to share information and promote good practice within an area. Make use of intranet facilities.

CHAPTER SUMMARY

- ❑ Enlist senior management support
- ❑ Involve staff from all areas of your organisation
- ❑ Give your environmental programme a high profile
- ❑ Monitor the programme and give regular feedback
- ❑ Make sound environmental practice part of the company culture

CHAPTER 8

Environmental Management

INTRODUCTION

This Manual guides you through the areas where your office has an impact on the environment and the practical actions you can take to reduce this. A common experience of organisations that have reached this stage is that as time gets tight and initial enthusiasm runs out, environmental initiatives can fade. To avoid this pitfall many organisations have formal procedures to implement their commitment to responsible practice.

The formal approach has a number of advantages. By integrating responsibility for environmental issues into day-to-day work it makes sure that initiatives last beyond initial enthusiasm. It also helps organisations to identify all their environmental effects and potential risks in a structured and systematic way rather than responding to outside pressures on an ad hoc basis.

Environmental management has received a great deal of support from policy makers. Agenda 21, the programme for action agreed at the Earth Summit at Rio, states that 'Business and industry should recognise environmental management as among the highest corporate priorities and as a key determinant to sustainable development.' The UK Government is committed to promoting a proactive approach to environmental management in order that businesses realise their own responsibilities in meeting international commitments and targets.

This chapter guides you through the principles of formal environmental management for an office. It explains how to systematically review your current position, develop an environmental policy and set out a programme to implement your policy. The chapter does not aim to guide you through a specific management standard but is applicable to any formal environmental management system. Information on key industry initiatives and sources of guidance is also provided.

Standards

The international environmental management system standard (ISO 14001) was developed from the first such standard: British Standard (BS7750) which has now been withdrawn. In addition there is a European Regulation, the Eco-Management and Audit Scheme (EMAS), and a local authority version of this (LA-EMAS). These

Case Study 8.1

SUBJECT: **Environmental Management in an SME**

ORGANISATION: **Shot in the Dark**

LOCATION: **Brighouse, West Yorkshire**

STAFF: **16**

Background

Shot in the Dark is a video production, multimedia and publishing company dedicated to providing environmental training materials for industry and commerce. They provide corporate environmental training and awareness raising videos, and market environmental programmes and services. The Shot in the Dark team includes in-house writers and directors experienced in environmental issues. Shot in the Dark are long standing members of Sheffield Regional Green Business Club and have strong links with BiE and a number of other environmental initiatives. The company philosophy is based on an application of the principles of Total Quality Management, and Shot in the Dark are currently working towards attaining ISO 14001.

Action

As an example of a small, office-based organisation implementing an EMS and working towards ISO 14001, the company is establishing an environmental policy statement which will demonstrate their commitment to the continual improvement of their environmental performance. The company is currently sending staff members on a training course for ISO 14001 in order to gain the necessary skills to implement the system themselves.

The policy and training will help establish targets and objectives for the EMS to adhere to. An initial environmental review of Shot in the Dark's activities has already led to a number of environmental initiatives which have now become common practice in the workplace. These include:

- Incorporating environmental considerations into purchasing. Shot in the Dark now buy in only recycled paper and have purchased a plain paper fax machine to eliminate the need for photocopying for future reference. Environmentally friendly products such as washing-up liquid and recycled toilet tissue are bought in. Shot in the Dark are developing a purchasing policy to ensure buying only from sustainably managed forests and buying in bulk, for example buying videotapes in boxes of 50 rather than 10, avoiding unnecessary slipcover waste.
- Waste minimisation. Double-sided photocopying has been introduced and the use of scrap paper for printing non-essential or draft copies. 'Tick and pass on' memos printed on scrap paper are used rather than individual

copies. Mugs rather than plastic cups, and a water cooler with large refill-able water bottles, are provided for staff.

- Recycling. Shot in the Dark recycle used envelopes, sending them to a play scheme to be re-used. Shredded confidential papers are used for packing or collected for recycling. Recycling bins are placed in the most accessible positions. Aluminium drinks cans are collected for recycling. All packaging is re-used and cardboard boxes unsuitable for re-use are turned into compost at a local farm! Printer cartridges are sent for recycling.
- Energy efficiency. Staff switch off any lighting that is unnecessary. When necessary, fluorescent tubes are replaced with slim-line low energy versions.

Results

As well as improving the environmental performance of the office, these initia-tives have also proved to be cost-saving exercises. All these initiatives were developed after identifying the environmental impacts of Shot in the Dark's activities, and those areas in which performance could be improved. In summary, moving towards implementing an environmental management system has already had a number of benefits for Shot in the Dark. These include:

- cost savings in both purchasing and energy use;
- the raised awareness of customers and suppliers (for example all Shot in the Dark products state if they are from recycled sources);
- reduction of waste and more efficient resource use;
- good links with neighbours such as the community farm.

These achievements are in accordance with the business aims of Shot in the Dark: to raise awareness on a greater scale and to continue as a successful business producing media dedicated to environmental issues. Certification to ISO 14001 will improve environmental management at Shot in the Dark and allow them to demonstrate their commitment to the environment to their customers. ■

management standards have created an international blueprint for integrating environmental issues into the management structure of an organisation. They are by no means the only possible designs for a management system but they do provide an opportunity for independent certification of an organisation's commit-ment to responsible environmental practice.

Who can implement a management system?

Environmental management systems provide a structure for managing the environ-mental effects of any organisation, though this book obviously concentrates on offices. If you are implementing a management system for an office and factory together on one site, the guidance will remain valid, though you may require more specific manufacturing based guidance.

Environmental
Management

Environmental management systems are flexible enough to be applied to a whole organisation, an operational unit such as a head office, or even a particular activity. However, the unit implementing the system must have management responsibility for all significant environmental effects. For instance, if you share a building with other parts of your organisation you are unlikely to have control over areas such as waste, energy and air-conditioning. This will make it difficult to implement a system independently.

To date, management systems have been implemented almost exclusively by larger companies. However, they are equally beneficial for smaller organisations. See the guest article by Dr Ruth Hillary. ISO 14001 and EMAS are being progressively updated to make certification more applicable to small and medium sized enterprises.

Advantages of a systematic approach

No successful organisation leaves the management of areas like sales and performance to chance. Successful management involves setting clear goals and a strategy to meet them. A management system provides a structure in which to set these goals, implement a programme to achieve them and monitor the progress achieved.

Environmental performance is no different from other corporate goals in benefiting from this systematic approach. The fast changing nature of the issues and the range of interested stakeholders, from the public to insurance companies, make a systematic approach essential. The benefits to be gained are set out below.

Legislative compliance

Legislation remains the key driver behind responsible environmental practice for business. A management system will ensure that you are aware of current and forthcoming environmental legislation and the impact it will have on your organisation and it sends a clear message to regulators such as the Environment Agency that you are taking environmental issues seriously.

Competitive advantage

It is extremely difficult to win contracts within industry without a quality assurance system. Environmental performance is following a similar path. A formal policy and management system is already necessary to win contracts from organisations such as British Telecom. Ford and General Motors announced that they want their suppliers to have environmental management systems in place by 2003, which will affect 10,000 companies.

Environmental procurement policies increasingly affect the service sector. This is changing as requirements move down the supply chain from major purchasers in business and local authority sectors. B&Q, for instance, delists suppliers who do not show a commitment to environmental improvement. *See Chapter 4, Purchasing, for more information on supply chain pressure*

Guest Article

Why Have SMEs Been So Slow Taking Up EMS?

by Ruth Hillary, Network for Environmental Management and Auditing (NEMA)

Small business have traditionally been very slow in adopting environmental management systems, claiming that there are no market benefits to be had, and that the systems are costly and irrelevant as small companies have no effect on the environment. Ruth Hillary of the Network for Environmental Management and Auditing investigated the adoption of formal environmental management systems in SMEs and found that while the external benefits and drivers for adopting an EMS do exist, take-up is slow because:

- not everyone understands how EMSs work and what can be gained;
- it is difficult determining what your impacts are and which are most important.

Generally the problem is the lack of expertise and knowledge rather than cost. Guidance is available to small companies (have a look at Chapter 10, Contacts and Resources) and there are pipeline schemes to help SMEs up the management system ladder.

The study confirms that SMEs which have implemented an EMS have gained real benefits, including:

- A range of financial savings and payback periods for investments as diverse as the sector itself.
- Enhanced image and improved relationships with stakeholders.
- Improved environmental performance, assured legal compliance and resource use.
- Spin-off management and organisational benefits.
- Improved skills and knowledge.
- Attraction of new business and customers and the satisfaction of customer requirements.

The study found that positive personal attitudes towards the environment are too often not translated into actions in SMEs; staff enthusiasm on environmental issues is a valuable driving force to improvement and should be encouraged and rewarded!

Also, many still feel that their firms have low environmental impact or face no environmental issues. We hope this book convinces you this is not true!

For details of the report and Dr Hillary's new book, see Chapter 10, Contacts and Resources ↴ ■

Environmental Management

Maximising achievement

All business activity has an effect on the environment. It is clearly not possible to manage all of these effects. An environmental management system will identify those areas of most significant effect, ensuring that the effort you put into your environmental programme is spent on your main effects rather than wasted on minor issues.

Identifying potential liabilities

By systematically identifying all your environmental effects, actual or potential, you will ensure that you are aware of any areas that might lead to liability for environmental damage. Contaminated land, for instance, is potentially very expensive to remedy. Many insurance companies and banks now include environmental risk in their assessments of companies that they insure or lend to. The Co-operative Bank has ethical and environmental criteria for funding projects, and a number of investment banks incorporate environmental liabilities into merger and acquisition decisions.

Systematic assessment of your environmental effects can also alert you to any potential public relations issues. Public environmental campaigns can develop very quickly and have a major impact. In recent years biotechnology companies have spent a significant amount to counter negative publicity campaigns.

Maintaining progress

Once environmental responsibilities are integrated into procedures and job descriptions it is much harder for initiatives to fade away after the initial start-up. If targets are not met, this will be flagged up by review and auditing procedures.

A management system gives staff environmental responsibilities as part of their day-to-day work. This avoids the problem common to those following a less structured approach where environmental initiatives are loaded on to one keen individual.

Getting your house in order

One of the first steps for a local authority or government department encouraging a community response to environmental initiatives is to put its own house in order. A management system will help with a systematic approach to improving environmental performance in council buildings and to integrating sustainable development into the services the council provides. The government and Local Government Management Board have identified environmental management for local authorities as a major part of the LA21 initiative.

⚠ Common problems

Bureaucracy

The key problem of a formal system is that a lot of time, and paper, can be spent on bureaucracy that could have been spent on actual improvements. Vague policy statements and action plans can be drawn up without any real improvements taking place.

There are three key steps to preventing your environmental programme turning into a paper chase. The first is to integrate new procedures into the existing management culture of your organisation rather than creating a large pile of new documents. The second is to encourage ownership of procedures by the staff who are going to be carrying them out. The third is to use a system to improve your management rather than seeing the end result as a badge, such as ISO 14001.

Small businesses

Very few small companies have environmental policies let alone environmental management systems. Environmental issues are often recognised as important but they are outweighed by other pressures. The everyday pressures of running a business in a competitive world tend to leave little time to respond to anything not seen as an immediate priority.

Small companies can, however, gain considerable benefits from environmental awareness. Energy efficiency and waste minimisation measures can be implemented with no capital investment and can produce surprising savings. A simple environmental policy and action programme can have marketing benefits and may well become essential for selling to some companies and local authorities.

Summary of benefits

Formal environmental management systems will help:

✔ develop a systematic approach
✔ ensure compliance with environmental legislation;
✔ develop competitive advantage
✔ identify potential liabilities
✔ develop effective, targeted objectives to manage environmental effects

ENVIRONMENTAL MANAGEMENT SYSTEMS

EMS standards

There are two independent formal EMS standards. The standards set out an approach to environmental management that has been widely taken up even where formal certification is not being sought. The advantage of independent certification of your environmental programme is that it will give your customers and the public confidence that you are taking real steps to improve your environmental performance. The disadvantage is that these standards can require high levels of bureaucracy to comply with their requirements. An organisation that does not already have an ISO 9000 quality system in place needs to consider very carefully whether it is ready to work in this way.

Environmental management standards are part of a general European move to encourage companies to improve voluntarily. The first environmental management system standard was the British Standard BS7750, which was based on the approach of the widely used quality standard BS5750. In Europe EMAS was developed specifically for manufacturing companies. The International Standards Organisation has now developed a standard, ISO 14001, that has replaced BS7750 and is recognised worldwide.

Environmental
Management

227

ISO 14001

The International Standards Organisation's ISO 14001 is an international environmental management system for ensuring and demonstrating compliance with stated environmental policies and objectives. ISO 14001 is part of the ISO 14000 series, other parts of which are detailed in Chapters 4, Purchasing, and 9, Environmental Reporting.

ISO 14001 is designed to enable any organisation to establish an effective standardised management system, as a foundation for sound environmental performance and to ensure compliance with environmental legislation and regulations. It does not specify absolute levels of environmental performance, with the exception of compliance with legislation and a commitment to continual improvement. Thus two organisations carrying out similar activities but having different environmental performance may both comply with its requirements.

The responsibilities of staff in implementing the policy and objectives must be documented in a set of procedures. These procedures should set out who is responsible for achieving what and when.

The standard requires that your system is regularly audited to ensure that the procedures are being followed. Periodic management reviews of the success of the system in achieving the aims of the environmental policy must also be carried out.

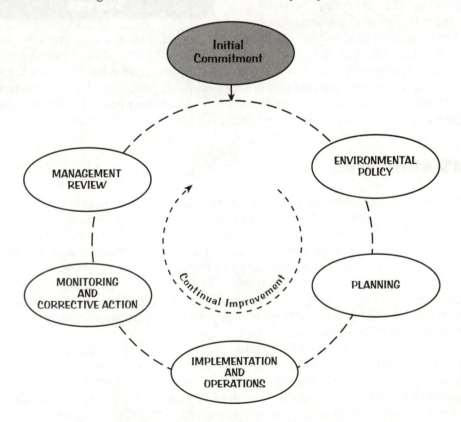

Figure 8.1 *Stages in the implementation of ISO 14001*

Certification for compliance with the standard is carried out by external certifiers who are formally accredited under a scheme run by UK Accreditation Services (UKAS). Companies are certified to ISO 14001 on a three-year basis, after which they are audited again if they want to retain the standard.

EMAS

The Eco-Management and Audit Scheme is a voluntary European Union scheme which aims to encourage evaluation and improvement of environmental performance and the provision of relevant information to the public. Unlike ISO 14001, EMAS was initially only available to industrial companies and local authorities. However EMAS is due to be extended to all types of organisation in the first half of 2000. *See EMAS Revisions below* ↘

EMAS is compatible with ISO 14001 but requires the publication of a concise and comprehensible statement for each participating site to ensure that the public and interested parties understand the environmental impacts of the site and how they are being managed. Publication is usually yearly and should contain up to date information on progress against the objectives and time scales agreed by the site's management team.

This environmental statement must be verified by an independent, accredited environmental verifier at the end of each cycle. The policy, programme, management system and audit procedure also have to be validated. Verifiers are accredited under a scheme run by UKAS on behalf of the DETR.

EMAS revisions

Revisions to the legislation which set up EMAS in 1993 were proposed in 1999. The main changes proposed were:

- The standard would be applicable to **all types of organisation**, although the organisation must make the case that its environmental effects are significant. The standard would be applicable to the *organisation* rather than to a site (an organisation is defined as anything with a central administrative control). The organisation applying for EMAS can treat each branch separately or apply for certification for all branches (a 'corporate EMAS') if it can demonstrate sufficient control over other branches.
- the **EMAS logo** could be used in advertisements for products, activities and services, and on letterheads.
- SMEs would be required to have **less frequent verification statements** made. SMEs would be able to work in partnerships with local authorities on a regional basis in gaining EMAS and there may be potential for a stepped process towards certification, as is the case in Belgium, which has a five-step staging process towards achieving certification.

Additional requirements for registration:

- Organisations would be required to make publicly available **detailed objectives and targets** for environmental performance, as well as their performance against them.

Environmental Management

- Organisations need to demonstrate their efforts to communicate with the **public and interested stakeholders**, and how they have secured the **active involvement and training of employees**.
- Environmental statements published by EMAS-registered organisations must include data which allow the reader to make **year on year comparisons** in performance.
- On defining significant environmental aspects, organisations would have to demonstrate how their **criteria for defining significant environmental aspects** have been selected, and also that the significant environmental aspects of their **procurement procedures** have been identified.

(The best source for updates on EMAS in the UK is www.emas.org.uk which includes details on the regulations, and the register of certified bodies.) These changes to the legislation should come into force in the first half of 2000 if approved by the European Commission.

The EMAS-ISO 'Bridging Document'

The EMAS Bridging Document sets out the issues which need to be addressed by organisations with ISO14001 who want to progress to EMAS. The document has three major aims:

1 To identify those areas where EMAS requires EMS and auditing procedures not covered by ISO 14001.
2 To highlight those areas where ISO 14001 and EMAS already agree which may not be readily apparent.
3 To identify further requirements of EMAS outside the scope of the ISO 14000 series.

Copies of the document are available from the EMAS Competent Body. *See Chapter 10, Contacts and Resources* The document will be of less relevance when the proposed changes to EMAS are introduced.

Local Authority (LA) EMAS

The DETR, in association with the Local Government Management Board (LGMB), has established a version of EMAS for local authorities called LA-EMAS. The system is voluntary and is aimed to help local authorities improve their management of environmental issues. A number of councils have already been validated to LA-EMAS. The scheme is closely modelled on the industrial version but has three key differences:

1 The standard EMAS scheme was specific to a particular industrial site; for LA-EMAS a management unit is a department or division.
2 The industrial scheme can be achieved by one site in a company. A local authority can also register one department; however, a corporate overview and coordination scheme is also required and the whole authority must commit itself eventually to seek corporate registration.

3   The industrial scheme focuses on the environmental effects of production activities such as energy use and air pollution. These direct effects are also applicable to local authorities but the main impact of, for instance, a planning department, is likely to be in the way the service is delivered. LA-EMAS would be ridiculed if it concentrated on the energy use of the planning department and ignored the effect of a planning decision on an application to open a large quarry. The local authority scheme therefore also aims to manage these service effects.

Which standard?

You may choose not to aim for certification to a standard. You may not feel they are relevant to your company structure or size. However, should you choose to, ISO 14001 and EMAS are both applicable to any office and service sector company. Only ISO 14001 is internationally recognised, however.

For local authorities LA-EMAS is the best option. It has been specifically adapted and there is a dedicated help desk run by the LGMB to assist authorities with the process.

For manufacturing companies the choice between ISO and EMAS is more difficult. A company should take into account that EMAS is a more demanding scheme, which requires a detailed public statement and should, therefore, have greater credibility. The choice, however, will probably rest on which is most recognised in the particular market sector in question.

You are not tied to the standard to which you first choose to be certified. EMAS and ISO 14001 have many similarities and once you have achieved one standard it will be a much simpler process to fulfil the criteria of the other.

Industry initiatives

Sustainability management systems

There has been a lot of independent work done on managing the economic, social and environmental aspects of organisations but very little on drawing together these three areas of corporate responsibility into an integrated management system. This could be the next generation of management systems, especially with the progress being made on TBL and sustainability reporting.

Research began in 1999 through a government contract awarded to Forum for the Future and the British Standards Institute on a programme to develop a Sustainability Management System.

However, there is still much room for improvement in the take-up of established environmental management systems in most sectors of industry in the UK and abroad.

Environmental Management

CBI Environment Business Forum

The Environment Business Forum (EBF) is a service for all businesses that want to aim for environmental excellence. The Forum provides an opportunity to further promote your environmental position. The EBF is open to any company with a stated aim to improve its performance.

It is a two-way commitment:

* by the CBI, to help businesses improve their environmental performance; and
* by business, to demonstrate the action which they are taking.

The Forum has a voluntary agenda which businesses should work towards. This includes designating a board level director with responsibility for the environment, publishing a corporate environmental policy statement and report and having a management system in place.

In return, businesses get a regular update on developments in environment, health and safety (EHS) news, access to regular regional events and Contour, a members' service that allows you to benchmark your EHS practice and performance.

The Business Charter for Sustainable Development

The International Chamber of Commerce runs the Business Charter for Sustainable Development. The charter consists of 16 principles for environmental management which the ICC encourages enterprises and associations to use as a basis for pursuing environmental improvements. These principles include:

* Integrated management. To integrate environmental policies, programmes and practices fully into all business as an essential element of management.
* Process of improvement. To improve corporate policies, programmes and environmental performance, taking into account technical and scientific developments, consumer needs and community expectations, and to apply the same environmental criteria internationally.
* Prior assessment. To assess environmental impacts before starting a new activity or project and before decommissioning a facility or leaving a site.
* Products and services. To develop products or services that have no undue environmental impact and are safe in their intended use, that are efficient in their consumption of energy and natural resources, and that can be recycled, re-used, or disposed of safely.
* Research. To conduct or support research on the environmental impacts of raw materials, products, processes, emissions and waste associated with the enterprise and on the means of minimising such adverse impacts.

Some of these principles are quite demanding, but the Charter is focused on helping businesses achieve sustainable development, and so is quite forward thinking in its approach.

STEPS TO A MANAGEMENT SYSTEM

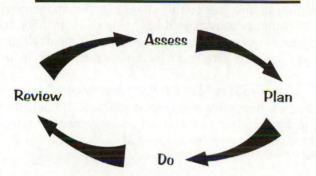

Figure 8.2 *The improvement loop*

An environmental management system is a tool. It does not set levels of performance but a structure in which to achieve the performance targets you set yourself. The approach follows the simple cycle of planning what you will do, doing it, checking that it is working and reviewing your approach.

The details of the system you implement must fit in with the way your organisation works but the basic steps are more or less the same for all systems.

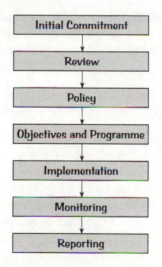

Figure 8.3 *Steps to a management system*

Step 1: Initial commitment

The successful development of a system is dependent on commitment from the highest level to carry it through. An environmental management system is a programme of change. It will take significant resources to develop and will have an impact on all areas of your organisation and the way all managers and staff carry out their jobs.

Before committing themselves to this change, top management will need an understanding of the implications as well as the benefits. If there are members of your senior management who are sceptical about environmental issues, a presentation covering the key business drivers outlined in Chapter 1 can help to bring them on board.

It is equally important to keep staff informed and involved from the start. When you ask staff to take on new roles and responsibilities, the benefits must be very clear if it is not to be dismissed as another management gimmick. *A guide to successful communication is given in Chapter 7* ↰

Step 2: Review

Your office has a range of effects on the environment, some of which you may not have been aware of until picking up this Manual. For many of these effects you will already have management procedures due to legislation and cost. To develop a system to manage and reduce these effects you need to know what they are and how you currently deal with them. Thus the second stage for an organisation developing a formal environmental management system is a structured assessment of its current position.

Most offices that have decided to consider a management system will already have taken some action on environmental issues. Having worked through this Manual you will have identified a range of practical actions you can use to improve on your performance. This work can be used as part of the more structured approach of a formal review.

How to plan a review

Establish a coordinating group
The first step of a review is to establish who is going to carry it out. One successful approach is to set up a project team of staff who cover the key areas of your organisation. You may already have a group looking at environmental issues on a less formal basis on which you can draw. Using a team-based approach will draw in a wide range of knowledge and spread the load. It will also involve a range of staff in the environmental programme at an early stage and improve communication between areas.

Decide on training needs
Consider whether the group has the necessary range of skills and expertise to conduct the review. If you have no staff who have experience in environmental management and auditing, then training in these areas will add value to the review. Knowledge gained at this stage will also be helpful in developing the rest of the management system. If training is required then you need to identify what the needs are, how staff will be trained and who will conduct the training.

Plan scope of review

The project team should define carefully the scope and aims of the review before starting. Different areas of the review can be allocated among the members of the work group.

Guidance on what topics to cover within the review is dealt with in more detail below.

Consider a two-stage review process

If you are dealing with a large, complex office it can be helpful to divide the process into a scoping and detailed review. The aim of a scoping review is to do a first stage assessment of all of your environmental effects and to identify those that merit further investigation. Once you have identified key areas you can undertake a detailed review focusing purely on those areas.

The two-stage review is recommended for local authorities in the LGMB guidance. Local authorities have a wide range of environmental effects and a scoping review can make the process less daunting and can save time costs.

Decide on methods

It is best to use a range of methods to gather information. For instance if you are examining your existing recycling scheme, a simple check of waste bins will tell you a great deal. The most common methods are questionnaires/worksheets which require staff to fill in information, interviews with key staff and direct observation.

When deciding on your methods you should consider how similar projects work in your organisation, the area you are examining and what information you already have. To minimise your work, make sure you do not duplicate this information.

What to cover

Your review should cover the following key areas:

Main environmental effects

Identify your key environmental effects. This is a key part of the review and is looked at in more detail below.

Legislative and regulatory requirements

Record all the environmental legislation relevant to your operations. Each chapter in the Manual contains a section on legislation which will help you to identify these regulations. This information should not be taken as a comprehensive listing of environmental legislation. Where legislation applies to your organisation, seek further details from the appropriate regulatory body.

The Environment Agency is responsible for enforcing a large amount of environmental legislation and can provide further information on specific areas.

Record any policy commitments by any wider corporate body or industry sector of which you are a part.

Existing management procedures

You will already have procedures or practices to manage important cost areas such as energy use, or health and safety measures for items such as hazardous chemicals.

Recording these will help with designing your environmental management system to make the best use of existing procedures rather than imposing a completely new system.

Previous incidents or problems

Previous incidents can provide valuable information as to current weaknesses in your control of environmental issues. For instance your recycling company may have complained about contamination of paper for recycling with other wastes such as plastic cups and food wrappers.

Assessing environmental effects

The assessment of the effects you are having on the environment is the most time-consuming and challenging part of a review. These effects, or impacts, can be wide ranging but are defined by the BSI as 'Any change to the environment, whether adverse or beneficial, wholly or partially resulting from activities, products and services of the organisation'.

Your approach to assessing these needs to be comprehensive but focused on the key areas rather than getting bogged down identifying the environmental effects of every last Biro. Wherever possible you should seek to measure and quantify the effect; this will enable you to set targets and measure the progress you are making.

Direct and service effects

This Manual covers the direct effects of the office; however, many offices will also have effects arising from the services they provide. The difference between these two types are illustrated by the example of a solicitor's office:

1   'Direct effects' are those which result not from the nature of the service provided, such as legal advice, but from the general activities required to provide that service, eg energy use, transport use, paper purchasing, etc. These areas are covered in detail in the Manual.
2   'Service effects' are those which arise from the actual service, such as legal advice provided in areas like takeover bids, contaminated land and environmental law. These are specific to the organisation and are outside the scope of the Manual.

For some office-based organisations, such as an office attached to a factory, service effects will not be relevant.

Identifying effects

Stage 1 Divide your operations into activities, products and services as appropriate to your organisation. For direct effects you can divide your offices by the chapters of this Manual: office waste, purchasing products, purchasing services, office equipment, building and energy management, and transport. To assess service effects you can use the different departments in your office. For instance, a solicitor's office could be divided into the different legal areas it deals with.

Stage 2 Identify the inputs and outputs from each of the areas you have divided your activities into. For example, inputs for transport would include cars and fuel and the outputs would include carbon dioxide emissions and waste tyres. You should make sure you have covered inputs and outputs in the following areas:

- emissions to air;
- discharges to water;
- waste;
- contamination of land;
- use of raw material and natural resources; and
- other local environmental issues.

Some inputs and outputs such as office waste will arise as part of your normal daily operations. Others may only occur during abnormal conditions or in an emergency such as a fire causing release of hazardous cleaning and building maintenance chemicals. It is important that you consider these potential issues as well as the normal ones.

You should also take into account past incidents and future plans. For example, if you are planning office relocation the effects of your energy and transport may change dramatically.

Stage 3 Identify the environmental effects of the inputs and outputs, both positive and negative. For instance, the key environmental impact of carbon dioxide release is contribution to the greenhouse effect.

Concentrating on the important areas

Following this assessment process, focus on the effects that are important enough to require more detailed consideration and management. Keep in mind the following criteria when assessing your inputs and outputs to determine whether they give rise to effects that are significant.

- Whether there is any relevant legislation.
- The scale of the effect.
- The importance of the environmental issue.
- The chance of the effect occurring.

Recommendations

The review should include recommendations for improvements. While reviewing your environmental position, the project team is likely to have plenty of ideas which will help to set objectives and targets. At this stage the review does not need to contain polished and costed initiatives but a wide range of ideas to take forward.

The review is also a good time to encourage ideas from other members of staff. It is usually those carrying out a particular activity that have the best ideas as to how it can be done better.

Environmental
Management

Reporting the review

The review report

The review report will be used in all the stages of your management system. It should contain a clear presentation of the review. In particular it should detail environmental effects in a systematic way to allow objectives and targets to be developed to set your organisation on the path to continuous environmental improvement.

The effects register

You can take your review of significant environmental effects a step further by compiling a formal register of all your effects based on your earlier assessment. This is a major component of EMAS.

The advantage of this approach is that you can clearly justify the objectives you set and evaluate and report progress objectively against the register of effects. For organisations with a high environmental profile, such as manufacturing companies or local authorities, this is a major advantage. For other organisations it is important to carefully weigh the advantages against the resource demand.

SWOT analysis

A useful way of summarising the finding of your review is by analysing the strengths and weakness of your organisation and the opportunities and threats environmental issues present. Table 8.1 illustrates how you might present your analysis.

Table 8.1 *SWOT analysis of A. Model Investment Bank*

Strengths	Weakness
A. Model has committed itself at top level to an environmental management system A. Model has in place procedures to ensure environmental liabilities are considered in investment decisions	There is a lack of knowledge and measurement of the organisation's environmental effects Environmental management is currently on an ad hoc basis There is a lack of knowledge of relevant environmental legislation
Opportunities	**Threats**
Environmental issues not taken seriously by middle management Environmental improvements would show A. Model as a responsible company Environmental management will assist in competing for contracts. Environmental measures could provide cost savings by cutting waste	There is increasing pressure from customers for A. Model to demonstrate that it is an environmentally responsible company An environmental management system could create bureaucracy

⚠ Common problems

Getting a positive response

Staff may well see someone giving them questionnaires or interviews about how they do their job as a threat. If this is the case you are unlikely to get the information you are looking for. It is important to involve all staff from the beginning so they see it as a positive exercise which they want to contribute to rather than a threat.

Identifying the information you need

Since all aspects of your organisation have some effect on the environment there is a danger of being swamped in information when undertaking your review.

The key is to follow a structured approach such as that outlined above so that you know what information you are looking for and can ignore anything that is not relevant.

Summary guidelines

- ✔ Establish a review coordinating group and plan scope of review
- ✔ Decide on any training needs
- ✔ Decide on methods you will use
- ✔ Assess your environmental effects using a structured approach
- ✔ Review relevant legislation, existing management procedures and previous incidents
- ✔ Make recommendations based on your findings

REVIEW

Step 3: Environmental policy

An environmental policy is a mission statement for your whole organisation and is integral to your company's management system and environmental principles. Its aim is to set out and communicate key environmental commitments to all stakeholders. The policy should therefore be a clear statement of the organisation's overall aims and approach.

It should be possible to implement the overall aims in the policy through practical action. It is important to realise that your aims may be subject to close scrutiny and you should make sure that you are ready to fulfil them. For instance, a broad policy commitment to minimise air pollution from your activities will need to be implemented with specific actions and measurable improvements. It is not necessary for the specific actions or targets to be detailed in your policy; these should come in the environmental management system you put in place to implement it.

How to compile your policy

Involve senior management

Senior management should be involved in initiating, designing and supporting the environmental policy. They should fully understand the business reasons behind the policy and the resource commitment that is required to implement it.

Environmental Management

Review your environmental impacts

The review, outlined in the previous section, will give you a good idea of your main areas of environmental impact. These should serve as the basis for the specific areas to be covered in the policy.

Review existing policies and guidelines

Most large organisations have publicly available environmental policies. Obtaining a selection of these can help you with ideas of layout, style and content for your own policy. Those in your own sector of business will be particularly relevant.

Both the CBI and the ICC Charter provide guidance on what the content and principles of your policy should be. *See Chapter 10, Contacts and Resources*

The Local Government Management Board EMAS Help-Desk produces guidance notes for LA-EMAS. These provide some of the most useful guidance to all the stages of a management system. They are aimed at local authorities, but the principles will be valuable for any organisation.

Key features of a policy

Complies with corporate policy

If the organisation is part of a broader corporate body your environmental policy should comply with any corporate policy. However, you should not just copy the corporate approach but ensure you take account of specific issues which affect your organisation or division. The environmental policy should also be consistent with health and safety policies.

Has senior management commitment

A policy that is not clearly endorsed by the senior management of the organisation will have no credibility for staff members or for stakeholders such as customers and the public. Your policy should therefore be signed by a senior manager.

Covers the main environmental issues

To have credibility your policy must cover the key environmental issues affecting the organisation. The policy of a nuclear power station, for instance, will not be taken seriously if it does not mention potential radioactive emissions. Equally a policy for a bank which did not mention investment would have little credibility.

Includes a commitment to continuous improvement

Environmental management should not be seen as a one-off process but an ongoing move towards an environmentally sustainable organisation. The policy should therefore include a commitment to continuous improvement of environmental performance. This should be taken to mean an improvement each year in overall environmental performance rather than an improvement in all areas at all times.

Includes a commitment to comply with legislation

A commitment to meet all relevant legislative and regulatory commitments is required by environmental management standards. More ambitious companies often set a policy commitment to aim to exceed the requirements of legislation.

Makes clear commitments

To be credible, your policy should include clear environmental commitments that can be implemented through practical action.

Is publicly available

Openness to the concerns of the public is a key principle of an environmentally aware business. You should publicise your policy within the local community, perhaps through local media or by providing local authorities with a copy. The policy should also be available to anybody that requests a copy.

Is clearly written and concise

The policy should be written clearly and concisely with the minimum of jargon. This will encourage people to read it and help to ensure that it gives a clear message of your aims and values.

Model policy

We have outlined a model policy (see box) to provide an example of how these key features and the CBI and ICC guidance can be put together in a policy. The policy is nominally for a banking organisation. It therefore focuses on the environmental impacts of the banking service provided as well as of the operation of the business.

A. Model Office Environmental Policy

The A. Model Corporate Environmental Policy states that 'We regard ecological protection and sustainable development as key priorities for all organisations and as essential for the future success of our business.'

This Policy sets out how we aim to fulfil this commitment in the office by continuously improving our environmental performance. We will:

- assign responsibility for implementing the office environmental policy to a senior manager;
- minimise our use of resources by applying the hierarchy of 'Reduce, Re-use and Recycle';
- dispose of any remaining waste safely, and in accordance with all relevant legislation;
- minimise our energy use in all areas of our office through staff awareness and the use of energy-efficient heating, air conditioning, lighting and office equipment;
- consider the environmental impact of products and services in our purchasing decisions and purchase environmentally preferable products where practicable;
- reduce the environmental effect of commuting to work and business travel by efficient use of travel and by encouraging cycling and public transport; and
- encourage staff ideas and keep staff informed on new environmental initiatives.

To implement the environmental policy we will put in place an environmental action plan each year setting out our environmental objectives and target dates for that year.

Signed Ms Big Cheese ∎

Environmental Management

There is, of course, no ideal policy; your policy needs to reflect the main issues for your business, to be realistic as to what you can achieve and to fit with the style of your organisation.

Office environmental policy

If your office is part of a wider organisational environmental management system it can help to have a specific office policy to make sure that specific issues relating to the office are not ignored. An office policy does not need to cover areas that do not come under its remit. The model office policy provides an idea of what this might look like.

⚠ Common problems

Waffle

Some organisations use their environmental policy to reassure everybody about how wonderful they are and fail to make any meaningful commitments. Such a policy will have no credibility within or outside the organisation.

All organisations have scope to improve their environmental performance. A recognition of the impacts your organisation is having, and credible commitments to improve, must be at the heart of your policy.

Lack of Understanding of the Consequences

Organisations and individuals can sometimes fail to realise that a policy statement means what it says. Meaningful environmental commitments will mean change in all areas of the organisation. Once you have made a public commitment then failure to fulfil the policy will mean you lose credibility and you will be open to negative publicity.

You must make sure that all your staff are aware that policy statements will have to be carried through and are not just meaningless standard statements to appease the green lobby.

Summary guidelines

✔ State clearly the aims and values of your organisation
✔ Have top level management endorsement
✔ Cover the main environmental issues
✔ Make clear commitments to ongoing environmental improvements
✔ Be publicly available

ENVIRONMENTAL POLICY

Step 4: Objectives and Programme

The basic aim of any environmental programme is to reduce your impact on the environment. Your environmental policy will have committed you to this aim. The objectives and action programme are where you turn these words into real change.

The environmental effects identified in your environmental review will provide you with the basis for setting your objectives.

Not all significant effects need to be addressed at once but they will need to be managed in due course. Each objective should have an implementation programme with management responsibility and resources identified together with targets and performance indicators to monitor progress.

Objectives

It is important to set demanding objectives that are seen to be making a real change rather than just reinforcing the status quo. They must also be achievable. Failure to achieve your objectives will be demoralising, so consider carefully whether you are being realistic or whether you need to concentrate on a smaller number of key issues.

Criteria

Objectives should closely reflect the policy commitments they are designed to implement. In setting objectives you should take into account the following criteria:

- policy commitments;
- the review of environmental effects;
- legislation and compliance issues;
- ease of implementation;
- views of interested parties; and
- cost, time and potential savings.

Environmental programme

Each objective should be supported with a specific action plan, detailing who is going to do what and when they are going to do it. This will link the objectives into the management system you use to implement your policy by establishing management control and monitoring procedures.

Types of actions

It is important to be clear exactly what each of your actions is trying to achieve. Confusion can arise between those which aim to achieve an actual improvement, such as reducing energy use, and those which aim to gather further information or achieve better control. The LGMB EMAS guidance notes (EMAS Help-Desk, 1996) divide actions into three categories:

- Improvement actions that directly fulfil your commitment to continuous improvement, such as installing energy efficient lighting.
- Further analysis actions that improve the information you have in order to judge the importance of an environmental effect, such as surveying how staff commute to work.
- Control actions that ensure an actual or potential environmental effect is properly controlled to minimise risk, such as a procedure to ensure hazardous waste is properly stored and disposed of.

If you are clear as to what type of action you are setting it will make it much simpler to define and monitor it. An extension of this approach is to have three separate

Case Study 8.2

SUBJECT: **ISO 14001 – Implementing through Innovation**

ORGANISATION: **Dudley UK Limited**

LOCATION: **London**

STAFF: **2000**

Background

Dudley Stationery was founded over 50 years ago and has grown to become the UK's largest independent commercial stationers, and a one-stop-shop supplying office products, bespoke printing, business services, furniture, and office automation services. Dudley supply offices nationwide and in Europe.

Although Dudley's commitment to the environment has been integral to the company since establishment, this has been formalised in a comprehensive environmental management system (EMS). Established in 1994, the system has enabled Dudley to ensure continuous improvement in all aspects of their environmental impact. The framework for the EMS is founded in Dudley's environmental policy. In September 1998, the company gained accreditation to BSEN ISO14001 and now has three sites certified, including their new state-of-the-art national distribution centre. The company has and continues to win a number of high profile environmental awards.

Action

Dudley have approached environmental challenges in three areas:

Environmental management system development

In identifying environmental aspects and their effective management, a number of initiatives have been developed including:

- Certification of Environmental Management System to ISO 14001.
- Extension of environmental management across new acquisitions.
- Establishment of Environmental Intranet and on-line environmental database.
- Action plan development for continuous improvement.

Product and supply chain management

Dudley has many suppliers and products and has invested in a number of initiatives to reduce the impact that our influence on our suppliers may have on the environment including:

- A supplier assessment and audit programme and vendor assessment questionnaire.

- Environmental product development such as wood and paper products sourcing through WWF95+ Group membership and FSC.
- Communication of environmental specifications and development of on-line environmental enquiry facility.
- Environmental seminars and training.

Customer relationship development

In addition to a responsibility for environmental impacts in the supply chain and within internal operations, Dudley feel they have a responsibility to customers to reduce the impact they have on the environment and have initiated a number of programmes:

- Customer environmental enquiry database development.
- Provision of environmental consultancy to customers, eg environmental policy development/review.
- Provision of support to identify material inefficiencies in the order/delivery process.

Results

The key results of these activities are:

Environmental management system development

- Control and reduction programmes established for waste streams, emissions, energy consumption and resource use (see www.dudley.co.uk).
- Three sites certified to BS EN ISO 14001 in 13 months
- Four further sites with environmental reviews under way.
- Extensive environmental information available on intranet accessible from every computer in the company.
- Database management system for environmental programmes, aspects, register of legislation and enquiries available to all staff.
- Key performance indicators set on environmental management established for group management board. Responsibilities clearly defined to cover management of all environmental aspects.

Product and supply chain management

- 75 per cent of products now sourced from suppliers with environmental policies.
- Introduction of FSC certified products including the first ever FSC A4 copier paper.
- Environmental seminars at Dudley Business Show.

Customer relationship development

- More efficient system for handling of environmental enquiries.
- Increased involvement with sales force in providing an environmental service function to customers.
- Reductions in packaging use through collaborative initiatives with a number of customers. ∎

Environmental
Management

Table 8.2 *A. Model UK Ltd environmental programme 2001*

Policy commitment:	We will minimise our waste, our consumption of natural resources and our energy use in all areas of our business
Objective 1:	To reduce office waste arisings by 5% by January 2001
Project leader:	A Manager
Monitoring procedure:	Total figures of different waste streams and progress against previous figures, to be recorded on a monthly basis
Baseline:	kg per person

Action programme	Target date	Respons-ibility	Performance indicator	Resource cost	Non compliance and corrective action taken
Develop general good housekeeping guidelines for staff	1 June 2000	Office Manager	Production of guidelines	2 days	Completed on time
Place poster above all photocopiers to remind staff to double side	1 March 2000	Clerk	Production of poster	1 day	Completed on time
Train all staff in use of electronic mail for internal communication	1 January 2000	IT Manager	Number of staff trained	1 hour training for 300 staff	Training of 50 staff delayed – lack of resources. Completed 1 March
Assess all computer report print-outs to examine whether information could be accessed on-line	1 June 2000	IT Manager	Number of reports assessed	1 day	Completed on time

programmes: improvement, control and further analysis.

Criteria

Actions you set should fulfil the following criteria.

- Be clearly designed to achieve the objective you have set.
- Have a specific person responsible for achievement.
- Have an identified timescale.
- Be measurable so that progress and achievement can be assessed.
- Have adequate resources allocated.

In Table 8.2 we have set out a model programme structure with some example actions. The actual structure you choose should be tailored to fit in with your existing management practices.

Summary guidelines

Your objectives should:
✔ implement your policy commitments
✔ be demanding but achievable
✔ cover your main environmental effects
✔ cover any issues of legislative compliance you have identified

Your action programme should:
✔ have responsibilities and resources defined
✔ be monitored against a given timescale
✔ achieve the objective you have set

OBJECTIVES AND PROGRAMME

⚠ Common problems

Under-ambition

Your policy should include a commitment to the overall objective of continuous improvement as well as specific aims. You do not need to tackle all areas at all times but your objectives need to be sufficiently ambitious to show you are making a real commitment to improvement. Objectives that just reinforce the status quo will undermine the credibility of your programme and the morale of those implementing it.

Over-ambition

Setting hundreds of objectives that you do not have the time or money to fulfil will undermine confidence in your environmental programme. You should concentrate on a relatively small number of demanding targets.

Step 5: Implementation

Procedures and documentation

An environmental management system requires that you document the key procedures needed to implement your policy. In most people's minds documentation means bureaucracy, and bureaucracy is to be avoided at all costs. Yet all organisations use letters, filing systems and records as part of their day-to-day work. The key is to not shy away from developing procedures but to ensure they form a streamlined system with only essential documents.

Environmental Management

What to cover

Your documented procedures need to translate the environmental policy and objectives into specific responsibilities for staff. In other words who does what when to make sure that the policy is met. Procedures also need to cover what happens when things go wrong and the corrective action that will be taken. This documentation will help to ensure that staff are aware of their responsibilities, provide continuity when staff take up new jobs and give you a set of procedures against which the system can be audited. The documents could include organisational charts, emergency plans and procedures describing specific tasks.

Your environmental programme links into this system by documenting who is responsible for implementing environmental objectives, how they are going to do it and when they are going to do it.

Training

There will inevitably be some nervousness amongst your staff about the change of culture that environmental management will bring. The aim of a training programme is to overcome this concern by giving staff a clear idea about their roles under the new system and to equip staff with the skills they need to make that system work. The previous chapter outlined a number of methods for raising staff awareness which will help you to implement the training which you need.

To implement training for all your staff you will need a structured programme which ensures that all staff are trained, including induction training for new recruits. You will need to identify what training staff are going to receive and who is going to deliver it. Training programmes for staff should cover the following areas:

- The system and what it means to staff. All staff in your organisation should feel involved in the development of your system from day one and understand the business reasons for environmental management. As you put the system in place, train your staff in how your environmental policy and procedures will function and the importance of conforming with these. This training must emphasise the potential environmental consequences of not following the procedures. Staff also need to understand their individual role and responsibility in the system.
- The environmental effects of their work. In your review you will have identified your key environmental effects. The staff who are carrying out the activities that give rise to these effects should be aware of them and why they are important. They need to understand how improved performance of their activities will reduce these environmental effects.
- Specific skills. In some areas specific skills training will be required to enable staff to put in place an objective. For instance an office with a product design team will need to train designers in considering environmental issues in the design process.

Ease of use

You should aim to complement existing management procedures rather than set up an entirely new management system. Very often it will be a case of signposting existing documents concerned with areas like health and safety or emergency procedures. This should avoid the development of a weighty tome stuffed with procedures. For organisations that have a quality system in place, this will provide a base on which to add environmental procedures. It can be of help to create a central manual as an overview of the system.

⚠ Common problems

Procedures that nobody follows

The danger is that you will create procedures that sit on a shelf and which everybody ignores until there is an audit. To avoid this, each document should be owned by a specific job holder who is responsible for keeping it up to date and making any changes. That person should be involved in writing the procedure so that it reflects what they actually do. Any documentation should be clearly written with a minimum of jargon and have a clear purpose.

Step 6: Monitoring

A management system needs to be self-repairing to be successful. Monitoring and corrective action when problems arise are key features of a successful system. There is little point in setting objectives if you never check to see they have been achieved. Checking should occur at three levels:

Day-to-day monitoring

On a day-to-day basis the management system should include checks on compliance. For instance, your environmental objectives and programme are to a set timescale. Where targets are not met, this should trigger corrective action.

Management system audits

The purpose of a regular audit is to have a more comprehensive and independent assessment of how the system is working. Auditing will highlight areas of weakness in your system and the strengths that you can build upon. The audit programme should cover:

- whether environmental management activities are happening as planned; and
- the effectiveness of the system in fulfilling your environmental policy.

Audits should be carried out by a trained person who is independent of the area he or she is auditing. If you do not have a specific audit team you should train a range of staff to carry out auditing. This has the additional benefit of being an effective method of increasing understanding of environmental management.

Environmental Management

Management review

The management review is a periodic strategic review of the effectiveness of your system by the top-level management. It provides an opportunity to examine the success of the policy and management system in responding to the business drivers that led to its adoption.

 **Common problems**

Reviews may not be carried out frequently enough to result in performance improvements. Even when they do, the results may not be followed up. The audit should monitor why failings have occurred and targets have not been met, whose responsibility this is and what remedial action will be taken.

Step 7: Reporting

Openness to the concerns of interested parties is an important principle of an environmentally aware organisation. We have looked at the importance of internal training and communication for the success of the system in the previous chapter. Equally important is external communication with stakeholders. Chapter 9, Environmental Reporting, contains detailed information on an increasingly common means of communicating with stakeholders, the publicly available environmental report. However, there are other ways in which organisations report on their environmental performance:

Openness to concerns

The first principle of environmental reporting is to be open to complaints and communications from interested parties, such as the public and customers, regarding your environmental effects and to respond promptly. When setting your environmental policy and prioritising your objectives, take these communications into account to ensure you are tackling the issues of concern to stakeholders.

Publicly available policy and statement

A publicly available policy provides a basic tool for taking a more proactive approach to demonstrating your environmental awareness and commitment to responsible practice. It sets out your aims and values in a short and clear format which will be accessible to a wide range of people. Many organisations now have their environmental statement available on their website, or incorporated into their annual reports or product brochures.

Local authorities have also seen benefits of a public environmental statement which enables them to report back to residents on their environmental position in a rigorous way. Sutton Borough Council and Hereford City Council have both published statements as part of their EMAS programmes. These have the added advantage of being independently validated. *Common problems and summary guidelines for environmental reporting are given in detail in Chapter 9, Environmental Reporting* ↴

Pulling it all together

Reporting your environmental performance is the last step in implementing an environmental management system and should draw together the efforts your organisation has made to improve its performance. An environmental management system should deliver two things:

- A continually improving system for managing your environmental impacts
- Ongoing improvements in your environmental performance.

Essential to this is the careful running of the system and its elements. You may decide that you would like to employ a consultant. If so, bear in mind you will get much more value from your consultant's work and be in a better position to evaluate competitive tenders if you:

- have a clear understanding of the structure and aims of the management system you are implementing; and
- are able to provide a consultant with a clear brief of the work you want them to carry out.

The consultant you choose should, as a minimum, have:

- experience of implementing environmental management systems; and
- understanding of your business area.

Alternatively, or in addition, you may decide to use an electronic support system to document and organise your system, or to work with an external organisation to implement or improve your system. Some possibilities are listed in Chapter 10, Contacts and Resources. Chapter 9, Environmental Reporting, also gives some ideas on how you can use an environmental report to document the successes of your system, and to let interested parties know you have one in place!

Environmental Management

CHAPTER SUMMARY

- Decide whether a formal management system will work for your organisation
- Decide which independent standard is most appropriate for your business
- Get senior management support for the programme
- Make sure that everybody in your organisation is aware that implementing a management system will involve significant changes in the way they work
- Integrate your system within your existing management structure
- Keep all staff informed of the programme, and get their ideas and feedback
- Aim for real, continuous, improvement in your environmental performance
- An effective management system does not have to follow ISO or EMAS formats

CHAPTER 9
Environmental Reporting

INTRODUCTION

Environmental reporting is the public disclosure of a company's environmental impacts and performance, and has increased significantly in recent years. This growth reflects a shift in corporate culture, which recognises the benefits and necessities of adopting a more accountable approach to the way in which companies operate. Being open in providing reliable information on environmental performance for target setting and communication purposes is also accepted as good business sense. A growing number of organisations now publish information about their environmental performance: from carbon dioxide emissions and paper consumption to staff training and partnerships with local community groups. This trend can be attributed to a growing acceptance that companies do not operate in isolation – responsible only to their shareholders – but under a 'license to operate' granted by a much wider range of interested stakeholders.

> *'Virtuous but uncompetitive companies will not be part of our future. Socially or environmentally destructive companies must not be part of our future. The challenge is to create the conditions where social and environmental benefits go hand in hand with competitive advantage.' Making Values Count* (ACCA, 1998)

This chapter explains how to take the first steps towards monitoring and reporting your environmental performance. The business case for environmental reporting is discussed, followed by a general assessment of reporting practice in the UK, Europe and internationally. This chapter tells you what to report on, how, and who to report to. The issue of verification and giving credibility to your data is then discussed, and the chapter concludes with advice on how companies can maximise their returns and make the most out of their reporting efforts. Specific guidance is given for small companies, and priority is assigned to those steps which will be of most benefit to the company.

Legislation

As we mentioned in the introduction, the UK government has taken a long-term view with regards to introducing future legislation. Internationally, other governments have moved more quickly in this area. The Dutch and Danish governments have introduced mandatory reporting requirements on particular industrial sectors. These companies must annually report their key emissions to air, land and water, and amounts of energy, water and raw materials used, along with the polluting substances in products and wastes. Dutch companies must produce a report for the regulators and one for the public, which must be actively promoted.

In the US, the federal government has taken three approaches to reporting: federal environmental laws, information for emergency response requirements, and broad 'right-to-know' laws such as the Toxic Release Inventory (TRI), a computerised database that includes information from over 22,000 facilities.

Government and industry initiatives

This section gives a brief rundown of reporting practices on a global and UK level. Then the quality of reports is discussed, with reference to the UK FTSE 350.

The Global Reporting Initiative

The Global Reporting Initiative (GRI) is a multi-stakeholder initiative that aims to develop a common framework for sustainability reporting which can be adopted by companies around the world. The guidelines for reporting are being piloted by companies who will be giving their views on the usability of the guidelines as a framework for their future sustainability reports. Two companies, Bristol Mayers Squib in the USA, and Eastern Group here in the UK, have already used the guidelines as a framework for their own 1999 reports. It is hoped that the GRI will incorporate a range of disparate reporting initiatives around the world into one universally adopted standardised approach to reporting.

The UNEP Engaging Stakeholders Programme

The Engaging Stakeholders programme is run by the United Nations Environment Programme and uses a list of 50 key indicators to gauge company performance. These include more advanced measures like 'eco-efficiency' and life cycle analysis (LCA). Eco-efficiency measures the energy and resources required to produce a unit of product and the waste produced, in a measure of the ecological efficiency of the production process. *LCA is explained in Chapter 4, Purchasing*↱

ISO 14031

ISO 14031, which gives guidance on what measures and indicators companies could use for reporting, has just been added to the international environmental standard series ISO 14000. The list contains over 100 indicators; however, it makes no demands on compulsory information which companies must report for ISO 14001 certification. EMAS, on the other hand, makes quite specific demands on companies certified to it to report certain information annually to the public.

Tomorrow's Company

The Centre for Tomorrow's Company runs a programme with the ultimate aim of ensuring that the UK encourages and fosters an environment which creates world-

Guest Article

The ACCA Environmental Reporting Awards

by Rachel Jackson, Social and Environmental Issues Manager, ACCA

A national scheme that highlights and rewards the best environmental reports is the Environmental Reporting Awards scheme (ERA), founded by the Association of Chartered Certified Accountants. The objective of the ERA is to identify and reward innovative attempts to communicate corporate environmental performance, but not to report on good performance itself, and has significantly improved the standard of environmental reporting in the UK. Companies who have produced relevant, reliable, complete and verified information in their reports have been rewarded with the Award.

Previous award winners for best overall environmental report have included British Telecom, British Airways and Anglian Water, and other award categories have included best first time reporter, best small and medium sized reporter and more specific categories for site reporting and supply chain reporting. The scheme is open to both private and public sectors, and any size of company or organisation in the UK.

The ERAs are now a major national initiative, reflecting the growth in corporate environmental reporting and increased demand from stakeholders for corporate environmental accountability. In 1999, a record 64 companies took part in the scheme. The Awards scheme has proved influential in the development of corporate environmental accountability around the world, and has been mirrored in many other countries.

The ERA also identifies trends in the development of reporting practice. Many companies are responding to pressure to widen the scope of corporate public accountability by including social data in their environmental reports. Examples of social measures include: employee statistics and conditions, community support and involvement, and stakeholder consultation information. The scheme has also identified other trends such as a move to Internet reporting and the production of other types of environmental communication media, for instance CD ROM and video.

The ACCA Environmental Reporting Awards judging criteria are mentioned later in this chapter in Getting the Most out of Your Report.

Pensions and Investment Research Consultants (PIRC)

The Pensions and Investment Research Consultants (PIRC) survey assesses information provided in both companies' annual report and accounts and separately produced environmental reports. They produce a very detailed analysis of leading companies' reporting practice on environmental and social issues in the UK, covering the FTSE 350. See Chapter 10, Contacts and Resources ⤷

Environmental Reporting

Key findings of the 1999 PIRC survey
* The proportion of FTSE 350 companies that 'report' has risen from 65 per cent to 70 per cent. (This includes companies which provide a one-sentence statement in the report and accounts, to those giving a fully fledged and comprehensive report with external verification.)
* Some sectors have improved dramatically; the proportion of the financial sector reporting rose from 52 per cent to 70 per cent.
* 35 per cent of the companies reporting used websites to promote their report.
* The proportion of companies using some form of external verification for their report rose.

Source: PIRC (1999) ∎

class businesses. The Centre's work is based on the principle that to create sustainable businesses the company of tomorrow will operate differently from yesterday's company. This means constantly adapting to meet the demands of stakeholders and adopting an inclusive approach to management, identifying the needs of business partners and measuring the company's success in doing this. This ties in to research into sustainable development, and the Centre aims to provide businesses with practical guidance on becoming 'Tomorrow's Company'. *See Chapter 10, Contacts and Resources* ❧

The BiE annual index of environmental engagement
Business in the Environment (BiE) runs an annual survey of the FTSE 350 in which they ask a series of questions on a company's engagement in environmental issues. The response to this survey is in effect a wide-ranging but simple environmental report, and BiE publishes an annual survey of findings which gives a picture of the efforts of the FTSE 350 to improve their environmental performance.

DETR reporting guidance
The DETR has been producing a steady flow of guidance, beginning with a brief guide to getting started on reporting, then a detailed guide on reporting greenhouse gas emissions and waste. This will be followed by further guidance on water reporting. *See Chapter 10, Contacts and Resources* ❧

Green Officiency
Green Officiency is a useful booklet which aims to help with running a cost-effective, environmentally aware office. Throughout the guide there are tables to complete which form the basis for a simple environmental report and will help you benchmark your performance. The free guide is available from the ETBPP. *See Chapter 10, Contacts and Resources* ❧

Guidelines for company reporting on waste

Following the DETR's guidelines for company reporting on Greenhouse Gas Emissions in 1999, the new waste guidelines are a useful and comprehensive guide for businesses who wish to report in a meaningful way on their waste figures. The guidelines contain eight steps to lead companies through the reporting process, from identifying a waste champion responsible for driving the programme forward to reporting progress to a range of audiences. There is also useful information on contacts and sources of help and conversion tables to work out the volumes and weights of your bins.

Copies of the guidelines can be downloaded from www.detr.gov.uk or ordered by telephone on 0870 1226 236.

Why report?

Environmental reporting has a number of benefits. Most of these come from satisfying pressures which will eventually come to bear on most companies.

Raise staff awareness
Staff are interested to know about their employer's environmental performance. Raising awareness of the importance of individual action will encourage participation and improve your results.

Find out where you are at!
Assessing your environmental position will identify whether you are complying with relevant legislation and addressing stakeholder concerns. Stakeholders are the organisations and individuals that literally have a stake in your business and commonly include customers, regulators, media and a range of interested or campaigning groups. The first step in both of these cases is being aware of your current performance.

Improved management information
The well-recycled phrase 'what you can't measure you can't manage' underlies one of the key benefits of reporting. Collating and reporting key performance information in a meaningful format will provide a periodic snap-shot or a longer-term track of consumption trends, environmental impacts and operating costs. The report provides a strategic view of your operations and allows managers to incorporate the environmental dimension into decision-making.

Reduced business risks
Reporting puts in place a mechanism for addressing the concerns and enquiries of a range of stakeholders and reduces future business risks by identifying areas of weaknesses. These may be in your own environmental performance or that of your suppliers.

Environmental Reporting

257

Public image

A report is a means of communicating with customers and the wider community. It allows a company to promote its efforts to attain high environmental performance, and to exceed government requirements. A report can be used to satisfy the concerns of a range of stakeholder groups, and is therefore a valuable public relations tool. Some companies distribute their environmental reports to customers or make them available through the Internet, which is an efficient means of reaching a large audience.

The environment report gives a positive public image of the company, and perhaps a competitive edge over its non-reporting rivals. This is likely to become more important as the government continues its policy of naming and shaming the non-reporters, as it did for the first time in 1999.

Demonstrating efforts to regulators

For the first-movers in the reporting field, mainly utility and chemical companies, reporting arose as a response to direct pressures from outside; to demonstrate to regulators and other key stakeholders that they were making positive moves to account for their operations. While reporting cannot be used as a defence in cases of legislative breach, it will help support any case with quantified data and an auditable recording system.

Summary guidelines

✔ Environmental reporting is on the increase and is here to stay
✔ Starting to report now leaves you better placed to meet future legislation
✔ Reporting forms a key part of an effective environmental management system
✔ Reporting will increase staff awareness and enhance public image

ENVIRONMENTAL REPORTING

ISO and EMAS links

Both ISO 14000 and EMAS contain guidance on environmental reporting and encourage it as a key element of an effective environmental management system. Companies registered to EMAS must produce an environmental statement that includes environmental performance data which allows the reader to make year on year comparisons. ISO 14000 suggests guidance only on the possible choices for environmental performance indicators which could be used for monitoring and reporting purposes. *Chapter 8, Environmental Management, contains more information on integrating reporting into the management system* ⤴

WHAT AND HOW TO REPORT

☞ **Practical action**

Having gained board-level support for reporting your performance, you need to make sure that you direct your energies and resources into the most cost-effective and appropriate way of reporting. Bear in mind the following before deciding on which approach to use:

Target audience

Be clear about your target audience and make sure that what you report on is what they want to know. It is important to recognise that an environment report does not have to be a flash, glossy publication. It is more important to make sure that the content is of high quality and relevant to the audience. For most office-based service companies, key stakeholder groups will be: shareholders, lenders, investors, insurers, employees, suppliers, customers and local communities.

How will you report?

Decide how you are going to report and how it will be disseminated. You may include a section in your annual report or produce a separate environment report. Identify communication mechanisms such as websites, shareholders' meetings and staff. Many companies publish an environmental report during the end of the financial year, to supplement the Annual Report. This will be determined by your corporate priorities and the amount of resources available.

Setting boundaries

Decide at the outset exactly which areas of your business and which regions of your operations your report will cover and make sure it is clearly defined. For example, decide if you are going to cover all your offices and include your supply chain. Set targets for when to extend the scope of coverage. Decide what timeframe of your company's operations your report will represent, otherwise you will not be able to track performance accurately year on year. For example, CGU plc began reporting in 1999 with an environmental statement covering their UK operations. In 2000 they will produce their first full environmental report including data on their worldwide operations in over 60 countries.

Coverage

Don't attempt to cover everything! It is far better to progress towards a fully comprehensive report in planned stages than to produce a flimsy report which promises more than it can cover. The key is to prioritise the data you do report to ensure you cover your key environmental impacts. The most commonly reported areas are energy, water, waste and travel and the existence of company environmental policies or initiatives.

Environmental Reporting

259

Case Study 9.1

SUBJECT: **Environmental Reporting**

ORGANISATION: **EMI Group plc**

LOCATION: **Worldwide (48 Countries)**

STAFF: **10,000**

Background

The EMI Group is one of the world's major music companies, with interests in both recorded music and music publishing. The Group employs over 10,000 people in 48 countries and more than 200 business locations, which range from small marketing offices with 10 or 20 staff to large, round-the-clock manufacturing facilities.

In the early 1990s, as THORN EMI and with a much wider mix of businesses (including rental of home entertainment products, lighting, etc), the Group adopted an environmental policy and introduced annual environmental reporting.

Action

It was decided at the outset that the primary audience for the report would be the Group's own staff, although the interests of other stakeholders should be borne in mind. The content was scoped against these requirements, and annual information collected through a detailed questionnaire sent to operating companies around the world.

The reporting process itself acted as a mechanism for the businesses to begin to grapple with their issues: identifying their main impact areas for life-cycle assessments, measuring their performance in those key impact areas, and committing to a plan of action for the coming year.

Early published reports necessarily reflected the broad mix of the Group's employee base in their design – A4 and somewhat 'corporate' in feel. Some content, such as targets and commitments for individual operating companies, was quite detailed from the outset; other information, such as year-on-year tracking of a set of normalised performance measures, came as a result of a better understanding of the key impact areas.

In 1996, after four years of reporting, THORN EMI demerged. The EMI Group's main businesses were now music and music retailing and with that came an opportunity to produce a more focused report that could engage more directly with staff. The core content – hard data and performance trends, individual company commitments, etc – still formed a key part of the report, but both the editorial approach and the design concept could be directly linked to the business of music. Additionally, translations of parts of the report were made available (six languages).

A staff survey was conducted after the 1998 report, to try to determine whether the approach was working. Two dominant responses were that electronic delivery would be more resource-efficient and that employees wanted something more tailored to their own part of the business. The 1999 report tried to address those needs – the full report was on the web, with a search function in the section on worldwide activities; its print companion was a brief review of EMI's environmental footprint and issues by business area, printed entirely on waste sheets from CD booklet production.

Results

The reporting process has:

- acted as a continuous mechanism to raise awareness;
- provided impetus to introduce change and sustain local programmes; and
- enabled better management (equipped with measurement) of key impact areas.

Public recognition of early reports (one ACCA award as Best First Timer and two as Overall Winner) provided a further boost to awareness raising, motivation and commitment.

Staff feedback to the 1998 internal survey, with a 14 per cent response rate, indicated that:

- 54 per cent had first become aware of the environmental programme through reading a report;
- close to 60 per cent were encouraged by the report to find out more about and/or implement environmental initiatives in their company;
- 78 per cent were encouraged by the report to be more 'environmentally friendly' themselves.

Based on prior years' consumption, the move to the web in 1999 saved two tonnes of paper.

Contributed by Kate Dunning of the EMI Group ∎

Triple bottom line

The triple bottom line (TBL) approach combines social, economic and environmental performance in a single report. The majority of companies producing TBL or sustainability reports (such as Shell and BP) have done so as an extension of their environmental and health and safety reporting systems. TBL may represent the future of corporate reporting, combining financial accounts, environmental and social performance of a company in a single report. These types of reports are becoming increasingly complete in addressing the impacts of the company's operations and in particular tackling issues such as investment and supply chain assessment. They will also become increasingly relevant with further requirements for companies to disclose information such as the Statement of Investment Principles required from pension funds from July 2000.

The Co-operative Bank produced their first 'Partnership Report' in 1997 and now produce an annual report with three key sections: Delivering Value; Social Responsibility and Ecological Sustainability.

Prioritise

Not all potential information will be easily obtainable when reporting for the first time. Prioritise which information is of most use in reporting terms. Key figures for reporting are energy and water consumption, tonnage of waste to landfill and recycling rate. To reflect DETR concerns, report corporate travel distances and energy and transport related CO_2 emissions if the data are available.

Getting started

Greenhouse gas emissions

The government recently published its greenhouse gas reporting guidelines and is encouraging all sectors to contribute to achieving the international targets agreed to at the Kyoto Conference on Climate Change in 1997. The DETR guidelines enable carbon dioxide and other gas emissions to be associated with travel and energy use, for example 0.44 kg of carbon dioxide is emitted in the generation of one kilowatt of electricity (based on grid average for 2000). This process is not quite as daunting as it sounds and requires the use of simple conversion factors to make estimates.

Energy use

Energy use is one of the most important contributors to your organisation's carbon dioxide emissions. Electricity, gas and other fuels are consumed for heating, lighting and appliances, on the premises. You can calculate your emissions from your electricity and gas bills.

Water consumption

This is the total volume bought in for catering, sanitation and other purposes. Calculate from your water bills.

Transport

This splits into corporate travel and commuting. For corporate travel, quantify the number of business trips made, distances travelled and transport mode. For commuting, quantify the staff numbers travelling to your premises by transport mode, and their journey distances. Many companies have facilities for joggers and cyclists, and operate car-share schemes for getting to work. To quantify your travel, look at mileage details kept, or estimate the number of vehicles in your fleet, or the number of business trips made and by what mode. Monitor how colleagues travel to and from meetings, for example 50 per cent of national journeys by rail, 50 per cent by petrol car, average trip length in km, and so on.

Waste

Often handled by a range of contractors, monitoring your waste production will require details on the types of waste produced, how it is disposed of, and what quantities are disposed of. Any recycling schemes also need to be detailed, with the aim of quantifying landfill tonnage, recycling and incineration rates. Guidance will be available from the DETR along the lines of that produced for greenhouse gases. Contact your waste disposal contractor to determine the amounts collected from your premises each year or use the ready-reckoners in Chapter 3, Office Waste.

Environmental policy and management systems

Just as important as the quantifiable impacts of your organisation are the processes you have in place to deal with these. Some companies have a comprehensive environmental management system (EMS) in place. Report any systems you have in place and any certificated standards you are working towards attaining. Does your company have any formal environmental policies, or are environmental considerations incorporated into existing procedures for various departments; for example, do purchasing or banking policies include environmental criteria?

Many companies now have general environmental policies, but some have separate policies for integrating environmental criteria and considerations into corporate travel decisions or purchasing procedures, for example.

Best practice

Best practice on reporting includes reporting on those areas mentioned earlier under sustainable development, such as financial investments and impacts. The actual expenditure made on environmental initiatives, such as new technology and staff training, is a positive indicator of your commitment to the environment. Some companies report their charitable donations to local communities, staff costs, and the financial institutions they deal with for pensions, insurance, banking and investments. Are any of your financial services such as company bank accounts, insurance or pension funds held with 'ethical' financial institutions or funds, such as The Co-operative Bank and Friends Provident?

Summary guidelines

- ✔ Be aware of the reasons for and potential benefits of reporting – these will help to keep you focused on why you are doing it
- ✔ Be realistic about the resources you can devote to the task. Plan your report in stages so as not to take too much on at first. Prioritise key areas
- ✔ Define the scope of your report clearly, aiming to incorporate all areas and aspects of business eventually
- ✔ Make use of readily available information but make sure you prioritise reporting on key figures such as energy use and waste

GETTING STARTED

Environmental Reporting

⚠ Common problems

Bear in mind some common weaknesses of environmental reports:

- Producing a glossy, attractive report with little accurate and meaningful data.
- Attempting too much, and not reporting on the key aspects of environmental impact.
- Making it too long and inaccessible to the audience.
- Not reaching the audience.
- Lack of feedback

Benchmarking

Benchmarking is now well established as a means of assessing a company's performance. Systematically monitoring and reporting your performance will help you to develop a picture of the environmental 'footprint' of your office, which can be compared with industry benchmarks. By this method, areas of strong or weak performance can be highlighted.

Benchmarking organisations and initiatives have become a prominent feature in the national press and are being used increasingly by the government in its effort to encourage environmental improvements from industry. For example, the results of BiE's Index of Environmental Engagement usually result in high profile articles with headlines such as 'Turning the tables on the green slackers'.

In Table 9.1 we have included some key benchmarks against which to compare your own environmental performance and, for demonstration, that of a fictitious service company. Obviously benchmarks change annually with improving industry performance and changing environmental policies and priorities. All the benchmarks referred to in this Manual represent only accepted industry benchmarks available at the time of publication. The grey boxes represent the grey areas! These are areas of corporate environmental performance where good or typical practice benchmarks are yet to be established.

Tables 9.2–9.8 allow you to summarise the effects of your activities in key areas. Taken together, these provide a limited picture of your environmental performance. Industry benchmarks are given where relevant, against which you can assess your current performance.

Waste

Use the tables in Chapter 3, Office Waste, to calculate your baseline figure for waste. The Good Practice Benchmark is 200 kg per member of staff per year. You should also calculate your recycling rate, the proportion of your total waste stream that is recycled.

Table 9.1 *Comparison of A. Co Ltd current performance and industry benchmarks*

Environmental impact	Unit of measurement	A.Co Ltd: current status	Good practice	Typical practice	A.Co Ltd: target for end of 2000
Electricity	kWh per m^2	345	234	358	15% reduction in
Gas	kWh per m^2	67	114	210	total energy use
Air travel	km	3,232,325			5% reduction in
Rail travel	km	77,005			total km travelled
Courier deliveries	% of domestic deliveries by bicycle	7.9			20% increase in London deliveries by bicycle
Carbon dioxide emissions					
Electricity	kgCO$_2$/m^2	150	103	158	
Gas	kgCO$_2$/m^2	37	22	40	
Total	kgCO$_2$/m^2	210	103	158	5% reduction in total energy use-related CO$_2$ emissions
Travel	tonnes CO$_2$	5000			5% reduction in transport-related CO$_2$ emissions
Water	m^3/employee/pa	16	7.7	11	15% reduction
Waste	kg/per employee	370	200		20% reduction
Recycling	% of total waste recycled	5.0			10% increase
Purchasing	Integration of environmental criteria into procurement procedures	Formal environmental assessment of suppliers Environmental purchasing policy	Around 50% of FTSE 100 companies work in partnership with their suppliers to meet their environmental requirements		Work with suppliers to develop environmental policies
Communication and reporting	Channels of communication and stake-holders engaged	No staff communication Participation in BiE survey	A large proportion of the FTSE 350 produce a separate environmental report		Increase external communication of the Environmental Policy and improve internal staff communication channels

Source: Benchmark figures for utilities (Energy Efficiency Best Practice Programme, 1998)
Note: The benchmark figures given are for an air-conditioned 'prestige' office building (4000 to 20,000m^2).

Environmental Reporting

265

Case Study 9.2

SUBJECT: **Environmental Reporting**

ORGANISATION: **Schroders [London Group]**

LOCATION: **City of London**

STAFF: **2500**

Background

Schroders are an international investment banking and asset management company with their London Group (now Schroder Salomon Smith Barney) activities based in the City of London. Schroders have a number of environmental initiatives in place including paper and glass recycling, energy use monitoring and environmental purchasing criteria, and have responded to the annual Business in the Environment Index for Environmental Engagement since 1997.

Action

For the 1999 Business in the Environment Index survey, respondents were asked to provide quantified information on environmental performance and to detail the extent of their monitoring systems. To respond fully to the Index and to become more aware of their own environmental impacts, Schroders carried out a full audit of their offices, restaurants and staff facilities and examined the future scope for assessing their core business activity: the environmental impacts of their financial products and services. Also covered were the environmental impacts of corporate travel, the environmental performance of a new office block and Schroders' effectiveness at communicating with stakeholders on environmental issues.

This allowed Schroders to report its waste figures including types, disposal routes and recycling rates; electricity, gas and water consumption; and annual travel distances for corporate rail and air travel. Energy and transport-related carbon dioxide emissions were also calculated using DETR reporting guidance

Results

Schroders have benchmarked their data on environmental performance against industry standards to highlight strengths and weaknesses in performance. Targets have been agreed for various impacts including:

- 10 per cent reduction in waste by 2001.
- 10 per cent reduction in energy use by 2001.
- 5 per cent reduction in water consumption by 2001.
- Transfer of 5 per cent of central London courier deliveries from van and motorbike to bicycle by 2001.

Schroders also set themselves targets to improve the quality of information for reporting, for example ensuring over 75 per cent of data is based on actual readings not estimates. The exercise also suggested new ways of measuring communication, such as hits on environmental websites, the number of video-conferences held and the number of groups Schroders communicate with on environmental issues. ∎

Table 9.2 *Benchmark waste per person (kg/year) from Chapter 3, Office Waste*

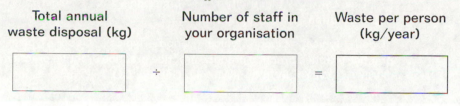

Total annual waste disposal (kg)		Number of staff in your organisation		Waste per person (kg/year)
	÷		=	

Table 9.3 *Benchmark recycling rate (%) from Chapter 3, Office Waste*

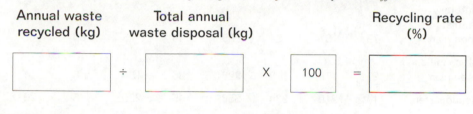

Annual waste recycled (kg)		Total annual waste disposal (kg)				Recycling rate (%)
	÷		X	100	=	

Energy use

Carbon dioxide emissions

A key indicator of the environmental effects of energy use is the amount of carbon dioxide released. Carbon dioxide is generated by the burning of fossil fuels and is the main gas contributing to the greenhouse effect.

Table 9.4 *Total CO_2 emissions (kg per m^2 per year) from Chapter 5, Building Management*

	Annual kWh		Treated floor area (m^2)		Annual kWh/m^2		CO_2 conversion factors		CO_2 emissions kg/m^2/year
Gas		÷		=		X	0.19	=	
Oil		÷		=		X	0.25	=	
Coal		÷		=		X	0.30	=	
Total fossil fuel kWh/m^2									
Total electricity kWh/m^2		÷		=		X	0.44	=	
Total CO_2 emissions kg/m^2/year									

Table 9.5 *Industry benchmarks for energy use*

	Gas/Oil consumption		Electricity consumption		Emissions		Cost	
	Good practice kWh/ m²	Typical practice kWh/ m²	Good practice kWh/ m²	Typical practice kWh/ m²	Good practice kg CO₂/ m²	Typical practice kg CO₂/ m²	Good practice £/m² tfa	Typical practice £/m² tfa
Smaller office	79	151	33	54	33	59	3.50	6
Naturally ventilated open plan	79	151	54	85	44	75	4.50	7
Air-conditioned open plan	97	178	128	226	86	154	8	14
Headquarters	114	210	234	358	145	229	13	20

Source: Energy Use in Offices (ECON.19) (Energy Efficiency Best Practice Programme, 1998)

Benchmarking your performance

Compare your baseline figures with the Good and Typical industry averages above. Use these benchmarks when setting your targets.

Water use

Calculate your baseline figure for water use. A good practice benchmark is 7.7 m³ per member of staff per year (Environment Agency, 2000). *See Case Study 9.3* ↘

Transport

The amount of carbon dioxide released is also a key indicator of the environmental effects of transport. See the Ready Reckoners section in Chapter 6, Transport, to calculate your total transport emissions. Levels vary too much by type of organisation to provide a performance benchmark but the total will enable you to monitor your progress.

Table 9.6 *Water use (m³) per person per year from Chapter 5, Building Management*

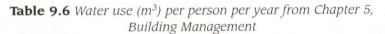

Annual water use (m³)		Number of staff in your organisation		Water use per person (m³/person/year)
	÷		=	

Case Study 9.3

SUBJECT: **Water Use Benchmarks**

ORGANISATION: **NWDMC, Environment Agency**

LOCATION: **Worthing, West Sussex**

STAFF: **200**

Background

The principal aim of the Environment Agency is to protect and enhance the environment while contributing towards sustainable development. It is committed to conducting activities and operations in a manner that reflects best environmental practice. An important part of minimising the impact of the EA's activities is establishing, measuring and reporting on performance targets.

Action

In recent years water consumption at the Agency's various premises has been calculated per employee basis (per FTE – full time equivalent). This was then compared with an Agency-wide target of 7.7 m^3 per FTE per year, based on a 30 per cent reduction on the accepted norm for office buildings (of 50 litres/person/day). The failing of this generic approach is that the Agency operates a large number of sites, ranging from standard office buildings through to laboratories and vehicle depots. The different sites have different water use requirements and consequently the application of a uniform target based on the number of employees is not necessarily the best method for setting a realistic target.

The Agency's National Water Demand Management Centre was asked by the Environmental Management Unit, which monitors the Agency's environmental performance, to come up with a tool that will enable each site to calculate its 'benchmark' water consumption, based on site-specific information. The benchmark calculation will be derived principally from washroom use but will be sensitive to factors such as the presence of canteen facilities and even the proportion of male to female staff!

Results

The process of developing the benchmark tool has necessitated each site completing a water use questionnaire. This has helped site managers think about the ways in which water is used on the site, which is a useful exercise in itself. An important decision to make in calculating the benchmark is where to set the target. In general we have adopted the approach that water-using appliances should be more efficient than average but not necessarily the most efficient on the market. This keeps the resulting targets challenging, yet realistic. The tool is still undergoing development and the data collected so far suggest that benchmarking water use in the Agency's laboratories and fish farms will require further investigation and possibly detailed sites audits.

Environmental Reporting

However, the Agency aims to set new site-specific targets for water use using the benchmarking approach for the majority of its offices in 2000. Once the benchmarking tool has been set in place, future targets can be calculated by altering the assumptions to reflect changes in technology, for example the re-introduction of dual-flush toilets. This would then have the effect of setting a more stringent benchmark.

In 1998/99 the Environment Agency met its target of 'reducing water use in offices and depots to 30 per cent below accepted norm for office type or 1996/97 consumption, whichever is the higher'. During the year the Agency actually used 65,400 m³ of water, which represented a reduction of 30.4 per cent on 1996/97, or a saving of over £40,000 based on industry average water and sewerage charges.

Contributed by David Sayers, NWDMC ■

Environmental footprint

Table 9.7 will provide a summary of your environmental position, at least for your quantitative impacts. Insert your key performance figures in the empty boxes after working through the relevant guidance in the chapters. By updating this yearly you can develop an objective measure of the success of your programme in reducing the environmental footprint of your organisation. It is important, however, that you also compare your performance on qualitative aspects like purchasing and communication. The benchmarks given in Table 9.8 can be determined yourself by keeping up to date through the information sources provided in Chapter 10, Contacts and Resources.

Table 9.7 *Total annual distance (km) and CO_2 emissions (kg) per year from Chapter 6, Transport*

Transport mode	Annual distance (km)		CO_2 emission factor (kg per vehicle km)		Total CO_2 emissions (kg)
Bus		x	1.28	=	
Petrol car		x	0.20	=	
Diesel car		x	0.12	=	
Transport mode	Annual distance (km)		CO_2 emission factor (kg per passenger km)		Total CO_2 emissions (kg)
Short haul flight		x	0.18	=	
Long haul flight		x	0.11	=	
Train		x	0.06	=	
Total annual distance and CO_2 emissions					

Table 9.8 *Environmental footprint*

Activity	Our performance	Good practice benchmark	Units
Waste		200	kg per member of staff per year
Recycling		70	Percentage of total waste
Energy use		See Table 9.5	Total kWh
Energy-related emissions			Total CO_2 (tonnes)
Water		7.7	m^3 per member of staff per year
Transport		No established benchmarks available	km per staff member/total transport-related CO_2 emissions

Getting help

There is a range of help available to companies, from Internet-based texts to free booklets, which are accessible and useful. *See Chapter 10, Contacts and Resources*

Small- and medium-sized companies

The majority of the most active reporters are admittedly larger organisations, for whom the process of reporting is a logical extension of an EMS they already have in place. For smaller companies who would like to report, the good news is that a lot of the information you require is already easily available from records you currently have, or can obtain easily. Wastebusters are publishing their first annual environmental report in 2000. *See Chapter 10, Contacts and Resources*

Making your report meaningful

Tracking and normalising are both crucial elements of an effective reporting strategy, enabling consistency and comparability in the data you report.

Track your environmental performance

Track the performance of your company over time, using key environmental performance indicators (EPIs). EPIs are a group of measures which quickly give an idea of a company's performance in key areas. Common examples are annual energy consumption and waste generation. The environmental report is not a snap-shot of a company's impacts, but a means of actively following the trends of a company's operations. Are your office premises consuming more energy and water and pumping out more waste each year, or are they becoming leaner, slimming their bins, and 'greening the office'?

Table 9.9 *Examples of normalised units*

Environmental impact	Normalised units
Travel	km per person per year
Waste	kg waste per person per year
Water	m^3 water per person per year
Electricity	kWh per person per year
Lighting	kWh per m^2 per year
Greenhouse gases	CO_2 emissions per m^2, CO_2 emissions per km travelled

Normalising your data

Business is constantly changing, staff numbers will alter, premises may expand, and you may install different heating, lighting or air-conditioning systems. It is therefore necessary to ensure that wherever possible you normalise reported data. Normalising data involves using units of measurement which are appropriate to the quantity being measured. Data should indicate the key factors which influence performance, making year on year data much more comparable. For example, GDP is measured per capita, not land area. If we measured GDP per square kilometre, we would have no direct measure of whether the average citizen was becoming wealthier, as variations in figures would reflect population densities also. Similarly, water consumption is not measured per square metre of office space, but per person – a square metre of office space doesn't have any water requirements!

Table 9.9 gives examples of normalised data, though you will have other units of measurement which are more appropriate to your organisation. It is important that any measures used will show any change in performance, and will not become meaningless when circumstances change.

External verification

After going to the trouble of collecting and presenting data on your environmental performance, it would be nice to think this was enough! Unfortunately, it is not always. Although you may have disclosed plenty of information on your organisation's activities, there is no guarantee that this will be accepted as accurate at face value. Reported information holds far more credibility if it has been independently verified by an external party. Most companies have sought some degree of independent endorsement of their review along the lines of the independent audit of a business's financial accounts. An in-depth public report is a requirement of EMAS and validation of the report is an important part of achieving EMAS.

The aim is to give the reader a measure of assurance that the data presented are accurate, present a comprehensive view of operations, and are clear in their scope and limitations. There are a number of ways in which you can achieve this. Two techniques in use are:

1   Independent assessments of reports by environmental or quality assurance consultants (such as BSI and Lloyds Register Quality Assurance), which involve examining the report contents and process and site visits. The consultants will produce a verification statement which can be included in your environmental report, but only after assessing both the systems used to collect the data and the traceability of the data itself.

2   Stakeholder panels included at some or all stages of the reporting process. This helps ensure the information you report is relevant, and that you communicate on what they would like to see. For example, in a chapter on conservation initiatives or ground maintenance, it may be useful to have a wildlife group involved in the reporting process to determine what is the key information to report.

The more imaginative ways of assurance-providing are likely to yield better results as they satisfy companies' needs to engage stakeholders at the same time as giving credibility to the final report.

Getting the most out of your report

Make your environmental report accessible. Even where companies have spent a lot of money and staff resources developing an environmental report, the target audience may still not find it easily accessible.

Make it available
Place links to your environmental report on the homepage of your organisation's web-site, have a specific telephone number that people can call to have a report sent out to them; don't spoil your efforts to report by making it difficult for people to get hold of it!

Include in tender submissions
Include copies of your environmental report when tendering for new contracts; even if a customer does not specifically ask for environmental credentials, being able to demonstrate your proactive approach will give you a competitive edge.

Promote within your organisation
Ensure all staff have access to the report and invite their feedback on the contents and any areas they feel can be improved. Employees often tend to be the most active users of environmental information and are keen to know what their employers are doing to improve performance. The report can also be used as an awareness-raising tool, informing staff of your organisation's strengths and environmental initiatives, and allowing them to respond to any queries their families and friends may have on your performance. Your staff can be a valuable source of positive publicity!

Participate in environmental reporting awards and initiatives

See the details in Government and Industry Initiatives on ACCA's environmental reporting awards ➥

ACCA use the following criteria as a basis for judging the merits of different reports. The criteria also give suggestions as to what a good report should contain.

- **The corporate profile:** Does the report frame the environmental profile of the organisation within the context of its corporate profile – product, financial, group, geographical and employment details, etc?
- **Scope of the report:** What locations and activities does the report cover? All significant aspects, direct *and* indirect effects? Is it limited to discussing only environmental aspects? What about health and safety, social and ethical issues, and sustainability?
- **Environmental management issues:** EMS and accreditation objectives; integration of environmental management into the business process; internal and external audit; environmental goals and targets; compliance/non-compliance record.
- **Stakeholder relations:** Corporate communications policies and practices; feedback and engagement actions; employees; customers and consumers; contractors and suppliers; regulatory bodies and NGOs; voluntary initiatives.
- **Communications and design issues:** Rationale behind choice of EPIs; layout and appearance; clarity; communication and feedback mechanisms; variety of approaches.
- **Environmental impact information:** Inputs (by category of resource used); emissions (air/water/land); waste/other non-product output; packaging; transportation; land contamination and remediation. Are the EPIs reported to be of any use to the financial services sector? How are direct/indirect effects treated? Explanation of results against previous year(s) objectives or targets.
- **Finance related data:** Environmental costs, liabilities, contingent liabilities, provisions and investments; financial penalties, fines etc; impact of government financial instruments; financial quantification of benefits; opportunities and risks; future costs; investment needs.
- **Sustainability and eco-efficiency:** Product stewardship/life cycle design discussion/report; eco-efficiency EPIs; eco-financial EPIs; sustainability indicators; industry focused discussion of sustainability issues and the company's position; evidence of move towards integration of/reporting of social and ethical issues.
- **External independent verification:** A third party statement (one or more) which gives an independent assurance of the accuracy of the content: mention of standards used, shortcomings found, etc; credibility (see later in this section).

⚠ Common problems

Despite the growing case for companies to report on their environmental performance, many companies in the UK and worldwide still do not release any information on their environmental performance.

Not seen as relevant

Many firms do not see reporting as relevant to them and do not realise the benefits of addressing environmental issues positively. However, with environmental awareness on the increase, and as more businesses attempt to reach certification to an environmental standard such as ISO 14001 or EMAS, they are seeing the relevance of monitoring and reporting their performance.

Lack of board-level support

Having high-level support, ie board-level support for environmental policies and initiatives, is essential to ensuring environmental improvements and policies are taken seriously. Getting board-level support for reporting will ensure that the resources and attitudes required for generating the information needed in the report will be forthcoming. Without support, your reporting efforts may fall at the first hurdle.

Confusion

There are so many different formats and indicators to use, so many initiatives to follow, that companies may feel confused as to which to adopt. The important thing to remember is to ensure accuracy and consistency by progressing gradually towards a complete report in planned stages.

Limited time and resources

Even where management accept the value of practices like environmental reporting, they may be unwilling to commit extra time and resources to an additional task. However, the benefit of approaching reporting early on is that a company can progress gradually towards producing a full report. The first steps can be very small, but as long as these are built on over time and targets are made, with a process in place the report can gradually be expanded across regions and business activities.

Summary guidelines

✔ Benchmark your results and see how you're doing! This will also highlight where your strengths and weaknesses are
✔ Ensure tracking and normalising are in-built elements of your reporting programme

MAKING YOUR REPORT MEANINGFUL

Environmental Reporting

CHAPTER SUMMARY

- ❑ Reporting is of most benefit to you! It is not an altruistic exercise and many companies have found real, quantifiable benefits from making the effort
- ❑ Take a planned and gradual approach to reporting
- ❑ Look at ways of giving credibility to your data and outside groups who you might bring into the reporting process
- ❑ Identify opportunities to use your report for marketing and PR benefits
- ❑ Let the report evolve as your reporting systems improve and you get feedback on the effectiveness of your approaches

CHAPTER 10

Contacts and Resources

INTRODUCTION

There is now a mass of information available on environmental issues. Any quick library or Internet search will reveal a list of promising but often unusable materials. This chapter has been compiled as a selective guide to those websites, telephone helplines, books and other information resources and contacts that do contain useful and relevant information for greening the office.

Resources have been listed for each chapter heading and under the following additional areas:

*   Major support organisations.
*   Environmental legislation.
*   Sustainable development and environmental issues for business.

Each section contains key contacts and a list of other useful resources in that area.

KEY SUPPORT ORGANISATIONS

This is not an exhaustive list of support organisations and every care has been taken to ensure that the information is correct at the time of printing. Details may change and Wastebusters Ltd. cannot be held liable for any errors, omissions, or variations in the details supplied or the service provided. Inclusion does not imply a recommendation.

Department of the Environment, Transport and the Regions (DETR)
The Department of the Environment, Transport and the Regions is an important source of information on UK policy and research on a large range of environmental issues. View their website or contact them at:
DETR Free Literature
PO Box 236
Wetherby LS23 7NB
T: 0870 1226236
W: www.environment.detr.gov.uk

Department of Trade and Industry (DTI)
The Department of Trade and Industry has the overall aim of increasing industrial competitiveness and scientific excellence, to promote a healthy economy.
Department of Trade and Industry
Environment Directorate
151 Buckingham Palace Road
London SW1W 9SS
T: 020 7215 1018
W: www.dti.gov.uk

Environment Agency (EA) and Scottish Environment Protection Agency (SEPA)
The EA and SEPA were created by the 1995 Environment Act and are working together to protect the environment. They are charged with safeguarding and improving air and water quality and with ensuring that waste management activities do not cause pollution or harm to human health.

UK General Enquiry Line and Local Offices
T: 0645 333 111
Emergency Hotline
T: 0800 80 70 60

Environment Agency (EA)
Head Office
Waterside Drive
Aztec West
Almondsbury
Bristol BS32 4UD
T: 01454 624 400
W: www.environment-agency.gov.uk

Scottish Environment Protection Agency (SEPA)
Head Office
Erskine Court
Castle Business Park
Stirling FK9 4TR
T: 01786 457 700
E: info@sepa.org.uk

Energy Efficiency Best Practice Programme (EEBPP)
The EEBPP is the government's principal energy efficiency information, advice and research programme for organisations in the public and private sectors. Funded by DETR and managed by ETSU and BRESCU, it is designed to help organisations cut their energy bills by 10–20 per cent. EEBPP services include advice, support, publications and events. For further information contact the Environment and Energy Helpline:

T: 0800 585 794
E: etsuenq@aeat.co.uk (industrial issues) or brecsenq@bre.co.uk (buildings issues)
W: www.energy-efficiency.gov.uk

Environmental Technology Best Practice Programme (ETBPP)
The ETBPP is a government initiative funded by DETR and DTI, and managed by ETSU, that aims to promote better environmental performance while increasing the competitiveness of UK industry and commerce. The Environment and Energy Helpline gives free up-to-date information on a wide range of environmental issues, legislation and technology. If your query cannot be answered on the spot, a specialist will contact you and can work on your enquiry

for up to two hours free of charge. The ETBPP also produce *Green Officiency*, an extremely useful guide to greening the office. To obtain copies, call the Helpline and quote GG256.

Environment and Energy Helpline
ETSU
Harwell
Oxon OX11 0RA
T: 0800 585 794
E: etbppenvhelp@aeat.co.uk
W: www.etbpp.gov.uk/index.html

Regional waste minimisation clubs and Green Business Clubs
The ETBPP is promoting and supporting the establishment of regional waste minimisation clubs or 'Green Business Clubs' throughout the UK. These can be an invaluable source of support and information and offer a chance for smaller companies to get together to discuss environmental improvement and share ideas.

There are a number of benefits to joining a Green Business Club such as sharing information on tried and tested environmental improvement techniques, information on wider environmental issues and legislation, and contact with initiatives, suppliers and contractors in your area.

Local authorities
Local authorities have a key role in determining the way we deal with waste. As well as their statutory responsibilities for waste collection, disposal and planning, the Waste Minimisation Act 1998 allows local authorities to promote waste minimisation to the public and work in partnership with businesses to reduce their waste

Consultants and expert help
Environmental Data Services (ENDS)
ENDS provides expert knowledge on environmental policy and business issues. The *ENDS Environmental Consultancy Directory* lists UK consultancies, their areas of expertise, competencies and full contact details. Available from:

ENDS
Finsbury Business Centre
40 Bowling Green Lane
London EC1R 0NE
T: 020 7814 5300
E: post@ends.co.uk
W: www.ends.co.uk

Key campaigns
Are You Doing Your Bit?
The Are You Doing Your Bit? campaign is a DETR initiative that aims to communicate key 'quality of life' messages. It encourages people to take simple everyday action to help protect their local and global environment. The campaign focuses on four key areas: travel, energy, water and waste and is funded for the next three years.
W: www.doingyourbit.org.uk

Going for Green
Going for Green is the biggest environmental campaign ever to be aimed at the British public. Its Green Code aims to do for environmental behaviour and attitudes what other public awareness campaigns have done, for instance, for drink-drive, anti-smoking and seatbelt issues. Its five-point Green Code is: Cutting Down Waste, Saving Energy and Natural Resources, Travelling Sensibly, Preventing Pollution and Looking After the Local Environment. Going for Green was launched with government help and all-party support, with its slogan, 'Do your bit', being the focus of the campaign. The basic message is that one person alone cannot make much difference to the environment, but if everyone carries out many small actions together, it can make a big difference.
W: www.gfg.iclnet.co.uk

CONTACTS AND RESOURCES

Environmental legislation
Cedrec Professional and Cedrec CD
Provide full access to UK and EC legislation, updated every 13 weeks. Ideal for use as part of ISO 14001 and EMAS. Demonstration CD available from:
International Marketing Enterprises Ltd
North East of England Business and Innovation Centre
Sunderland Enterprise Park (East)
Wearfield, Sunderland SR5 2TA
T: 0191 516 6125/6
E: steven.Armstrong@imeuk.co.uk
W: www.imeuk.co.uk

www.edie.net
CD-ROM with specialised environmental information.

www.environment-agency.gov.uk/epns/
The Environment Agency's website for regulatory guidance for industry.

www.europa.eu.int/pol/env/index_en.htm
European Union environment (DG XI) legislation in force and in the pipeline, and details on how European legislation is implemented.

ENDS
ENDS is a good source for information and queries on environmental legislation. *See Consultants and Expert Help* 👌

The NSCA 1999 Pollution Handbook
Detailed and user-friendly guide to UK and European Pollution Control Legislation. Available from:
National Society for Clean Air and Environmental Protection
136 North Street
Brighton BN1 1RG
T: 01273 326313

Environmental Health and Safety Handbook
Step-by-step procedural guidance on legislation available in print and on CD-ROM from:
GEE Publishing Ltd
100 Avenue Road
Swiss Cottage
London NW3 3PG
T: 020 7393 7400
W: www.gee.co.uk

Sustainable development and business issues

Confederation of British Industry
Centre Point
103 New Oxford Street
London WC1A 1DU
T: 020 7379 7400

International Chamber of Commerce UK
14–15 Belgrave Square
London SW1X 8PS
T: 020 7823 2811

Local Government Management Board
Woyden House
76–86 Turnmill Street
London EC1M 5QU
T: 020 7296 6600

Environment Council
212 High Holborn
London WC1V 7VW
T: 020 7836 2626
E: environment.council@ukonline.co.uk

Environmental Industries Commission
45 Weymouth Street
London W1N 3LD
T: 020 7935 1675
F: 020 7486 3455

The Centre for Tomorrow's Company
19 Buckingham Street
London
WC2N 6EF
T: 020 7930 5150
W: www.tomorrowscompany.com

www.ifi.co.uk
Information for Industry's website with concise coverage of policy, regulation, waste, air, water and business, legislation and suppliers of environmental goods and services.

www.envirosearch.com
The Stationery Office's environmental website sorts out the good from the bad environmental websites and is a one-stop shop for a range of environmental issues. If you cannot find information on what you want in the resources here, try it out!

www.SustainAbility.org.uk
Policy guidance, case studies, tools and techniques to show how the principles of sustainable development can be put into practice at a local level.

iisd1.iisd.ca/about/prodcat/default.htm
The International Institute for Sustainable Development's good but not recently-updated publications catalogue for corporate environmental and sustainability texts.

www.nef.org
Website of the New Economics Foundation, a research and consultancy organisation concerned with sustainable development, especially social and environmental accounting.

www.wri.org/wri/meb/sei/perspec.html
Part of Greenware (see Environmental Management below) site giving access to a handful of interesting articles and discussions on sustainable business issues.

Natural Capitalism
Widely praised book by Paul Hawken and Amory and Hunter Lovins on new models for sustainable business, published in 1999. Available from Earthscan:
Earthscan Publications Ltd
120 Pentonville Road
London N1 9JN
T: 020 7278 0433
E: earthinfo@earthscan.co.uk
W: www.earthscan.co.uk

Office waste

Recycling contractors

A W Lawsons & Co
55 Lant Street
London SE1 1QP
T: 020 7407 5296
Range: Within M25

BPB Recycling UK
Folds Road
Bolton BL1 2SW
T: 01204 364 141
Range: SE England

Greener World Ltd
Airport Business Centre
427 Great West Road
Hounslow
Middlesex TW5 0BY
T: 020 8571 0100
Range: Within M25

London Recycling
4D North Crescent
Cody Road
London E16 4TG
T: 020 7511 8000
E: recycle@london-recycling.co.uk
Range: Within M25

Paper Round Ltd
Room 428
London Fruit and Wool Exchange
Brushfield Street
London E1 6EL
T: 020 7247 0470
E: info@paper-round.co.uk
Range: Within M25

Pearce Recycling Group
Pearce House
Acrewood Way
St Albans
Herts AL4 0JY
T: 01727 861522
Range: SE England

Severnside Waste Paper
The Pines
Heol-y-Forlan
Whitchurch
Cardiff CF14 1AX
T: 029 20544215
Range: National

SCA Recycling
543 New Hythe Lane
Aylesford
Kent ME20 7PE
T: 01622 883000
Range: National

Materials Recycling Handbook and
Materials Recycling Weekly
19th Floor
Leon House
233 High Street
Croydon CR0 9XT
T: 020 8277 5540
E: recycling@maclaren.emap.co.uk

Confidential waste

Hayes Secure Destruction Ltd
James Arthur House
90 Camford Way
Sundon Park
Luton Beds LU3 3AN
T: 0345 078319

Organic waste

The Composting Association
National Centre for Organic Gardening
Ryton-on-Dunsmore
Coventry CV3 4ER
T: 024 7630 8222

Crisis Fareshare
296/302 Borough High Street
London SE1 1JG
T: 020 7403 8588

Operates in London, Birmingham,
Southampton, South Yorkshire, Huddersfield
and Manchester.

Vending cups

Save-A-Cup
Suite 2
Bridge House
Bridge Street
High Wycombe
Bucks HP11 2EL
T: 01494 510167

Metal: cans

**Aluminium Can Recycling Association
(ACRA)**
5 Gatsby Court
176 Holliday Street
Birmingham B1 1TJ
T: 0121 633 4656
E: alucan@dial.pipex.com

Local Cash for Cans Recycling Centre
T: 0845 7 227722

**Steel Can Recycling Information
Bureau**
69 Monmouth Street
London WC2H 9DG
T: 020 7379 1306

Electrical and Electronic Equipment

Charity Logistics
1 Bower Terrace
Tonbridge Road
Maidstone
Kent ME16 8RY
T: 01622 673 678
W: www.charitylogistics.com

Industry Council for Electronic Equipment Recycling (ICER)
6 Bath Place
Rivington Street
London EC2A 3JE
T: 020 7729 4766
W: www.icer.org.uk/

Intex Shields
Eurocourt
Oliver Close
West Thurrock
Essex RM20 3EE
T: 01708 683400

MIDEX Europe Ltd
Unit B, Manawey Industrial Estate
16 Holder Road
Aldershot
Hampshire GU12 4RH
T: 01252 338 414
E: pbroadbent@midex-europe.com

R Frazier
Irongay Business Park
Lochside Industrial Estate
Dumfries DG2 0NR
T: 01387 723000
E: gary@rfrazier.co.uk
W: www.rfrazier.co.uk

Shield Environmental
Kerry Avenue
Purfleet Industrial Park
South Ockendon
Essex RM15 4YE
T: 01708 684000

Silver Lining
Richmond Works
Garforth
Leeds LS25 1NB
T: 0113 286 2323

Williams Environmental
Unit 3, Charles Street Industrial Estate
Charles Street
Silvertown
London E16 2BY
T: 020 7474 1100

Unwanted Computer Equipment: A guide to reuse
Published by the DTI (see Key Support Organisations above).

Batteries and Mobile Phones

British Battery Manufacturers Association
26 Grosvenor Gardens
London SW1W 0GT
T: 020 7838 4800

Energizer UK Company
Recycling
Freepost LOL2311
Dunstable
Bedfordshire LU5 4YY
T: 01582 478 182

Independent Services Waste Management Ltd
Greenways Business Centre, Unit 18
10 Pencroft Way
Manchester M15 6JJ
T: 0161 233 1977

UK NiCd Battery Recycling Group
c/o International Cadmium Association
42 Weymouth Street
London W1N 3LQ
T: 020 7499 8425
W: www.rebat.com/collectionwebpage.htm

Fluorescent Tubes and Sodium Lamps

Biffa Waste Services Ltd
See Waste Management Companies below.

S Grundon (Services) Ltd
See Waste Management Companies below.

Mercury Recycling Ltd
Unit G, Canalside North
John Gilbert Way
Trafford Park
Manchester M17 1DP
T: 0161 877 0977
E: info@mercuryrecycling.co.uk
W: www.mercuryrecycling.co.uk

Furniture

Furniture Recycling Network
c/o SOFA
Pilot House
41 King Street
Leicester LE1 6RN
T: 0116 233 7007
E: frn@btinternet.com
W: www.btinternet.com/~frn/FRN

OFFERS
Unit 3 Sumner Workshops
80 Sumner Road
London SE15 6LA
T: 020 7703 5222/ 7701 3324
(South London area only)

Recycling Containers

Greenback Recycling
PO Box 54
Welwyn Garden City
Hertfordshire AL8 7DA
T: 01707 332525
Can Banks and Crushers

Straight Recycling Systems
31 Eastgate
Leeds LS2 7LY
T: 0113 2452244
W: www.straight.co.uk

Waste Management Companies

Biffa Waste Services Ltd
Head Office
Coronation Road
High Wycombe
Bucks HP12 3TZ
T: 01494 521221
W: www.biffa.co.uk

Cleanaway
Bedfont Road
Feltham
Middlesex TW14 8EP
T: 020 8890 2440

Cory Environmental
25 Wellington Street
London WC2E 7DA
T: 020 7331 2130

Onyx Aurora Limited
Onyx House
401 Mile End Road
London E3 4PB
T: 020 8983 1000

S Grundon (Services) Ltd
Lakeside Road
Colnbrook
Berks SL3 0EG
T: 01753 686777

Shanks Waste Solutions
Dunedin House
Auckland Park
Mount Farm
Bletchley
Milton Keynes MK1 1BU
T: 01908 650650

UK Waste Management Ltd
Head Office
Gate House
Castle Estate
Turnpike Road
High Wycombe
Bucks HP12 3NR
T: 01494 449944

Associations

Local Authority Recycling Advisory Group (LARAC)
PO Box 116
Chichester
West Sussex PO19 1XU
T: 01243 534619

Community Recycling Network (CRN)
10–12 Picton Street
Bristol BS6 5QA
T: 0117 942 0142

Energy from Waste Association
26 Spring Street
London W2 1JA
T: 020 7402 7110
W: www.efw.org.uk

ENTRUST
(Regulator of Environmental Bodies under the Landfill Tax Regulations)
Pofex House
25–27 School Lane
Bushey
Herts WD2 1BR
T: 020 89502152

Environmental Services Association (ESA)
154 Buckingham Palace Road
London SW1W 9TR
T: 020 7824 8882

Going for Green *and* Tidy Britain Group
PO Box 2100
Wigan WN3 4FF
T: 0800 783 7838
E: gfg@dircon.co.uk
W: www.gfg.iclnet.co.uk

Institute of Waste Management (IWM)
9 Saxon Court
St Peters Gardens
Northampton NN1 1SX
T: 01604 620426

Independent Waste Paper Processors Association
19 High Street
Daventry
Northants NN11 4BG
T: 01327 703223
E: iwppa@fsbdial.co.uk

National Household Hazardous Waste Forum
74 Kirkgate
Leeds LS2 7DJ
T: 0113 246 7584

Save Waste and Prosper (SWAP)
74 Kirkgate
Leeds LS2 7DJ
T: 0113 243 8777
E: mail@savewaste.freeserve.co.uk
W: www.wasteweb.com/swap

Waste Watch
Europa House
13–17 Ironmonger Row
London EC1V 3QG
T: 020 7253 6266
Waste Watch Wasteline: 0870 243 0136
W: www.wastewatch.org.uk

World Wide Fund For Nature (WWF)
Panda House
Godalming
Surrey GU7 1XR
T: 01483 426 444
W: www.wwf-uk.org

Recycler Review
Periodical available from:
19a Crawley Mill
Witney
Oxfordshire OX8 5TJ

Purchasing

Buy Recycled Programme *and* National Recycling Forum
Europa House
13–17 Ironmonger Row
London EC1V 3QG
T: 020 7253 6266
W: www.nrf.org.uk/buy-recycled/database/index

The Chartered Institute of Purchasing and Supply (CIPS)
CIPS Bookshop
Easton House
Stamford
Lincolnshire PE9 3NZ
T: 01780 756777
E: bookinfo@cips.org
W: www.cips.org

Toner Cartridges

Greencare
Greencare House
Sharpness
Gloucester GL13 9UD
T: 01453 511366

Office Green Limited
Sovereign House
Dorma Trading Park
Staffa Road
London E10 7QX
T: 020 8592 9998

Timber Products

Business Seating (Renovations) Ltd
Units 1 & 2
Wilnecote Lane
Tamworth
Staffordshire B77 2LE
T: 01827 261 599

Corporate Furniture Solutions (FSC approved)
New Rock Industrial Estate
Chilcompton
Somerset BA3 4JE
T: 01761 232997

Forests Forever
Clareville House
26–27 Oxendon Street
London SW1Y 4EL
T: 020 7389 0136
W: www.forestsforever.org.uk

Forest Stewardship Council (FSC) UK Working Group
Unit D Station Building
Llanidloes
Powys SY18 6EB
T: 01686 412 176
W: www.fsc-uk.demon.co.uk

Occasional Furniture (Manufacturing) Ltd (FSC approved)
Mitchell Building
Woodside Way
Eastfield Industrial Estate
Glenrothes
Fife KY7 4ND
T: 01592 774 485

Sven Christiansen plc
21 First Avenue
The Pensnett Estate
Kingswinford
West Midlands DY6 7PP
T: 01384 400120

WWF 95+ Group
Branksome House
Filmer Grove
Godalming
Surrey GU7 3AB
T: 01483 419 278

Wood Substitutes

Save Wood Products Ltd (Durawood)
Amazon Works
Three Gates Road
West Cowes
Isle of Wight PO31 7UT
T: 01983 299 935

Paper

Brand paper
Swift Valley
Rugby CV21 1QN
T: 01788 540 303

Curtis Fine Papers Ltd
Guardbridge
St Andrews
Fife KY16 0UU
T: 01344 839 551
E: exchange@curtisfinepapers.com
W: www.curtisfinepapers.com

Inveresk Plc
Head Office
Kilbagie Mills
Alloa
Clackmannanshire
T: 01259 455 000
W: www.inveresk.co.uk

National Association of Paper Merchants (NAPM)
Hamilton Court
Gogmore Lane
Chertsey
Surrey KT16 9AP
T: 01932 569 797

Paperback
Unit 2 Bow Triangle Business Centre
Eleanor Street
London E3 4NP
T: 020 8980 2233

Robert Horne
Head Office
Huntsman House
Mansion Close
Moulton Park
Northampton NN3 1LA
T: 01604 495 333

The Paper Federation of Great Britain
Papermakers House
Rivenhall Road
Swindon SN5 7BD
T: 01793 889 600
E: fedn@paper.org.uk

Stationery

Dudley Stationery Limited
Crown Close
Wick Lane
London E3 2JT
T: 020 8980 7199

Paperback
See Paper above.

www.greenstat.co.uk/
Green stationery suppliers.

Miscellaneous

www.envirospace.com
General information on green purchasing and environmental issues from The Stationery Office.

www.biothinking.com
Guidance on the techniques of sustainable product development and information on eco-efficient products.

www.cat.org.uk
Specialists in renewable technologies for domestic and commercial use.

www.oneworld.org
OneWorld's website which has a useful section for ethical shopping.

www.ethical-junction.org/index.shtml
An 'ethical junction' for a range of products and services.

www.lmu.ac.uk/fin/envmnt/purchas/ green/greeng1.htm
A useful example of purchasing policy and assessment criteria from Leeds University.

www.barclays.co.uk
Barclays supply chain initiative.

Building management

British Institute of Facilities Management (BIFM)
67 High Street
Saffron Walden
Essex CB10 1AA
T: 01799 508608

British Fire Protection Systems Association
48a Eden Street
Kingston Upon Thames KT1 1EE
T: 020 8549 5855

Building Research Establishment (BRE)
Garston
Watford WD2 7JR
T: 01923 894040

Building Services Research and Information Association (BSRIA)
Old Bracknell Lane West
Bracknell
Berkshire RG12 7AH
T: 01344 426511

CADDET Centre for Renewable Energy
ETSU
168 Harwell
Oxfordshire OX11 0RA
T: 01235 432968
W: www.caddet-re.org

Centre for Alternative Technology (CAT)
Machynlleth
Powys
Wales SY20 9AZ
T: 01654 703409
E: orders@catmailorder.demon.co.uk
W: www.cat.org.uk

Construction Industry Research and Information Association (CIRIA)
6 Storey's Gate
Westminster
London SW1P 3AU
T: 020 7222 8891
E: enquiries@ciria.org.uk
W: www.ciria.org.uk

Environment Agency Emergency Hotline
T: 0800 80 70 60

Environment Agency Pollution Prevention Guidelines (PPG01 to PPG22)
Available from EA website and local offices (see Key Support Organisations above).
T: 0645 333 111
W: www.environment-agency.gov.uk

Energy Saving Trust
21 Dartmouth Street
London SW1H 9BP
T: 020 7222 0101
Hotline: 0345 277 200
W: www.est.org.uk

Future Energy
See Energy Saving Trust.

Halon Users National Consortium (HUNC)
46 Bridge St
Godalming
Surrey GU7 1HL
T: 01483 414125
E: halon@hunc.org

Network for Alternative Technology and Technology Assessment (NATTA)
c/o Energy and Environment Research Unit
Faculty of Technology
The Open University
Walton Hall, Milton Keynes
Bucks MK7 6AA
T: 01908 858 407
W: www-tec.open.ac.uk/eeru

Office of Water Services (OFWAT) *and* **OFWAT National Consumer Council (ONCC)**
Centre City Tower
7 Hill Street
Birmingham B5 4UA
T: 0121 625 1300
E: enquiries@ofwat.gtnet.gov.uk
W: www.open.gov.uk/ofwat/

Premises and Facilities Management
IML Group
Blair House
High Street
Tonbridge
Kent TN9 1BQ
T: 01732 359990

Refrigeration Users Group (RUG)
46 Bridge St
Godalming
Surrey GU7 1HL
T: 01483 414125
E: rug@hunc.org

Transport

Air Pollution Hotline
Up-to-the-minute information on air quality in your area.
T: 0800 556677
Ceefax pages 410–17 or Teletext page 106
W: www.environment.detr.gov.uk/airq/aqinfo.htm

Association of Car Fleet Operators (ACFO)
The Mint House
Hylton Road
Petersfield GU32 3JY
T: 01730 260 162

Department of the Environment, Transport and the Regions (DETR)
DETR Free Literature
PO Box 236
Wetherby LS23 7NB
T: 0870 1226236
W: www.local-transport.detr.gov.uk/gtp/index.htm or
www.detr.gov.uk/itwp/index.htm

Don't Choke Britain
Events and information.
W: www.dcb.org.uk

Electrical Vehicles Association
17 Westmeston Avenue
Rottingdean
East Sussex BN2 8AL
T: 01933 276618
E: eva@gwassoc.dircon.co.uk

Energy Efficiency Best Practice Programme (EEBPP)
See Key Support Organisations.

Environmental Transport Association (ETA)
10 Church Street
Weybridge KT13 8RS
T: 01932 828 882
E: gg@eta.co.uk
W: www.etc.co.uk

Fleet Driver Training Association
The Stables
Walton Lodge
Chesterfield
Derbyshire S42 7LG
T: 01246 568 953

Health Education Authority – Active for Life campaign
Lots of tips about walking and cycling instead of driving on short journeys.
W: www.active.org.uk

Liquid Petroleum Gas Association (LPGA)
Pavilion 16
Headlands Business Park
Salisbury Road
Ringwood
Hampshire BH24 3PB
T: 01425 461612
E: lpga@btinternet.com
W: www.lpga.co.uk

Natural Gas Vehicles Association (NGVA)
11 Berkeley Street
Mayfair
London W1X 6BU
T: 020 7355 5086

National Society for Clean Air and Environmental Protection (NSCA)
136 North Street
Brighton BN1 1RG
T: 01273 326 313
W: www.greenchannel.com/nsca

Powershift Programme
c/o Energy Savings Trust
21 Dartmouth Street
London SW1H 9BP
T: 020 7222 0101
Hotline: 0345 277 200
W: www.est.org.uk

Sustrans
35 King Street
Bristol BS1 4DZ
T: 0117 929 0888
E: info@sustrans.org.uk

Telework, Telecottage and Telecentre Association (TCA)
T: 0800 616008
W: www.tca.org.uk

Transport 2000
Walkden House
10 Melton Street
London NW1 2EJ
T: 020 7388 8386

Travelwise
Organises National Car Free Day.
T: 01992 556117

Vehicles Certification Agency
1 The Eastgate Office Centre
Eastgate Road
Bristol BS5 6XX
T: 0117 951 5151
Publish 'New Car Fuel Consumption and Emission Figures', also available from:
W: www.roads.detr.gov.uk/vehicle/fuelcon/index.htm

The ACBE Report on Transport
Gives advice to business on developing better, more integrated transport systems.
Available from:
ACBE Secretariat
Zone 6/E9
Ashdown House
123 Victoria Street
London SW1E 6DE
T: 020 7890 6568

Buying Into Greener Transport – 1999
A guide to help professionals ask the right questions when purchasing to minimise the impact of transport on the environment.
Available from CIPS (see Purchasing).

Communication

Conservers at Work
Environment Council
21 Elizabeth Street
London SW1W 9RP
T: 020 7824 8411

Eco Schools
Tidy Britain Group
Elizabeth House
The Pier
Wigan WN3 4EX
T: 01942 824620
E: enquiries@tidybritain.org.uk
W: www.tidybritain.org.uk

Friends of the Earth (FoE)
26–28 Underwood Street
London N1 7JQ
T: 020 7490 1555
W: www.foe.org.uk

Henry Doubleday Research Association
Ryton Organic Gardens
Coventry CV8 3LG
T: 024 7630 3517

Wildlife Watch
The Green
Witham Park
Waterside South
Lincoln LN5 7JR
T: 01522 544 400

Woodland Trust
Autumn Park
Dysart Road
Grantham
Lincolnshire NG31 6LL
T: 01476 74297

World Wild Fund For Nature (WWF)
See Office Waste above.

National Recycling Forum (NRF) *and*
Local Authority Recycling Advisory
Committee (LARAC)
See Purchasing.

Environmental management

Business in the Environment (BiE)
8 Stratton Street
London W1X 5FD
T: 020 7629 1600

British Standards Institution
389 Chiswick High Road
London W4 4AL
T: 020 8996 7665

International Chamber of Commerce
UK
14–15 Belgrave Square
London SW1X 8PS
T: 020 7823 2811

Institute of Environmental
Management and Assessment (UK
Competent Body for the EMAS)
Welton House
Limekiln Way
Lincoln LN2 4US
T: 01522 540069
W: www.iema.net and www.emas.org.uk

United Kingdom Accreditation Service
(UKAS)
Audley House
13 Palace Street
London SW1E 5HS
T: 020 7233 7111

BSI Electronic Manager for ISO 14001
Software for implementing and managing
ISO 14001. Available from:

Intelex Technologies Ltd
62 King Street
Maidenhead
Berks SL6 1EQ
T: 01628 770037

Granherne EQS
Software for moving your current EMS into
an electronic system to control documentation. Does not assess whether system is in
compliance with ISO 14001. Available from:

Granherne Information Systems Ltd
Chester House
76–86 Chertsey Road
Woking
Surrey GU21 5BJ
T: 01483 729661

Greenware Environmental
Management Systems
Greenware Software, based in Canada,
provides software tools in conjunction with
14000 & ONE Solutions Ltd (see Environmental Reporting below) for reporting
greenhouse gas emissions.
W: www.14001.com/software/index.html

Environment Business Magazine
18–29 Ridgeway
London SW19 4QN
T: 020 8944 2930

Evaluation of Study Reports on the
Barriers, Opportunities and Drivers for
Small and Medium Sized Enterprises in
the Adoption of Environmental
Management Systems
Report by Ruth Hillary, 1999. Available free
of charge from:

Network for Environmental Management
and Auditing
174 Trellick Tower
Golborne Road
London W10 5UU
T: 020 8968 6950
E: rhillary@nema.demon.co.uk

Small and Medium-sized Enterprises and the Environment: Business Imperatives
By Ruth Hillary. To order contact:
Greenleaf Publishing
Aizlewood Business Centre
Aizlewood's Mill,
Sheffield S3 8GG
T: 0114 282 3475
E: greenleaf@worldscope.co.uk
W: www.greenleaf-publishing.com

Environmental reporting

Environmental Reporting: Getting Started
Guidelines for Company Reporting on Greenhouse Gas Emissions
Guidelines for Company Reporting on Waste
Due Summer 2000. Available from DETR (see Key Support Organisations above).

Wastebusters Environmental Report
Available from:
Wastebusters Ltd
3rd Floor, Brighton Huse
9 Brighton Terrace
London SW9 8DJ
T: 020 7207 3434
E: lesley@wasterbusters.co.uk

Pensions and Investment Research Consultants (PIRC)
4th Floor
Cityside
40 Adler Street
London E1 1EE
T: 020 7247 2323
An overview of the findings of the 1999 survey is available at:
W: www.pirc.co.uk/pubs/env99.htm
The *PIRC Annual Survey* gives a complete report on the environmental reporting efforts of the FTSE 350.

Association of Chartered Certified Accountants (ACCA)
20 Lincoln's Inn Fields
London WC2A 3EE
T: 020 7396 5973
ACCA runs the UK environmental reporting scheme and supplies judging lists, guidance and a summary of the annual awards results on request. ACCA also produces the *Guide to environment and energy reporting and accounting* which includes specific company examples.

www.enviroreporting.com
This free Dutch-based website is devoted to corporate environmental information. The site allows visitors to easily access information on reporting, as well as a number of environmental reports such as:

* *The Copenhagen Charter: A management guide to stakeholder dialogue and reporting.* It details what stakeholder dialogue is, what can be gained from it, and ways of approaching it in your organisation.
* *The Corporate Environmental Report Score Card: A Benchmarking Tool for Continual Improvement.* It benchmarks your environmental report against several criteria based on international research and experience and highlights areas in which your report is weak.
* *Corporate Environmental Reports: a guide for environmental managers.* Leads them through the process and offers advice on how to get the best results from internal resources and external suppliers.

www.tomorrow-web.com
This website has links to corporate environmental reports from some of the most proactive companies from all sectors of industry.

www.cfsd.org.uk/eer/
Detailed discussion of electronic environmental reporting.

Greenware Software and 14000 & ONE Solutions Ltd
These organisations have developed in partnership software tools for automatically producing environmental reports, including specifically developed greenhouse gas software.
14000 & ONE Solutions Ltd
15a Chorley Old Road
Bolton BL1 3AD
T: 070000 14000
E: info@14001.com
W: www.14001.com

Ethical investing

Applying Sustainable Development
Provide an excellent overview of ethical investing in the UK and abroad in their website. Look under What's New and Making Change Happen.
W: www.applysd.co.uk

Glossary

Acid rain – rain with lower pH, caused by the presence of atmospheric pollutants such as oxides of nitrogen and sulphur. Acid rain has resulted in large areas of Scandinavian forestry and lakes being damaged and, closer to home, has also caused significant damage to limestone buildings.

Agenda 21 – arising from the Rio Earth Summit of 1992, Agenda 21 is an agenda for the 21st century, which aims to bring about environmental change through action at a local level. Agenda 21 is now enshrined in local authorities throughout the UK and many other countries which attended the Summit.

Benchmarking – a method used by organisations to stay competitive – to regularly compare their own services and business practices against others', and then use lessons from the best organisations to make improvements.

Best Value – this replaces CCT (compulsory competitive tendering) and requires local authorities to seek services on grounds not only of lowest cost but also of providing the best value service. Implies a move from low cost service provision to quality provision.

Controlled waste – a term to define any wastes arising from industrial, commercial or domestic activities in the UK.

Duty of Care – as part of the Environmental Protection Act of 1990, the Duty of Care regulations govern the way in which waste is transported and disposed of within the UK in order to ensure effective tracking of waste and avoid fly-tipping incidents and unnecessary damage to the environment.

Eco-Management and Audit Scheme (EMAS) – EMAS was introduced in 1995 and is a management system now available to all industry sectors. The requirements for certification are more stringent than ISO14001, especially in requiring a publicly available environmental statement from companies which must be actively promoted. EMAS is a European scheme, mainly adopted in Germany and other European nations.

Environmental performance indicator (EPI) – any of a range of measures such as waste arisings per year, or CO_2 emissions per cubic metre, which can be monitored over time to assess whether the environmental impact of an organisation is increasing or being reduced.

Eutrophication – the increase in biological activity in aquatic ecosystems which disrupts natural energy and nutrient flows. This occurs through influxes of nutrients (such as fertiliser leaching into rivers) or through energy influxes (such as hot water from the outlet pipes of a power station or factory).

Global Reporting Initiative (GRI) – an international initiative to develop a standardised framework and guidelines for corporate sustainability reporting.

Green transport plans – these have recently been drawn up by companies and local authorities in recognition of the impacts of commuter and business travel on local and global climates and communities. Plans may set targets to increase the use of public transport, encourage the provision and use of bicycles or walking, and promote car sharing and other less environmentally damaging forms of transport.

Greenhouse effect – the gradual increase in global climatic temperature through increases in greenhouse gases such as carbon dioxide and methane, which trap the sun's rays. The amounts of these gases present in the atmosphere are increasing as a result of the use of fossil fuels, deforestation and agricultural practices.

Greywater – water which arises from industrial processes and requires treatment before being released into ecosystems or fit for human use.

ISO 14001 – the International Standards Organisation environmental management system series which requires companies to systematically monitor and manage their environmental impacts.

Landfill gas – during the anaerobic breakdown of biodegradable substances dumped in landfill sites, gases such as methane arise which contribute to global warming and may lead to an explosion hazard.

Life cycle analysis (LCA) – a tool to assess the environmental impacts of a product or service through each stage of its design, manufacture, use and disposal.

Montreal Protocol – this concerns the use of ozone-damaging chemicals and was responsible for the world-wide phasing out of CFCs, previously widely used in refrigerant and aerosol products.

Non-fossil fuel obligation (NFFO) – this requires countries to reduce their dependence on fossil fuels for energy generation and promotes the increased use of renewable energy forms such as wind and solar power.

Special waste – this defines waste in the UK which is hazardous and liable to cause significant damage to the environment and human health. A long list of materials, including asbestos, are now classed as special waste, and require specialised disposal techniques and the issuing of Special Waste Consignment Notes for their collection and transport under the Duty of Care regulations.

Stakeholders – people affected by or interested in the activities of an organisation, such as community groups, shareholders and employees.

Total cost approach – a method which calculates a product or service's cost over its entire lifetime. Thus the total cost of a washing machine is not its retail price but its energy, water and detergent use, maintenance and disposal costs also.

Triple bottom line (TBL) – an extension of the bottom line, this includes the environmental and social performance of a company. TBL reports include information on these three 'pillars' of sustainability.

Volatile organic compounds (VOCs) – These are responsible for the formation of low-level ozone, a local pollutant, and also contribute to the global greenhouse effect.

Waste exchanges – these work on the principle that one organisation's waste is often a valuable resource for another organisation, eg a retailer would normally pay to dispose of the cardboard boxes which are left after unpacking new stock deliveries. Having these collected by local charity organisations that will use them to transport goods saves on the costs of purchasing new packaging materials, the disposal costs that having these taken to landfill would have incurred, and most importantly, saves natural resources.

References

CHAPTER 1: WHY GREEN YOUR OFFICE?

Audit Commission (1998) *Local Authority Performance Indicators 1998.* Consultation document

Department of the Environment, Transport and the Regions (1998) *Modern Local Government: In Touch with the People*, 30 July, The Stationery Office, London

Department of the Environment, Transport and the Regions (1999) *A Better Quality of Life: A Strategy for Sustainable Development for the UK*, The Stationery Office, London

Department of the Environment, Transport and the Regions (2000) *Waste Strategy 2000 for England and Wales*, The Stationery Office, London

CHAPTER 3: OFFICE WASTE

Department of the Environment (NI) (1998) *Shaping Our Future. Towards a Strategy for the Development of the Region.* Draft Regional Strategic Framework, HMSO

Department of the Environment, Transport and the Regions (1996) *Waste Management: The Duty of Care – A Code of Practice*, The Stationery Office, London

Department of the Environment, Transport and the Regions (1999) *A Better Quality of Life: A Strategy for Sustainable Development for the UK*, The Stationery Office, London

Department of the Environment, Transport and the Regions (1999a) *A Way with Waste: A draft waste strategy for England and Wales*, HMSO, London

Department of the Environment, Transport and the Regions (1999b) *Limiting Landfill: A consultation paper on limiting landfill to meet the EC Landfill Directive's targets for the landfill of biodegradable municipal waste*, DETR, London

Department of the Environment, Transport and the Regions (2000) *Waste Strategy 2000 for England and Wales: Part 1; and Waste Strategy 2000 for England and Wales: Part 2*, The Stationery Office, London

National Society for Clean Air and Environmental Protection (1999) *NSCA Pollution Handbook*, Brighton

Scottish Executive (1999) *Down to Earth: A Scottish Perspective on Sustainable Development*, The Scottish Office

CHAPTER 4: PURCHASING

Groundwork (1996) *Purchasing and Sustainability*, The Groundwork Foundation, Birmingham

CHAPTER 5: BUILDING MANAGEMENT

The British Fire Protection Systems Association (1995) *Code of Practice for Gaseous Fire Fighting Systems*, BFPSA, Kingston Upon Thames

Department of Environment (1996) *Circular 6/96-Environmental Protection Act 1990: Part II*, HMSO, London

Department of Environment, Transport and the Regions (1999) *A Way with Waste: A draft waste strategy for England and Wales*, HMSO, London

Department of Trade and Industry (1995a) *Refrigeration and Air Conditioning: CFC Phase Out: Advice on Alternatives and Guidelines for Users*, DTI, London

Department of Trade and Industry (1995b) *Fire Fighting: Halon Phase Out: Advice on Alternatives and Guidelines for Users*, DTI, London

Energy Efficiency Best Practice Programme (1995a) *Good Practice Guide 84: Managing and Motivating Staff to Save Energy*, ETSU, Harwell

Energy Efficiency Best Practice Programme (1995b) *Introduction to Energy Efficiency in Offices*, BRECSU, Watford

Energy Efficiency Best Practice Programme (1996) *Good Practice Guide 118: Managing Energy Use: Minimising running costs of office equipment and related air conditioning*, ETSU, Harwell

Energy Efficiency Best Practice Programme (1998) *Energy Consumption Guide 19: Energy Use in Offices*, ETSU, Harwell

Environment Agency (no date) *Water Wise: are you pouring money down the drain?* Environment Agency, Worthing

Intergovernmental Panel on Climate Change (1995) *Second Assessment Report*, Cambridge University Press, Cambridge

National Centre for Water Demand Management (1998) *On the Right Track: A summary of current water conservation initiatives in the UK, January 1998*, Environment Agency, Worthing

National Society for Clean Air and Environmental Protection (1999) *NSCA Pollution Handbook*, NSCA, Brighton

Natwest Group (1997) *Get Smart: Energy Management Workbook*, National Westminster Bank plc, London

CHAPTER 6: TRANSPORT

Committee on Medical Effects of Air Pollutants (1997) *Statement on Diesel v Pollution Engined Light Vehicles*, June, http://www.doh.gov.uk/comeap/diesel.htm

Department of the Environment, Transport and the Regions (1998) *A New Deal for Transport: Better for Everyone. The Government's White Paper on the Future of Transport*, The Stationery Office, London

Department of the Environment, Transport and the Regions (1999a) *Environmental Reporting: Guidelines for company reporting on greenhouse gas emissions*, DETR, London

Department of the Environment, Transport and the Regions (1999b) *Preparing your organisation for transport in the future: The benefits of Green Transport Plans*, DETR, London

Department of Transport (1993) *Road Traffic Statistics of Great Britain*, HMSO, London

Department of Transport (1996a) *Transport: The Way Forward*, HMSO, London

Department of Transport (1996b) *The National Cycling Strategy*, DoT, London

Energy Efficiency Best Practice Programme (1995) *The Company, The Fleet And The Environment*, ETSU, Harwell

Environmental Transport Association (1999) *Going Green Magazine*, ETA Services Ltd, Weybridge

London First (1996) *Clean Air Charter For Fleet Best Practice*, London First, London

Royal Commission on Environmental Pollution (1994) *Eighteenth Report: Transport and the Environment*, HMSO, London

Transport 2000 (1995) *Company Cars*, Transport 2000, London

Vehicle Certification Agency (1999) *New Car Fuel Consumption and Emission Figures*, Vehicle Certification Agency, Bristol

CHAPTER 8: ENVIRONMENTAL MANAGEMENT

EMAS Help-Desk (1996) *Writing an Environmental Programme*, LGMB, London

CHAPTER 9: ENVIRONMENTAL REPORTING

ACCA (1998) *Making Values Count: Contemporary Experience in social and ethical accounting, auditing and reporting*, ACCA Research Report No. 57, ACCA, London

Department of the Environment, Transport and the Regions (1999) *Environmental Reporting: Guidelines for company reporting on greenhouse gas emissions*, DETR, London

Energy Efficiency Best Practice Programme (1998) *Energy Consumption Guide 19: Energy Use in Offices*, ETSU, Harwell

PIRC (1999) *Environmental Reporting 1999: PIRC survey of FTSE 350*

Index

Page numbers in **bold** refer to figures; those in *italics* tables or boxed material